Contemporary Issues in Applied Economics

To Mum and Dad

Contemporary Issues in Applied Economics

Edited by

Graham Bird

Professor of Economics
University of Surrey

and Heather Bird

Lecturer in Economics
University of Surrey

Edward Elgar

Published by
Edward Elgar Publishing Limited
Gower House
Croft Road
Aldershot
Hants GU11 3HR
England

Edward Elgar Publishing Company
Old Post Road
Brookfield
Vermont 05036
USA

British Library Cataloguing in Publication Data

Contemporary issues in applied economics.
1. Economics
I. Bird, Graham *1947*– II. Bird, Heather
330

Library of Congress Cataloguing in Publication Data

Contemporary issues in applied economics/edited by Graham Bird and
Heather Bird.
    p.   cm.
  Includes index.
    1. Great Britain–Economic policy–1945– 2. Great Britain–
Economic conditions–1945– 3. Economic policy. 4. Economic
history–1945– I. Bird, Graham R. II. Bird, Heather, 1948–
338.9–dc20

90–27734
CIP

ISBN 1 85278 404 0
    1 85278 405 9 (paperback)

Printed in Great Britain by
Billing & Sons Ltd, Worcester

Contents

Figures

Tables

Abbreviations

CBI	Confederation of British Industry
CEGB	Central Electricity Generating Board
dc	Developed country
EC	European Community
EMS	European Monetary System
ERM	Exchange Rate Mechanism
esi	Electricity supply industry
GATT	General Agreement on Tariffs and Trade
GDI	Gross Domestic Investment
GDP	Gross Domestic Product
GNP	Gross National Product
ICA	International Commodity Agreement
IMF	International Monetary Fund
LDC	Less developed country
MoD	Ministry of Defence
MSB	Marginal Social Benefits
MSC	Marginal Social Costs
MTFS	Medium Term Financial Strategy
NIE	Newly Industrialized Economy
OECD	Organization for Economic Co-operation and Development
OPEC	Organization of Petroleum Exporting Countries
p.a.	per annum
PPP	Polluter pays principle
R&D	Research and Development
RPI	Retail Price Index
SDR	Special Drawing Right
UNCTAD	United Nations Conference on Trade and Development
WOCA	World Outside Communist Areas

Contributors

Graham Bird	Professor of Economics and Head of the Department of Economics, University of Surrey
Heather Bird	Lecturer in Economics, University of Surrey, formerly Senior Lecturer in Economics, Portsmouth Polytechnic
Tony Killick	Senior Research Officer, Overseas Development Institute, and Visiting Professor of Economics, University of Surrey
Paul Stevens	Senior Lecturer in Economics, University of Surrey
Colin Robinson	Professor of Economics, University of Surrey
Michael Utton	Professor of Economics, University of Reading
Michael Asteris	Principal Lecturer in Economics, Portsmouth Polytechnic
Peter Pearson	Lecturer in Economics, University of Surrey
Peter Ingram	Lecturer in Economics, University of Surrey
Geoffrey Maynard	Visiting Professor of Economics, University of Reading
Lester Hunt	Lecturer in Economics, University of Surrey
John Treble	Senior Lecturer in Economics, University of Hull
Roger Bootle	Chief UK Economist, Midland Montagu
Barry Naisbitt	Senior UK Economist, Midland Bank and Associate Lecturer in Economics, University of Surrey
Sheila Page	Research Officer, Overseas Development Institute
Christopher Flockton	Senior Lecturer in International Studies, University of Surrey
S Mansoob Murshed	Lecturer in Economics, University of Surrey

Preface

This book sets out to show how basic economic principles may be applied to many of the contemporary issues that are discussed regularly in the media. It is designed as a companion volume to a more regular introductory economics textbook such as *Economics* by Begg, Fischer and Dornbusch. Whereas many such texts have accompanying workbooks that go into more depth on key analytical techniques, this book attempts to provide the greater breadth and the applications which are often lacking. The level of discussion is set at that deemed appropriate for students taking first year courses in economics or related subjects at universities and polytechnics, but the book should also be accessible to GCE A level students as well as to the interested and motivated non-specialist reader.

The book has been developed from a lecture course on Contemporary Issues in Applied Economics which has been run, very successfully, at the University of Surrey for a number of years. This course is offered to first year economics undergraduates as a complement to the economic principles courses. It is also open to members of the general public, and local sixth formers studying for A level economics. The material covered by the course has been used as the basis for class discussion, and it is intended that this book could also be used as the core reference in the design of a tutorial programme. To this end each chapter is accompanied by some questions for discussion as well as by suggestions for further reading. The Surrey connection is reflected by the choice of authors, most of whom are lecturers at the University. But, where appropriate, contributions have also been drawn from a number of eminent 'guests'.

As editors we should like to thank all the contributors who participated in this project. We should also like to thank the Guildford branch of Peat, Marwick, McLintock for sponsoring the Contemporary Issues programme at Surrey; Liz Blakeway for her kind and efficient secretarial and administrative support; our children, Alan, Anne and Simon, who allowed us to disappear for a week in order to complete the necessary editorial work; and Nanny and Grandad who looked after them in our absence. Our grateful thanks also go to Mark Simpson who speedily prepared the index for us and helped us check the proofs.

We hope that at a time when much of economics seems highly technical and abstract, this book will show how simple analysis may be used as a means to more fully understand important contemporary issues. Hopefully it will be both an enjoyable and informative read.

It is intended to bring out new editions of the book every few years, so we would be pleased to hear from anybody with suggestions for future versions.

Graham Bird
Heather Bird

1. Introduction

Graham Bird and Heather Bird

There often appears to be a gulf between the economic principles and theories that students learn about in introductory economics courses, and the economic issues that they read about in the newspapers and hear about on radio and television. Yet to most students it is these current issues and the applicability of economic principles to them that makes economics an interesting subject to study. This book attempts to bridge this apparent gap by first identifying some of the most significant contemporary issues or problems in economics, and then showing how basic analysis can make an important contribution towards understanding them and reaching conclusions for policy.

The book is designed to provide an answer to a question often asked by students of economic analysis. Having mastered a piece of textbook theory, the student legitimately comments, 'Yes, I understand it, but is it relevant?' This book illustrates the relevance of basic economic principles to many of the complex issues that currently face societies throughout the world. It attempts to show how economic analysis may be used as a tool of the economist's trade, as a means to an end rather than as an end in itself. Clearly it may be expected that as a more sophisticated analytical tool kit is assembled, so more rigorous and searching applications may be made. Indeed this argument has frequently been used by people designing degree courses in economics, who choose to defer applied economics until the second or third year. Yet even elementary theory can get us a long way in developing and deepening our understanding of crucial policy debates. Indeed cynics might suggest that in many cases economic theory suffers from diminishing returns. This book shows how a significant output may in fact be generated from a relatively small analytical input. The book also shows that analysis does not have to be heavily technical in order to be useful. 'Low-tech' analysis may in fact provide greater insights than the professionally more respectable 'high-tech' alternative. Although graphs and algebra may help in working through and presenting ideas, complex mathematics can also cloud what is fairly straightforward economics.

Organizing a book such as this one is itself an exercise in economics.

Editors face problems of scarcity and choice. They have to use resources efficiently, maximizing output from a given input. Even the selection of contents reflects the interplay between demand-side and supply-side factors. Different economists will have different ideas about what are the most important contemporary issues in economics, or will at least have different rankings. On top of this, different editors will face different supply-side constraints. However, the fact that a different editor would have put together a different collection of chapters is thankfully unimportant. The point of the book is to show how economic analysis may be applied to a selection of real world problems; it is not to analyse every single contemporary issue that could be identified. Readers of the book should get a feel for the way in which analysis may be used and may then move on to apply it to issues that interest them, even if they are not covered here. At the same time, the editors trust that their choice of issues will not be at too much variance with the choice of others. Although not scientifically tested, our guess would be that the vast majority of issues that have received close media attention over the last couple of years find reflection in the contents of this book.

Two alternatives suggested themselves in terms of organizing the book. The first was, in effect, to abandon the idea of a structure at all and instead opt for an unrelated collection of essays. The second, and the one adopted, was to structure the book in such a way that the issues would follow a reasonably logical pattern in terms of the evolution of concepts and ideas, and at the same-time match the contents of most conventional introductory economics textbooks. The book is therefore divided into three sections – micro, macro, and international – although most economists would nowadays concede that the boundaries between these sections are poorly defined. Unemployment, which conventionally is seen as a topic in macroeconomics, involves the analysis of labour markets which uses tools of microeconomics; macroeconomic policy, traditionally analysed at the level of the individual (closed) economy, is increasingly seen as involving international analysis, given the interdependencies that exist in the modern world economy. Even so the distinctions remain useful if for no other reason than an organizational one.

The microeconomic section of the book begins by using demand and supply analysis to explain variations in commodity prices in general, and oil prices in particular. The chapters by Tony Killick and Paul Stevens draw on all the concepts introduced in the usual textbook treatment of this most fundamental of economic concepts. The next two chapters go on to look at two related aspects of market and industrial structure. Colin Robinson examines the question of privatization, taking the specific example of the electricity supply industry. Privatization not only involves changing the ownership of industry, it can also have a bearing on the degree of competition, something that is also affected by mergers. Merger activity and policy are discussed in Michael Utton's chapter. The case for public ownership and for active merger policy forms part of a broader argument for state intervention in the workings of the economy. The role of the state is investigated in more general terms in the next chapter by Tony Killick. Part of his discussion revolves around the resilience of the concept of 'market failure'. Two important sources of market failure relate to the existence of public goods and externalities. Michael Asteris and Heather Bird examine the financing and supply of a strategic public good in the form of defence, while Peter Pearson discusses the question of environmental damage and pollution, a crucial externality.

Each of the above issues has received considerable media attention. A great deal of recent policy in the UK as well as in other countries has been based on rolling back the boundaries of the state. Privatization has been a world-wide phenomenon. The increasing electoral appeal of the Greens, in the wake of Chernobyl and fears over global warming and the ozone layer, has forced governments to take greater account of environmental issues. Meanwhile political events in Eastern Europe, the retreat from Communism and the changing interface between the Warsaw Pact and NATO, have called into question the appropriateness of current levels of military spending. The apparent decline in support for centralized planning and the greater emphasis placed on the market mechanism finds numerous specific applications. Peter Ingram in the final chapter in the micro section of the book takes the labour market as an example and examines the relevance of the various factors which may influence wage determination.

Beginning the macro section Geoffrey Maynard assesses claims that there has been a significant improvement in Britain's economic performance in recent years. In particular the substantial growth in labour productivity in manufacturing is seen by many as one of the success stories of the Thatcher administration. Lester Hunt evaluates this so-called 'productivity miracle'. Two central elements in assessing macroeconomic performance are unemployment and inflation. A feature of most of the 1980s was the increase in unemployment in many European economies. John Treble reviews much of the recent work that has been done in an attempt to explain current levels of unemployment. Governments have frequently argued that higher unemployment has been worth it in order to reduce inflation. This, of course, rests on the view that there are high costs associated with inflation and this is the question examined by Roger Bootle. Attempts to reduce inflation have relied very heavily on a strategy of high interest rates to squeeze demand at home and to prevent exchange rate depreciation. Monetary policy forms the subject matter of the chapter by Barry Naisbitt. Some observers have argued, however, that in an increasingly interdependent world it is more and more difficult to pursue independent macroeconomic policy. Graham Bird, in the final chapter in the macro section, reviews the arguments both for and against the international co-ordination of macroeconomic policy.

Co-ordination is normally talked about in the context of the major industrialized countries. The international section of the book starts with a chapter by Sheila Page which plots out the gulf between the rich and poor countries of the world. An important problem faced by many of the latter, and one which has captured the headlines during the 1980s, has been that of sovereign debt. The next chapter by Graham Bird provides a review of the causes of the problem as well as a preview of the ways in which the debt issue may evolve during the 1990s. Other dominant issues on the international scene have related to the continuing evolution of the European Community and the recent emergence of the economies of Eastern Europe. Christopher Flockton examines the arguments for and against European integration, not only covering trade but also exchange rate policy. In the final chapter Mansoob Murshed discusses economic reforms in the Soviet Union which have acted as a catalyst for reform throughout Eastern Europe, and have raised the question of whether the configuration of the European Community will change radically in the 1990s as former socialist countries become more heavily engaged in European integration.

This brief summary of the contents of the book hopefully illustrates how an attempt has been made to cover many contemporary issues in applied economics. The chapters are organized in an integrated way and the book can be read as one unit. However, each of the chapters also stands on its own and may be read in isolation. In anticipation that the book will be used as the basis for class discussion, and may provide the framework for a tutorial progamme, each chapter is followed by suggestions for limited further reading as well as by some questions for discussion.

2. Commodity Prices: Investing in Decline?

Tony Killick

Until recently primary product prices were, in real terms, lower than at any time in the twentieth century, with the possible exception of 1932. The weakness of commodity prices in the 1980s has added new fuel to arguments about the long-term prospects for primary products exported by the least developed countries (LDCs). Instability – fluctuations around the trend – has increased and in the 1980s the trend has been far worse than forecast, relative to other prices. This chapter is about the longer term and asks whether new investments in primary products are likely to offer reasonable rates of return. The 'special case' of petroleum is not considered; all references to commodities and primary products relate to non-oil products.

PRICE TRENDS AND PROSPECTS – AN INEXORABLE DECLINE?

Generalizations about commodity prices are complicated by the fact that the prices do not all move together because they are influenced by rather different supply and demand factors. In recent years, metals and foods have fared particularly badly and agricultural raw materials rather better, while beverages have been wildly unstable. Large differences also occur *within* each product grouping. Composite indices of 'commodity prices' have to be treated with caution, and there are sometimes major deviations from the average. Accurate measurement of long-term changes in real commodity prices is difficult. Changes in a composite index series are much affected by the system of weights chosen. Thus, commodity indices weighted on the basis of industrial country imports (*The Economist*), or on world exports (the IMF), or on LDC exports only (UNCTAD) can give substantially different results. And whichever system is chosen, the weights alter over time, sometimes quite radically, distorting results and necessitating periodic revisions.

Figure 2.1   Real commodity prices deflated by price of manufactures: 1870–1986 (Index: 1980 = 100)

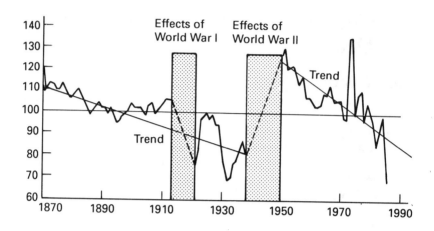

Then there have been changes in quality in both primary and manufactured goods. Some – not all – argue that improvements in the quality of manufactured products have been greater and, therefore, that an index of 'real' commodity prices deflated by an index of the prices of manufactures overstates the disadvantages of commodity exporters.

Price indices are, moreover, highly sensitive to movements in the currency in which they are denominated, commonly the US dollar. Here indices denominated in SDRs (based on a weighted average of leading currencies), are generally used, in order to minimize complications created by the fluctuating dollar.

On the other hand, the influences on supply and demand do have some strong common elements, so that there is a considerable degree of convergence in the long-term price experiences of most major primary products, see Figure 2.1. A few years ago commodity prices were widely expected to rise, propelled by the recovery of the OECD countries after 1982. Indeed, early in 1983 the IMF was confident enough to say that 'a broad-based recovery in commodity prices' was under way, and prices did indeed rise in 1983 and 1984. It didn't last, however. In 1984–86 a composite index of prices fell by 23 per cent in nominal terms. In 'real' terms, that is, deflated by the prices of manufactured exports, the fall was 28 per cent, although it would have been rather smaller for this period had the oil price been included in the deflator. In fact, the weakness of commodity prices in this period puzzled the forecasters. Thus, the annual forecasts of the OECD for 1982–86 were higher than actual outcomes in each of the five years, often by a substantial margin. As it turned out, average real commodity prices were by 1986 the lowest recorded in the twentieth century, with the sole possible exception of 1932, the trough of the Great Depression.

There was some apparent improvement in commodity prices during 1987 and talk that the long-awaited recovery was at last under way. Much of the seeming recovery was spurious, however – the result of a depreciating dollar. Thus, the IMF's dollar index of commodity prices by November 1987 was 28 per cent above the figure for 12 months earlier but was only up by 14 per cent in SDR terms. It was also misleading because there was a spurt in world prices for manufactures and the Fund estimates that in *real* terms there was actually a 13 per cent fall in 1987, on top of the 16 per cent decline in 1986. There were, moreover, fears that prices would remain weak indefinitely.

Since the early 1950s there has been controversy about the thesis that there is a long term tendency for real primary product prices to deteriorate, first put forward by Singer and Prebisch. The thesis found ready support in LDCs, but elsewhere their arguments were criticized; statistical studies threw doubt on the existence of such a deteriorating trend; and their viewpoint went out of fashion during the 1970s. However the record of the 1980s has brought it back into vogue again.

While most recent studies show a falling trend for the twentieth century, the rate of decline varies widely depending on how the 1940s are treated and the nature of the statistical tests used. Excluding the 1940s, the data underlying Figure 2.1 yield an average rate of deterioration in 1900–82 of 1.7 per cent p.a. but other tests reveal a range in trend values, down to a rate of decline of only 0.1 per cent p.a.

The experience of the 1980s has nevertheless added strength and numbers to the pessimistic school. Some have written of the primary products economy having come uncoupled from the industrial economy and others of the 'end of the Era of Materials'. Less cataclysmic but more influentially, the IMF does not foresee any major recovery in commodity prices, expecting them to remain roughly unchanged in real terms in the. medium term. On their last detailed projections, by 1991, prices would still be one-third below the 1980 level.

Looking forward to the end of the century, the World Bank expects real commodity prices to remain depressed for the remainder of the 1980s, to revive somewhat in 1990–95 and then to stagnate to the year 2000. By that year they expect the overall index to be 8 per cent above the 1986 nadir but still 25 per cent below the 1980 level. The forecasts just cited, moreover, were prepared before the global stock market crash, with its attendant recessionary risks.

THE UNDERLYING FORCES

To be able to take a view about future prospects it is necessary to go to the fundamental forces of demand and supply at work beneath the price trends. We deal with these in turn.

The Demand Side

The OECD slow-down

The level of economic activity in the major industrial countries remains the single strongest overall determinant of the state of demand for commodities. Indeed, its influence on commodity prices provides a powerful link between the economic performance of the OECD countries and the fortunes of LDCs; a major way, therefore, that booms and slumps are transmitted from the First to the Third World.

The 'income elasticity of demand' (the proportionate change in the quantity of demand for a good divided by the proportionate change in real incomes which brought it about) measures this linkage. The strength of the linkage naturally varies between product types. It is strongest for metals because they are demanded as industrial inputs. Agricultural raw materials, although also used as production inputs, have smaller elasticities. The smallest however, are for food and beverages. In fact, almost all estimates show elasticities of below 1.0 for all agricultural commodity groups – meaning that demand will grow proportionately less than incomes in the major consuming countries – but generally well above 1.0 for the metals group.

There are reasons for thinking that the size of the elasticities is tending to diminish over time. Moreover, the generally small elasticities for most commodities contrast strongly with the elasticities for many manufactured goods and for services. Demand for these latter items hence grows a good deal more rapidly than for commodities and helps to explain the persisting weakness of world primary product prices.

Nevertheless, the level of economic activity in the OECD countries remains a very strong influence; talk of 'decoupling' is much exaggerated. Aside from year-to-year fluctuations, the main fact about OECD growth in recent years is that it has slowed down. Industrial output and capital formation – which have a specially strong influence on demand for commodities – have been particularly affected. The following average annual OECD growth rates summarize the record:

	1970–79	*1980–86*
Gross National Product	3.3	2.2
Industrial production	3.4	1.8
Gross Domestic Investment	3.5	2.1

*Figure 2.2 World consumption of commodities per unit of GNP (Index:
1965 = 100)*

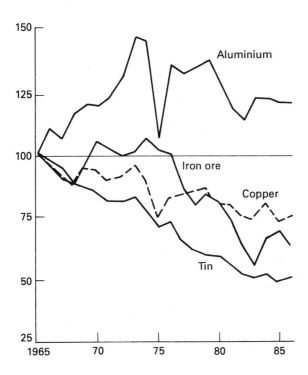

The impact of this deceleration has been severe. UNCTAD studied 19
commodities which have experienced declining demand growth in recent
years and found that over three-quarters of this decline was explained by
the more sluggish OECD performance. The crucial question for the future
is whether the West will return to the more expansionary days of the 1960s
and 1970s. The conventional wisdom is that it will not, in which case the
outlook for exports of commodities to these countries must be bleak, but
the case for accepting the conventional wisdom is not overwhelming.

Structural change
Among the factors tending to reduce income elasticities over time are
changes occurring in the patterns of industrial-country demand and production. There is, first, the widely-noted movement away from industrial

products in favour of services. Since the latter use far less by way of raw materials, that is bad news for the demand for commodities (see Figure 2.2). In Britain the share of manufacturing in GDP has fallen from 33.4 per cent in 1965, to 29.2 per cent in 1975, to 25.1 per cent in 1985. This is a particularly dramatic fall; partly because of the rise of North Sea oil, but there is a clear tendency for the share of manufacturing in GDP to decline for the industrial world as a whole. Even within manufacturing, changes are occurring which are unfavourable to primary product exporters, with a shift away from the heavy metal-using industries towards electronics. This helps to explain why in Britain the volume of sales of the mechanical engineering sector fell by 3.0 per cent p.a. in the period 1978–85, while electrical engineering sales expanded at 3.9 per cent p.a. At least in the more prosperous industrial countries, the demand for some items with high primary product contents is said to be nearing saturation, particularly for cars and consumer durables, and there are no significant new markets for consumer goods with a high primary product content.

Technological change
While most of its effects are on the supply side, the accelerated pace of technological change is reinforcing the demand trends just described. The traditional materials content of finished products has been substantially reduced, mainly in favour of plastics and other synthetic materials. In the USA, for example, the fraction of the average car made up of iron and steel fell from 81 per cent to 69 per cent in 1975–85; and the ratio of weight to power in a railway locomotive has fallen from about 100kg per horsepower at the beginning of the century to about 25 in 1950 and is now down to about 14.

Substitution of materials tends to work to the disadvantage of many traditional LDC producers, although not necessarily the more industrialized ones, thus, for example aluminium is widely substituted for other metals. Car engines and metal cans are cases in point. There is also much substitution of metals by plastics and ceramics; of man-made for natural fibres; of plastics and other materials for paper. Optical fibres are replacing copper in telecommunications (a 45kg length of fibre cable can transmit as much information as a tonne of copper wire).

The development of technologies for the re-cycling of materials is another factor. The increasing use of scrap metal is perhaps the most important instance. Thus, while the steel industry has been in decline worldwide, output from 'minimills', which use scrap as their 'raw' material, has been expanding rapidly – at 10 per cent p.a. in the USA. Modern information technology also permits the more efficient monitoring and management of inventory levels, meaning that a smaller quantity of stocks is now needed to maintain a given level of output.

Agricultural protectionism

The high levels of protection enjoyed by agricultural producers in industrial countries, and the intense competition between them leading to large export subsidies and 'price wars', necessarily reduce prices in third markets and place a potent damper on the demand for a number of LDC agricultural commodities[2]. The Japanese market is the most protected, with average agricultural producer prices a full 2.44 times higher than world prices in 1980–82; the ratio in the European Community was 1.54 and in the USA 1.16.

Not surprisingly, these countries have greatly reduced their imports in consequence. Thus, net EC grain trade has changed from net imports of 18m tonnes in 1970–71 to net exports of nearly 16m in 1985–86. While as importers, LDCs benefit from the lower world agricultural prices that result from this protectionism, as exporters they are big losers. A further factor is the escalation of protection according to stage of production, with even higher protective barriers against imports of processed goods, thus discouraging the higher value-added that LDCs could derive by undertaking more processing at home.

Other considerations

Nor have we quite finished the catalogue of gloom. It might be expected that the fall in relative commodity prices would itself stimulate the demand for these goods. So it does to some extent, but not very greatly. The responsiveness of the quantity demanded to a change in price is measured by the 'price elasticity of demand' (not to be confused with the income elasticity used earlier). With few exceptions, estimates of price elasticities for primary products are well below 1.0. Typically they are in the range 0.4 to 0.6, meaning that a 10 per cent fall in price will (other things being equal) only induce a 4–6 per cent increase in demand.

One other explanation that is sometimes offered for the adverse prices received by LDC exporters is that these prices are manipulated by the industrial countries (or transnational corporations) using monopoly power as buyers. This has certainly sometimes occurred. We have already discussed the case of agricultural protectionism. The market for bauxite is dominated by a few giant aluminium producers; and multinationals still dominate the production of some tropical fruits. But as a general explanation, the 'market manipulation' argument is difficult to sustain and the basic fact is that the underlying forces of supply and demand are moving to the disadvantage of LDC commodity exporters.

Various factors thus conspire to dampen the demand of OECD countries for primary products. Changes in the structure of demand and output, technological progress and agricultural protectionism are among the factors that have produced the steep decline in OECD consumption of these commodities relative to incomes illustrated in Figure 2.2. This is why we suggested earlier that there is a tendency for income elasticities – already low for many items – to decline. But while this decline in elasticities does weaken the link between OECD levels of activity and demand for primary products, that link remains powerful enough to mean that the slower OECD growth of recent years has compounded the weakness of demand.

The Supply Side

The tendency to over-supply

With prices drifting down, why does this not bring about a correction by discouraging production? One explanation is that there are strong pressures on LDCs to increase their production of primary products. The acute balance of payments pressure experienced by many of the exporting countries is one of the most potent. The world economic environment has become much less favourable for most LDCs during the last fifteen years. Many of them have run into acute shortages of foreign exchange owing to both a deteriorating balance of payments and burgeoning debt service obligations. 'Adjustment' programmes have been widely adopted, often in conjunction with the IMF and World Bank, and these have generally advised a strategy of export promotion. At the same time, avenues for the promotion of non-primary exports have been narrowed by increased protectionism in the OECD countries and by the successes of some of the early 'newly-industrializing countries'.

Faced with such a dilemma, an LDC government may regard the promotion of commodity exports as still the best option available to it, as indeed it might be were other governments not simultaneously making similar decisions. Thus, the Fund and Bank have been criticized for committing a 'fallacy of composition' by encouraging many individual LDCs into an essentially self-defeating process of export-led competitive adjustment (of which devaluation is a common ingredient). Their reply is that they are now paying more attention to food production and import substitution – and to ask, in any case, what else can they do in present-day conditions? Whatever the answer to that, balance of payments adjustment pressures surely help to explain the observed tendency to over-supply. And there remains a danger that LDCs seeking to adjust through the promotion of traditional exports are investing in decline.

A further factor helping to explain the downward movement of prices is that typically price elasticities of *supply* for primary products are small, especially in the short run. This means that even a small fall in demand will induce a large fall in price. In the short run the response of supplies to a fall in demand may be negligible, so that all the burden falls on prices. Estimates of short-term supply elasticities produce results of near-zero for the mining industries and values of 0.2 to 0.4 for other commodity groups. Even long-term elasticities are well below 1.0, generally in the range 0.3 to 0.8. For many products the time lags are lengthy and one of the factors in the commodities slump of the 1980s has been the delayed response of supply to good prices enjoyed in the mid and later 1970s.

The biotech revolution
Just as technological advances are affecting the demand for commodities, so developments in biotechnology are also threatening the competitiveness of traditional LDC producers. Two different techniques are being developed which between them may revolutionize farming. *Tissue culture* allows tissues and individual cells to be isolated and bred into whole plants, enormously accelerating the breeding of new varieties and hence greatly enlarging the possibilities of incorporating desirable characteristics such as disease resistance. *Genetic engineering* appears to offer even greater possibilities, for it enables a breeder to isolate desired genetic characteristics from one cell and incorporate them in another, opening up the possibility of changing the genetic characteristics of living matter.

Unilever has used tissue culture to reduce the time necessary to develop oil palm varieties to one-thirtieth of the previous time; the results have already raised average yields from new trees by 30 per cent; the expectation is that it will not be too long before yields are two to six times those obtained by older varieties, threatening the position of traditional cultivators and the producers of rival vegetable oil crops such as groundnuts and coconuts. Second, an American chemical firm has finished the first trials of a 'supertomato' which has resistance to parasites, viruses and herbicides built into it. It should soon be possible to extend these characteristics to tobacco, sugar beet and others.

One difficulty for LDC producers in these developments is that almost all biotech research is being conducted in the industrial countries, much of it now by private companies, so that a significant agricultural technology gap is opening up. With commercially-developed advances being subjected to the restrictions of patent laws, there is a danger that most commercial applications will arise in the industrial countries or be applied by multinationals based in them. It is already a feature of these developments that they rely for their commercial exploitation on very sophisticated methods of farming.

Relatedly, there is now the possibility of crops grown in the tropics being replaced by the output of factories in the West. Sugar and cocoa butter are currently being researched for factory production, as are tobacco and pyrethrum. The Soviet Union as well as Western European countries are busy developing a technique for producing protein from a petroleum base for animal feeds in factories to replace imports of soya beans, fish meal and cassava from various LDCs.

For those countries able to take advantage of these biotech advances there are large potential benefits to be secured from the higher productivities and lower costs. From the LDC viewpoint the dangers are that a high proportion of the applications will occur within, or to the benefit of, the industrial countries and that traditional producers which cannot keep pace with the technological advances will find themselves unable to compete, with devastating effects on their export earnings and economic prospects.

CONSEQUENCES

While it is obvious that the adverse trends described above will harm the economic prospects of commodity-exporting LDCs, it is necessary to trace the changing pattern of world trade in order to identify the consequences in more detail. Here it is important to recall that we are confining ourselves to *non-oil* commodities.

The Changing Pattern of Trade

Primary products make up a diminishing proportion of world trade; their share of world merchandise exports fell from 30 per cent in 1966–67 to 17 per cent in 1983–84. Within the primary products grouping, the share of food rose somewhat over the same period at the expense of agricultural raw materials, while minerals and metals roughly maintained their share.

The proportion of commodity exports produced by LDCs has also declined. Between 1966–67 and 1983–84 the share of LDCs in commodity exports fell from 33.9 per cent to 30.3 per cent, with a rather greater increase by the developed countries and a decline by Eastern European countries. Among developing countries, Asia has had the best export performance, having slightly increased its market share; the performance of Africa has been particularly weak, with a decline from 8.8 per cent to 4.9 per cent of world exports during the period 1966/67 to 1983/84, partly reflecting the stagnation of agriculture in many African countries during the period.

A rising proportion of raw materials produced in developing countries

Table 2.1 *Developing country dependence on primary product exports 1982–84*

Primary product exports as % of total exports	All LDCs	Low-income LDCs
Above 75%	48 (33%)	21 (47%)
50–75%	36 (25%)	11 (24%)
25–50%	24 (17%)	9 (20%)
Below 25%	37 (26%)	4 (9%)
Totals	145 (100%)	45 (100%)

Source: UNCTAD
Note: Figures are averages.

is being processed prior to export, so that the statistics on (unprocessed) commodity trade somewhat understate the value of this trade to LDCs; there were major increases in proportions processed in LDCs between the early 1960s and early 1980s for such items as cocoa, bauxite, phosphate rock and tin, and a general shift in metals production from industrial to developing countries. This development helps to explain the decline that is occurring in the importance of primary products in total LDC exports. Between 1973 and 1985 the share of commodities in total LDC exports fell from 38 per cent to 21 per cent, while the contribution of manufactured exports went up from 22 per cent to 34 per cent. Asia was particularly successful also in this expansion of industrial exports. Nevertheless, commodity exports remain crucially important for many LDCs, as Table 2.1 illustrates.

At the same time, the proportion of commodities entering LDCs as imports has been increasing, from 15 per cent in 1973 to 21 per cent in 1985. Indeed, the Third World has been the most rapidly expanding market for commodities; and there has been a major expansion in this type of South–South trade. And while observers in prosperous industrial countries may talk of a satiation of demand for metal-intensive consumer durables, the potential demand for such goods in Asia and elsewhere remains enormous. Increased South–South trade is probably an important way in which commodity markets will develop in future.

Balance of Payments Effects

Given the wide variations in the importance of commodities in developing-country exports, the influence differed greatly between countries, and it is easy to exaggerate the overall impact. According to one estimate, for example, for oil-importing LDCs as a whole, a 10 per cent decline in real commodity prices only results, on average, in a 3 per cent worsening in their overall terms of trade (an index of the prices of all their exports relative to the prices of all their imports). Country-level studies find great differences and emphasize the dangers of broad generalizations. It is agreed, however, that the impact on the low-income LDCs is dispropor-tionately severe because of their particular dependence on primary pro-ducts.

While it is difficult to calculate exactly, the magnitude of losses from the price falls of the 1980s has undoubtedly been great. Controversial UNCTAD estimates for all LDCs show a total loss from 1981 to 1986 of $42 *billions* when compared with average prices in 1979–80 – an amount equivalent to 40 per cent of their commodity earnings in the initial period. For the least developed the situation was even worse, with losses equiva-lent to 75 per cent of annual 1979–80 earnings. These figures probably exaggerate the true loss, but nobody disputes that the total cost has been very high.

In fact, the adverse price trend goes far to explain the worsening in LDC balance of payments deficits in the 1980s, as well as the emergence of the debt problem. For the countries of Africa and Latin America particularly, shortages of foreign exchange – partly the result of commodity price trends – have become the chief obstacles to resumed economic growth and development. Indeed, there have been major income falls in both regions. The deteriorating payments position has starved local industries of imported inputs and contributed directly to falling living standards; it has curtailed investment because of inability to import capital goods; it has reduced government revenues and exacerbated budgetary problems; it has depressed economic activity and employment. This situation and the need for associated adjustment programmes have imposed major economic and social costs, not least upon the poor.[3]

Policies which were able to reverse the downward drift of commodity prices would similarly add to LDCs' import capacities and thus help them to escape the foreign exchange constraint. Amex Bank has estimated, for example, that a return of prices simply to what they describe as the long-run average would raise import capacity by nearly a fifth.

IMPLICATIONS FOR LDC POLICIES

How ought LDC exporters to respond to the situation described in this chapter? Firmly-based policy choices are almost impossible in the face of the great uncertainties with which LDCs are confronted. Future structural change and growth in the OECD economies, and the pace and effects of technological developments, are particularly important and unpredictable factors. Nevertheless, policy decisions do have to be made and the key choice is about the extent to which it is prudent to invest major new resources in traditional export commodities. Governments and potential investors will note that there is an absence of optimism among the forecasters. There is still much scope for substitution away from traditional materials, for example of ceramics for metals in engines. There remains a tendency to over-investment in mining and the metals industries. Many of these industries survive economically by treating past investments as 'sunk costs' and thus do not require revenues to cover these costs and yield a return upon them, whereas new investments cannot be made on that basis. The Northern-based biotech revolution may bring important shifts in the global distribution of comparative advantage in agricultural products, to the disadvantage of the South.

Investment decisions on these matters tend to be made atomistically, by individual investors or governments who do not take into account decisions in other countries about investments in the same range of products. Balance of payments and adjustment pressures push each of them hard in favour of expanding capacity, with an aggregate effect on supply and thus price which prevent these investments from yielding adequate returns. Thus, the aggregated effect of the World Bank's country and project desk officers' assumptions about output and prices for primary products has in the past sometimes been inconsistent with the view taken by the Bank's commodities specialists – and has been strongly biased in an optimistic direction.

One policy alternative is to compensate for unfavourable prices by measures to raise productivities and lower costs, thus maintaining profitability. The danger, of course, is that many of the benefits of high productivities would be reflected in yet lower prices, thus raising once again the question whether productivity-improving investments would offer an adequate rate of return. On the other hand, LDCs certainly cannot afford to allow all the R&D work to be done in the West or in Western-based multinationals, especially in the area of biotechnology. A stronger set of policies in this area is needed.

Taking this line of thought further, a possible strategy, for products where LDCs and DCs are in competition, would be for LDC exporters to pursue aggressive cost-reducing, price-lowering policies to try to out-compete the DCs, as has already been happening for some of the metals. It is also important that LDCs keep a very close watch on the important economic changes now being initiated in the Soviet Union and other centrally planned countries, and seek to influence the design of the reforms so as to create new trade openings for themselves. The potential additional demand, especially for the products of tropical agriculture, remains great in most of these countries.

Decisions whether or not to invest in new (or rehabilitated) commodities capacity can only, of course, be taken in the light of what alternatives might be available. To simplify, three broad possibilities can be identified: to diversify exports from traditional into 'new' primary products; to diversify exports out of unprocessed commodities altogether, concentrating instead on manufactures and services (including tourism, and the processing of products previously exported as primaries) and to concentrate more on import-substitution, including the promotion of greater food self-sufficiency. These are not, of course, mutually exclusive but it is significant that the 1987 Geneva UNCTAD VII conference took a gloomy view of medium-term prospects for commodity prices and placed some stress on the 'horizontal and vertical diversification of (LDC) economies, as well as increased participation in the processing, marketing and distribution, including transportation, of their commodities ...'

The range of realistic options is greater for some LDCs than others, however, and the 'best' policies will vary from case to case. As a broad generalization, LDCs which already have some established manufacturing base have considerably more room for manoeuvre than countries whose output remains strongly based on agriculture and mining. And large countries generally face less acute difficulties than small ones, if only because the balance of payments gap is smaller relative to total economic activity. Those in the most unenviable position are the least developed countries with, typically, little of an industrial base and strictly limited scope for import-substituting manufacturing. As noted above, technological dependence on the North, and on Northern-based companies, is a further factor limiting the room for manoeuvre, particularly in agriculture.

There should be scope too for measures to expand South–South trade in commodities. As mentioned earlier, developing countries have already emerged as the most rapidly expanding market for metals and some other products and there is considerable scope for further expansion. There are also formidable obstacles, however. One of these is the high levels of protection which LDCs often afford their own farmers. Another is the inadequacy of the supporting international infrastructure for the encouragement of such trade, including transportation, insurance and export finance.

IMPLICATIONS FOR INTERNATIONAL POLICIES

What can the international community do if the downward trend in real commodity prices persists? Historically, much of the concern has been with the *stabilization* of prices, that is strictly, the reduction of fluctuations around the trend. The classical devices of International Commodity Agreements (ICAs) and compensatory finance schemes designed primarily to reduce, or offset, price instability are not well suited to coping with long-run decline, although the EEC's compensatory finance scheme, Stabex, does have potential for that purpose.

It would, however, be possible to link such mechanisms – and UNCTAD's Common Fund, intended principally to finance ICAs – to schemes for financing the development of new uses for commodities, greater LDC participation in the processing, marketing and distribution of commodities, and the diversification of output. The so-called Window II of the Common Fund has precisely these objectives and it is likely that, operationally, much of the Fund's work will focus on such activities. Financial support for such programmes would, however, amount to development aid and not all donors will think that much aid should be allocated solely on the basis of primary product dependence.

Improved market access and *reduced protection* by industrial countries could bring major benefits to LDC exporters, and much interest will thus attach to the outcome of the 'Uruguay Round' GATT talks.[4] Of special interest will be whether the negotiations succeed in reducing the pervasive escalation of tariffs and non-tariff barriers according to stage of production which discourages processing in the country of origin.

More fundamentally, can it be in the interests of the industrial countries not to reform a system which starves LDCs of the foreign exchange they would use to buy their exports? Measures to stimulate growth and avoid recession in the OECD countries would, of course, be highly beneficial to commodity markets but, given past experience are unlikely to be adopted simply for this reason. The aid community should be more cautious about urging the inclusion of potentially price-depressing, and hence self-defeating, investments for expanded commodity production in adjustment programmes.

NOTES

1. This chapter is a modified version of an Overseas Development Institute Briefing Paper, March 1988.
2. For a fuller discussion of this topic in relation to the EEC see 'The CAP and its Impact on the Third World', ODI Briefing Paper, June 1986.
3. See 'Adjusting to Recession: will the poor recover?', ODI Briefing Paper, November 1986, revised February 1988.
4. See 'The GATT Uruguay Round', ODI Briefing Paper, November 1987.

QUESTIONS FOR DISCUSSION

1. Why is it that not all commodity prices move together?
2. Explain the pattern of commodity prices shown in Figure 2.1.
3. In what ways do commodity prices serve to transmit booms and slumps from the First to the Third World?
4. Discuss the principal demand-side factors which influence commodity prices. Explain how certain influences may be more important in the case of some commodities than others.
5. In what way might export expansion by developing countries prove self-defeating?
6. What policies, if any, would be appropriate should the downward trend in real commodity prices persist?

3. Oil Prices – an Economic Framework for Analysis

Paul Stevens

THE BACKGROUND

For the past thirty years at least, crude oil and its products have been the largest single item in international trade in terms of both volume and value[1]. Energy prices in general (which are crucially influenced by oil prices) account for a significant slice of expenditure at a household, business and national level. For oil importers, the price is an important factor in determining the health of the current account of the balance of payments. For many Third World countries, revenues from oil exports represent their major source of foreign exchange, and this has a crucial influence both on their prospects for growth and development, and on their ability to service huge overseas debts. This in turn influences the health of the international financial system. The price of oil and expectations about the price strongly influence decisions to invest billions of pounds in energy projects all over the world. Finally, the price of oil will influence the rate at which various energy forms are burnt, and this will influence the rate of global environmental degradation. In short, oil prices are an important international variable.

On a more parochial basis, oil prices also matter to the UK economy. The explosion of oil prices in the 1970s made feasible the development of North Sea oil. Previous prices had been below the costs of finding and developing oil fields in such a hostile environment. Becoming an oil producer had many effects upon the UK economy although their significance remains controversial. It provided relief for balance of payments pressures, but also (some would argue) delayed structural changes in the economy essential to face the realities of the last two decades. It provided important sources of revenue for the government which was instrumental in allowing the initiation of a strategy of tax cutting in the 1980s. Many would argue that it led in the early 1980s to a gross overvaluation of the sterling exchange rate which led to a process of de-industrialization. The future prospects for North Sea development, the advancement or

21

Table 3.1 Oil prices

	Price ($) per barrel
1860	9.59
1880	0.95
1900	1.19
1920	3.07
1940	1.02
1950	1.71
1960	1.55
1970	1.25
1974	11.65
1981	34.00
1985	27.30
1986	13.44
1987	17.40
1988	13.54

Source: Gilbert Jenkins, (1989), *Oil Economists Handbook*. 5th edition, London: Elsevier Applied Science. Table 1.1

Notes: 1. For dates before 1950, the US price is quoted; 1950–1988 figures are Middle East prices.
2. Conventionally, oil is always priced in US dollars. Oil is not a homogeneous product. It is a product differentiated by its chemical characteristics. Different types of crude will refine into different proportions of products (more or less petrol, fuel oil and so on) and hence produce different values. For this reason the price is only a guide price. There is no such amount as *the* oil price, merely a structure of differentiated prices.

retrenchment of the current nuclear programme and a number of other key issues are all crucially linked to future oil prices.

The importance of oil prices has been justified mainly in macro-economic terms. However, as a 'price' it will be treated here as a micro-economic issue with macro overtones. Like any other price it can be analysed in the context of a demand and supply framework which enables us to identify and consider the many influences at work on oil prices. This allows us to explain the observable trends in oil prices over a long period of time.

Such an approach may be less useful to explain the short term dramatic changes in price which have become known as the Oil Shocks. Some would argue that this is because the Shocks were triggered by political events. The First Oil Shock of 1973 was launched by the Arab–Israeli war; the Second Oil Shock of 1979–81 followed the Iranian Revolution and the Third Oil Shock of 1986 was triggered by decisions within the government of Saudi Arabia. The argument then continues that political events cannot figure in supply and demand analysis. This is not true. Both demand and supply involve the notion of willingness and ability. Willingness has a political dimension. A desire for energy self sufficiency (a political motive) if acted upon will shift the demand curve for oil to the left. A desire to reduce the culturally damaging effects of access to large scale oil revenues will shift the supply curve to the left. There is a more plausible explanation of the limitations of supply and demand analysis to explain short term fluctuations in prices. As will be explained, perceptions and expectations are a crucial ingredient in determining oil price. Such beasts are notoriously difficult to capture with any precision although both implicitly underlie demand and supply curves[2].

THE DEMAND FOR CRUDE OIL

Of the two broad determinants of oil price, this is the dullest. The demand for crude oil and its products is a derived demand. Therefore, as well as being influenced by the expected determinants of price, income and so on, it is also in the short run crucially influenced by the size and nature of the stock of energy-burning appliances which use oil. If there were no petrol-burning engines, free petrol would face a zero demand until someone could invent an alternative use for it. The number of energy-burning appliances, their ability to convert energy into light, miles per gallon and so on, and the extent to which the capacity is utilized, determine the demand. In the short term, apart from behaviour with respect to capacity use (that is, driving fewer miles less quickly; turning down thermostats and so on), this leaves very limited flexibility on use. The pattern of demand is illustrated in Table 3.2. This shows energy consumption, which is the amount people were actually willing and able to buy, given prices and the other non-price determinants of demand.

Characteristics of demand can be picked up in the elasticities. The own price elasticity of demand for most oil products in the short run is inelastic, reflecting the fact that it is a necessity with limited substitutes. Technically, much substitution is possible, but an oil-fired power station can only be converted to burn coal at considerable expense over a period of time. In the longer run, greater elasticity is possible as the current stock of energy-using appliances can be replaced by ones which have a greater conversion efficiency or use different fuels. This may take a lot of time, perhaps a number of years to develop new fuel-efficient car engines or aerodynamic car bodies. The managerial decision to change car design and retool can itself take several years. Finally, assuming an average life for a car of ten years, each year only one-tenth of the car stock is turned over to more fuel-efficient cars.

Table 3.2   World commercial energy consumption

	1925	1950	1965	1975	1985
Total consumption (BBOE)	7.67	13.51	27.30	42.81	53.07
Source (%)					
Solid fuel	80.9	56.8	35.8	25.6	27.4
Oil	14.3	29.7	41.3	47.1	39.6
Gas	2.4	8.1	14.8	17.8	20.1
Other*	2.4	5.4	8.1	9.5	12.9

Source: Shell Briefing Service. Energy in Profile 1986 and Energy in Perspective 1977.

Notes: BBOE Billion barrels of oil equivalent
   * Mainly hydro and nuclear

Income elasticity for energy, at least prior to the Oil Shocks of the 1970s, was elastic. Growth of output and the economic development associated with higher incomes tended to be energy intensive. The richer the society, the more commercial energy was required[3]. The result, as can be seen from Table 3.2, was that energy demand grew rapidly.

Cross price elasticities of demand for oil products *vis à vis* other energy sources helps explain why gradually, (as is clear from Table 3.2) oil began to dominate the energy scene. In some areas, notably air and road transport, there are no close substitutes for oil products[4]. In these cases the cross elasticity, although positive, would be very low. In other uses such as the generation of electricity, there are a number of alternative substitutes including gas, coal, hydro and nuclear. Here the cross price elasticities would be positive and greater than one. As with the own price coefficient, elasticity rises over time. The rise in importance of oil in the energy market can be explained largely in terms of the declining real price of oil in relation to other forms of energy[5].

It is easy to conceptualize about the various elasticities, but difficult to come up with actual empirical estimates. The reason is a classic problem of partial equilibrium analysis which underlies the standard supply and demand exercise. In analysis it is possible to isolate variables and their effects by use of the 'other things being equal' assumption. In the real world the assumption cannot hold. After the First Oil Shock, many economists attempted to come up with an empirical measure of own price elasticity to explain the fall in the amount of oil used. However, it proved impossible to disentangle the effects of the higher price (own price elasticity), from the effects of the worldwide economic recession which followed the First Oil Shock (income elasticity) and the effects of fuel switching (cross price elasticities).

THE SUPPLY OF CRUDE OIL

This is a much more interesting subject than demand. It involves politics sometimes on a scale that makes Machiavelli look like Noddy. It involves the behaviour of oil company moguls and entrepreneurs who make television programmes such as Dallas look like Sunday school. Supplying oil is a rough, tough and extremely dangerous industry. It is also a good example of how simple economics can bring order and understanding to a horrendously complex subject. Three economic-based characteristics of oil have dominated the supply side of the industry since the first well was drilled in 1859. These are an overcapacity to produce crude oil, a very low marginal cost to produce crude oil and finally a crude oil industry with an oligopolistic structure. Before describing the consequences of these three factors when they meet in the market place, let me elaborate on each in turn.

Excess capacity to produce crude oil was created and maintained for a number of reasons. The first and most obvious point is that crude oil is hidden underground. A refiner who processes x million barrels cannot decide in the boardroom to find x million barrels. All that can be decided is to explore. They may find more than x or less than x. Capacity cannot be discovered to order. However, in theory it can be developed to order since that is an investment decision based upon reasonable knowledge of how much oil is in place. The second reason for overcapacity arises because oil is a fluid. Because oil can flow in three-dimensional space, it is subject to enormous economies of scale[6]. Because of this, oil producing, transporting, refining and distribution facilities are all highly capital intensive activities. Hence fixed costs represent a very high proportion of total costs. If capacity throughput of a refinery is below optimum, then these very high fixed costs are spread over a lower output. Average fixed costs rise and profitability declines exponentially. In such a situation the refiner must be assured of a secure supply of oil for his refinery. Operation below capacity severely impairs profitability. This encourages the securing of owned supplies of crude oil and transportation. In other words the operation becomes vertically integrated. It also encourages, as insurance, development of more supplies of crude oil than refining capacity requires. It is cheaper to store oil in its original underground reservoirs than above ground, hence excess capacity to produce is developed. Finally, excess capacity can be explained by a desire to prevent competitors gaining access to crude oil in the hope of limiting their ability to compete. At first sight, a refiner with access to more crude oil than currently required for refining would not seek further supplies. But if acreage became available for exploration there would be a temptation to take the acreage in the hope that oil discovered could be kept off the market and away from other refiners who might be short of oil. This was a major factor for the scramble for oil supplies before the Second World War. Taken together, all these factors meant that apart from a few occasions there was always a potential oversupply of crude oil.

The second characteristic of a very low marginal cost of production follows from the capital intensity of the industry already explained. Low variable cost equals low marginal cost, since in the short run the two are synonyms. To give some idea of the orders of magnitude, average total production costs vary throughout the world depending upon the hostility of the environment plus the size of the fields. Costs vary from a few dollars in parts of the Middle East to well over $10–15 per barrel in places like the North Sea. Variable costs however, are measured in terms of cents per barrel, since even costs normally regarded as variable such as labour costs are generally contracted and so may not vary with output in the short run. The significance of low marginal costs is that in the short run, the profit maximizer/loss minimizer will produce if marginal revenue exceeds marginal costs. Thus low marginal costs point to an inherent tendency to oversupply.[7]

The final key characteristic of supply is an oligopolistic structure. Until the 1970s, the international industry was dominated by the so-called Seven Majors,[8] of which three had derived from the legally enforced break up of the Standard Oil Trust in the USA in 1911, consequent upon the Sherman anti-trust legislation. The oligopolistic structure arose because the industry favoured large scale companies. This reflected the capital intensity, vertical integration and international nature of their operations. Bigness also provided barriers to entry, encouraged by technical barriers to entry arising from the complexity of the engineering (further enhanced by capital intensity). It also encouraged predatory behaviour. In the US, the Standard Oil Trust at the height of its power controlled over a third of US crude output, 85 per cent of US refinery thoughput and virtually all of the major pipelines in the US. Internationally, the picture was similar. In 1950 the Seven Majors owned 85 per cent of the world oil production, excluding North America and the Communist Bloc (WOCANA), 72 per cent of WOCANA refinery capacity, nearly 70 per cent of privately owned tankers and *all* the important pipelines! In the early 1970s, the oil producing governments took over much of the oil operations from the oil companies through nationalization. Thus the companies' oligopoly in crude oil was replaced by a government oligopoly. By 1978, of the 31.5 million barrels per day exported from WOCA (world outside communist area) countries, 70 per cent came from just six countries.

THE MARKET PLACE

Economic theory suggests that an excess capacity to produce, plus very low marginal costs in an oligopolistic structure would lead to price wars and a general collapse of prices. It would always be relatively profitable to push out the extra barrel. If you didn't, someone else would. After 1928, apart from the odd occasion however, such price wars did not happen. This absence of continual intense price competition requires an explanation. It lies in the creation and operation of a series of control mechanisms to contain the excess supply. The whole history of the international industry can be written in terms of these control mechanisms.

Prior to 1928 the industry performed according to the theory and was hit by a succession of price wars. The solution was the classic answer to oligopolistic uncertainty – cartelization. In 1928, during yet another price war the heads of three of the main competitors – BP, Exxon and Shell[9] – met in the Scottish Castle of Achnacarry (for a weekend of shooting!) and there they hammered out an agreement, subsequently joined by the other majors, to carve up the world oil market between them. It was an explicit cartel agreement aimed at securing the status quo. The Achnacarry agreement, reflecting this, is often called the 'as is' agreement. The agreement did not become public until the early 1950s, courtesy of the US Senate Committee hearings.

Price stability was based upon what became known as the Gulf Plus system. Before World War II, all oil trade was in products. This reflects a classic example of the economics of factory location. For example, a major reason for transporting products (that is, locating refineries on the oil fields) was that primitive refining lost a great deal of crude. All products outside the USA were priced as though they had been purchased on the Gulf of Mexico and shipped from that point. If they had been purchased from a cheaper source and/or shipped from a nearer destination then a phantom freight rate was added to equalize the landed cost of the product. During the Second World War, the British and American navies began to object to this practice since they were fuelling their warships at the Abadan Refinery in the Persian Gulf (where products were much cheaper than the US) and paying for it as though it had been shipped from the Gulf of Mexico. In response, the oil companies were forced to agree to introduce a second basing point at Abadan. This created two separate international markets surrounded by price watersheds, one supplied from the Gulf of Mexico and one from the Persian Gulf. Given the much lower production costs for crude oil in the Middle East the latter market expanded and the former contracted.

In the 1950s and 1960s, explicit cartels such as the Achnacarry Agreement were no longer acceptable behaviour. However, by then, the international oil industry had in place two control mechanisms which made explicit cartel agreements redundant. The first which we have already explained is that the industry was vertically integrated. This had two consequences. First it meant that there was no international market price for crude oil. Most crude oil was transferred between affiliates of the same company at a transfer price which was set as far as possible to minimize the global tax bill.[10] Vertical integration also meant that crude producers tended to produce only enough for their own refinery needs and not produce a surplus for sale at arms length in an open market.

The second control mechanism was joint ownership of crude supply – a form of horizontal integration. In the Middle East, which was becoming increasingly important in the oil trade, oil was produced by a number of companies. They were owned jointly by various combinations of the major oil companies. This had originally arisen largely because of pressure from the US and France to include their oil companies in developments in areas under British mandate, but partly also because of attempts by companies to absorb very large finds of crude oil into the international market without upsetting the supply balance. If a company found much more oil than it needed it would take as a partner a company which needed crude oil. This joint ownership had two effects. It meant that the major companies were immediately aware if one of their number attempted to cheat by lifting more oil to gain market share. This was because they all sat round the same table when production decisions were made. One of the great problems of oligopoly – uncertainty over rivals' response – had been eliminated. The second effect of joint ownership was that by means of the agreements under which crude oil was produced, the other companies could stop overlifting or at least make it economically unattractive. This solved the two great problems of all cartels – the ability to detect and the ability to deter cheating.

The system worked well, although in the 1960s an increasing number of new sources of crude oil were produced which were outside of these controlling mechanisms. Thus oversupply began to emerge, a crude oil market began to develop, and market prices weakened. This trend was shattered by the First Oil Shock of 1973 followed by the Second Oil Shock of 1979–81. The reasons behind these huge rises in price are complex. They are concerned with a fascinating interaction of economic forces and politics and require a story too long to be told here.

However, they can be summed up in the following way. In the 1950s and 1960s, the price of oil was an administered price set by the companies. Their sole right to set prices was jealously guarded. Between 1970 and 1973, the companies were forced to accept government involvement by oil-producing countries (at first individually and then collectively with OPEC, the Organization of Petroleum Exporting Countries) to set these prices in negotiations. In October 1973, the countries refused to negotiate and moved to a position of unilaterally setting price. Since then, the price of oil has been what it was (and is) because a group of individuals meeting in a room have stated a number, and enough people outside the room believed it.

This is all a far cry from notions of the intersection of supply and demand curves on a neat diagram. However, once the number had been set, supply and demand created the environment in which the price (or the belief in the price) had to be maintained. The normal state of affairs was pressure from the excess capacity to oversupply. After the First Oil Shock, this trend reasserted itself. The controlling mechanism of vertical integration remained but that of horizontal integration had gone, as the producing governments nationalized the producing companies in their countries.[11] It was replaced by Saudi Arabia taking up the role of swing producer in a dominant producer oligopoly. Thus imbalances between supply and demand were made up by Saudi Arabia absorbing the glut (reducing its production) or shortage (increasing its production).

We can now resume our story in October 1981 when OPEC (the 'individuals in the room') had set the price at $34 and those outside the room believed them. At this point, the problem of excess supply began to reassert itself with a vengeance. This was aggravated by the response to the higher prices of the 1970s. Both supply and demand responded in classic fashion, reflecting long term elasticity. Non-OPEC supply increased and the quantity of oil demanded fell. Demand for OPEC oil, effectively treated as the residual supplier, fell steeply. The only control mechanism now in place – the Saudi swing role – was proving insufficient and so for the first time (aside from a limited attempt in the mid 1960s) OPEC introduced production controls and became an explicit cartel.[12] In this role, OPEC faced two problems. The first was the classic cartel problem of cheating. It was always tempting for members to produce a few extra barrels. This is especially understandable when it is remembered that almost without exception, the OPEC members were (and are) poor Third World countries. The second problem faced by OPEC was a lack of information about supply and demand in the market. The importance of this was that OPEC was setting not only the quantity but *also* the price. The only way price and quantity could be set was if the precise point on the demand curve was known.

In the event, OPEC continued to produce more oil than the market wanted. Division of the production level into individual quotas was always contentious with everyone wanting more. If there is dispute over sharing the cake, then the bigger the cake, the easier it is to resolve disputes. Thus OPEC regularly set the total production level too high for demand, given price. Also, cheating was commonplace. While Saudi Arabia was willing to retain its swing role, cheating and error could be absorbed and the price structure held at $27–28 per barrel. However, the 'swing' was all in one direction to absorb more oil than the market wanted. Saudi Arabian production shrank. In the summer of 1985, Saudi Arabia announced it had had enough and was no longer prepared to act as swing producer. Furthermore they switched to market related prices rather than the officially administered price structure. In December 1985, OPEC put out an apparently innocuous statement that they would seek a 'fair share' of the market. The oil market interpreted that as a declaration of price war and within weeks, to everyone's shock, crude oil was trading at $8 per barrel and less. The people outside the room no longer believed.

After the price collapse of 1986, Saudi Arabia under pressure from the United States[13] changed its policy back (in October 1986) to one of defence of a price structure at $18 per barrel. This has resulted in considerable fluctuations, but oil since has averaged around the $16 per barrel level.

The future of oil prices can be divined from the framework developed. It will depend upon the effectiveness of OPEC as the control mechanism, or if OPEC were to collapse, on whatever control mechanisms replaced it.[14] This will depend upon the call on OPEC supplies, which will in turn be determined by what happens to the demand for energy in general, and oil in particular, and also by the supply of non-OPEC energy. The issue is very much one of economic analysis. Government policies will be of importance in terms of factors such as domestic pricing policies for energy or government need for oil revenues. Both supply and demand curves will shift under the pressures of economic, technical and political variables. Which way they will shift and how this translates into price remains an endless source of contention.

NOTES

1. Recently, it has been claimed that the international 'trade' in drugs (heroin, cocaine and so on) now exceeds that of crude oil in value terms. Problems of measuring the volume or value of such an illegal trade make verification of this claim impossible.

2. In the mid 1980s, a London trading firm had been caught out trading in the futures market for oil. Without a sudden increase in oil price, the firm stood to lose millions. The firm started a rumour (completely unfounded) in the City of London that Sheik Yamani (the Saudi Arabian minister of oil) had been assassinated. Within 24 hours, the price of oil rose significantly.

3. This statement requires many qualifications. For example, if traditional energy sources such as wood-based fuel or animal and vegetable residues (all widely used as fuel in the Third World) are included, most Third World countries are more energy intensive per dollar of output than industrialized countries. This simply reflects the very poor energy conversion associated with such traditional energy. In a simple fireplace less than 10 per cent of the heat produced actually heats the pan.

4. It is possible to run cars on non-oil based products such as chicken excrement. However, widespread switching to such fuels would require a lot of work, not least by the chickens.

5. The price advantage to oil is understated by simply looking at the price per unit of energy input. The ease of handling oil because it is a flowing liquid, plus the higher energy conversion efficiencies of oil-burning appliances set the actual end user cost per unit of useful energy well below those of substitutes in the period before 1973.

6. For example, the capital cost of a tank is a function of surface area, but the output (that is, capacity) is a function of volume. An exponential relationship exists between the two. If you have an enclosed tank measuring $2 \times 2 \times 2$ feet and increase it to a tank measuring $4 \times 4 \times 4$ the surface area has increased from 24 to 96 sq. ft, that is, capital cost increases by a factor of 4. Volume however has increased from 8 to 64 cubic feet. In other words, the 'value' of output has increased by a factor of 8.

7. For natural resources such as oil which are depletable, the production decision is complicated by the fact that costs and revenues incurred and gained today cannot be incurred or gained tomorrow and vice versa. Thus it is necessary to compare them over time.

8. To give them their modern names they were BP, Exxon, Gulf (taken over in 1984 by Socal), Mobil, Shell, Socal (Chevron) and Texaco. Sometimes, the French company CFP is included.

9. For convenience I am using their modern names rather than their names in 1928.

10. If the crude producing country had an easier tax regime than the country where the refinery was located, transfer prices were set to minimize refinery profits and give them all to the producing affiliate. In this period, few oil refineries in Europe made profits, yet new ones were being built at an increasing rate.

11. Vertical integration remained because although the governments now decided on production levels, the companies retained their crude oil marketing role at the request of the governments.

12. Whether OPEC in the 1970s was or was not a cartel is controversial. In my opinion because it did not set production and only rarely set price (other times price was set by Saudi Arabia) it was not a cartel.

13. Very low oil prices created a real problem for the United States. First, because it meant some oil producing governments might renege on their foreign debts, thus seriously damaging the US banking system who was the main creditor. Second, many US investment projects in other forms of energy would have become uneconomic at low oil prices. This would have further damaged the banking system which had lent for the projects and would have meant the USA became increasingly dependent upon oil imports. This was viewed as strategically undesirable.

14. Control mechanisms in this context are like some peoples' view of God – if they did not exist they would have to be invented.

REFERENCES

For a good straightforward and readable background to the whole issue an excellent introductory book is P. R. Odell, *Oil and World Power*, Penguin, London, eighth edition 1986.

For a more journalistic approach a highly enjoyable book (including sex, violence and dubious accounting practices) which provides a good sense of the interaction of politics and economics is A. Sampson, *The Seven Sisters – Great Oil Companies and the World They Made*, Hodder and Stoughton, Coronet, revised edition, 1988.

A useful reference source for many of the issues discussed above is P. Stevens (ed.) *The Oil and Gas Dictionary*, Macmillan, London. 1988. This excellent book is more of an encyclopedia than a simple dictionary and gives much greater detail in terms of the economics of many of the terms used above.

More statistical data about the industry can be obtained from BP, *Statistical Review of World Energy* produced annually by British Petroleum. The data contained is also available on spreadsheet disks for use with Lotus 123.

For those interested in further economic analysis of some of the issues described above the following are recommended: A. Roncaglia, *The International Oil Market*, Macmillan, London, 1985; P. Stevens, 'A Survey of Structural Change in the International Oil Industry 1945–1984', in D. Hawdon (ed), *The Changing Structure of the World Oil Industry*, Croom Helm, London, 1985, pp. 18–51; P. Stevens, 'The Price of Oil – The Prospects for the 1990s', *Natural Resources Forum*, **10**, (2), May 1986, pp. 165–72.

QUESTIONS FOR DISCUSSION

1. How might you try to disentangle the various elasticities of demand for oil to achieve some level of empirical measurement?
2. Would you agree that competition and the Gulf Plus system described above would produce the same result, that is, an equalization of landed prices?
3. How might OPEC overcome its problems as a cartel?
4. What rumour would you start (see note 2) to
   (a) increase the price of oil and
   (b) decrease the price of oil?
5. What specific factors might influence the future price of oil?
6. To what extent does economic analysis constrain the inclusion of political factors?

4. The Economics of Privatization: the Case of Electricity Supply

Colin Robinson[1]

WHY PRIVATIZE?

One of the principal driving forces behind privatization – which is a policy being followed in other countries as well as Britain – is the perceived failure of nationalization. There are few people today who would argue that nationalization in Britain has been successful, even though views differ on the relevant criteria for measuring success and on appropriate remedies. Powerful Government-created monopolies naturally formed their own objectives, based on the interests of management and workers. The lack of competition made it unlikely that those interests would be synonymous with the interests of the community at large. Such powerful monopolies, able to sway voters, were also able to sway Governments. After a brief honeymoon period, co-operative efforts (between workers and management, and between state corporations and Governments) were sadly lacking. Industrial relations were anything but harmonious. The corporations resented the constant interference from politicians which, despite Morrison's belief in an 'arms-length' relationship, seems inevitable when Government has an ill-defined responsibility for the activities of certain industries. Managerial objectives were confused by uncertainty over whether the nationalized industries should pursue 'commercial' or 'public service' aims. The public complained of bureaucracy within the corporations and failure to respond to consumers' demands. A succession of White Papers (in 1961, 1967 and 1978) did little to improve matters. Well-meaning pronouncements – such as the injunction to price on the basis of long run marginal social cost and to adopt test rates of discount comparable to those used for low-risk private sector projects – were over-ridden by the political calculus, by a lack of will within the nationalized industries and by the sheer practical difficulties of defining and putting into use such concepts of welfare economics.

Such failings in the nationalized industries are not, in themselves, suffi-cient reasons for returning those industries to the private sector. Other solutions could be tried – for instance, different forms of control, properly implemented by Government; or different forms of state ownership; or retaining the public corporations but subjecting them to more competition through imports and other means. At the other extreme from privatization, some economists would favour much tighter Government control of nationalized industries, extending in the ultimate to their direction as part of a system of central planning for all important activities.

Potential Benefits of Privatization

Doubts may be expressed about all the above solutions, but there are positive reasons to believe that a carefully executed privatization programme for many of the industries now nationalized would bring net benefits to society. The Government's privatization plan for any industry can therefore be judged by considering to what extent it is likely to realize the following potential benefits.

Wider share ownership
Provided one accepts a social organization which is essentially capitalist, there are advantages in spreading share ownership to a wide public so as to give as many members of society as possible a stake in its economic success. Nationalization gives the illusion of spreading ownership to society as a whole but in reality what is owned by everyone is perceived to be owned by no-one. Members of the public, nominal owners though they are, have no transferable property rights in nationalized corporations and no effective control of their managements. They cannot sell their shares if they believe the corporation is being mismanaged. Nor can they vote out management. In reality, the power of members of the public to influence the corporations they 'own' is so indirect as to be regarded as non-existent. Such control as exists is exercised by a small number of civil servants and politicians. Privatization, however, is capable of achieving a wider spread of true share ownership and control of management than is possible under nationalization.

Reducing waste from politicization of decision making
Under the form of nationalization practised in Britain, decision-making is highly politicized and the incentive to pursue economic efficiency, even by high-calibre management, is much less than it would be under private ownership. In the nationalized industries, as in all organizations, resources flow naturally into uses where expected returns are highest. Under nationalism, lobbying of Ministers and key civil servants and other political and quasi-political activities are seen to be potentially high return activities which occupy management time and therefore crowd out the

search for economic efficiency. Managers in nationalized industries may quite rationally conclude that time spent in persuading some key figure in Government that a particular course of action should be pursued will be more beneficial to the corporation than time spent in seeking to reduce costs. Because decision-making has been so politicized for so long in most of Britain's nationalized industries, it seems very probable that there are large efficiency gains waiting to be realized. Substitution of the incentives of the economic market place for those of the political market place seems to be a necessary (though not a sufficient) condition for those gains to be appropriated for the benefit of society.

Government revenue-raising

The sale of large corporations may raise substantial amounts of revenue for Government, with the amount depending primarily on the expected future profitability of the corporation and the probable risk attached to that return, which will be affected by the conditions of sale and the perceived probability of re-nationalization by a future Government. The proceeds can be used to reduce taxation or borrowing or to increase public spending. Provided they are used by Government in ways which bring net benefits to the community, privatization will be advantageous.

Liberalization

A significant positive benefit of privatization is that it is capable of promoting liberalization – that is, increasing competition both in the supply of the products in question and in the associated labour and capital markets, leading to increased efficiency, lower costs and prices and increased consumer choice. However, privatization will not necessarily lead to liberalization: in general, it will do so only if a nationalized monopoly is replaced by a number of competing private suppliers. There will generally be a conflict between the liberalization objective of privatization and the revenue-raising objective. A Government intent on revenue-maximization has an incentive *not* to liberalize. Selling a corporation with its monopoly power intact will make it more attractive to private investors than if it were in a competitive situation. Moreover, the sale will proceed more quickly because opposition from the corporation's management and unions is likely to be minimized if its market power is to remain untouched.

THE CASE OF ELECTRICITY SUPPLY

From Nationalization to Privatization

Nationalization of the British electric supply industry (esi) took place over forty years ago, under the Attlee Labour Government, when many 'commanding heights' of the economy were taken over by the state. In the intervening years, there have been several minor changes of structure and of name of the public corporations which run the industry. But, despite occasional suggestions for reform (mainly in the direction of increased central control),[2] there has been no substantial alteration in the structure of the industry.

In recent years, the esi in England and Wales has consisted of the Central Electricity Generating Board (CEGB), a monopoly generator also in control of long distance transmission of electricity; twelve Area Boards, which distribute electricity to consumers, as well as carrying out electrical contracting work and selling appliances; and the Electricity Council, which was established as the policy-making body of the industry. Most observers agree that the CEGB, which effectively controls most of the industry's investment spending, dominated the industry under nationalization.

The nationalized industry in Scotland was differently organized. There were two vertically integrated electricity supply companies – the North of Scotland Hydro-Electric Board (NSHEB) and the South of Scotland Electricity Board (SSEB). Each generated electricity, transported it and distributed it to consumers.

In 1986 the gas industry – a close competitor of electricity in some markets, also nationalized in the 1940s – was privatized. It was not surprising therefore, that in the Conservative Party Manifesto, the Next Move Forward, of May 1987 the government's intention to privatize electricity was announced. Two White Papers in February and March 1988 outlined the schemes for England and Wales[3] and Scotland[4]. The proposals were then turned into legislative form in the Electricity Bill of December 1988, supplemented in January 1989 by detailed draft licences for the generation, transmission and supply of electricity. Vesting day for the new companies was 1 April 1990 and flotation is scheduled for late 1990 and 1991.

The Privatization Proposals

Under the government's proposals for the industry in England and Wales, the CEGB will be divided into two generators and a transmission company. The larger generator (National Power) will have 60 per cent of existing fossil fuel capacity (excluding existing nuclear power stations). The smaller generator (PowerGen) will have the other 40 per cent of capacity. Nuclear power stations will be retained in two new state companies, one for England and Wales and one for Scotland. Long distance transmission of electricity will be in the hands of a third new company formed from the CEGB (the National Grid Company).

The government's expressed intention is to reduce generator dominance of the industry, moving away from the present 'cost-plus' arrangements which, in general, allowed the CEGB and the rest of the industry to pass on to consumers any costs they incurred. A principal aim of the privatization scheme is to give electricity distributors much more influence than they have had under nationalization. Distribution will be the responsibility of twelve supply companies, each based on an existing Area Board; they will, however, have much more extensive duties than the Area Boards which had to purchase their electricity from the CEGB and to pay whatever it charged them. The new area distributors will be able to contract for electricity with the two major generators, with other private generators, with foreign suppliers (most likely France), and with the Scottish generators. Both France and Scotland have surplus generating capacity at present: there is already a cross-Channel cable linking France and Britain with a capacity of 2000MW (about the same as a large modern coal-fired power station). The distributors will also be able to build their own generating capacity up to a limit of 15 per cent of their contracted capacity. Although the distributors will inherit the distribution systems in their areas, they will not have statutory monopolies to supply electricity in those areas; consumers will be able to contract for supplies with other distributors or (in the case of large customers) with generators, using the local distribution network to convey their supply.

In Scotland, unlike England and Wales, the industry will continue to be in the hands of two vertically integrated companies – one in the north (based on the NSHEB) with a high proportion of hydro-electric capacity, and a much larger company in the south (formed from the SSEB). There will be some reallocation of generating capacity among the two companies. The rest of this chapter concentrates on the privatization scheme for England and Wales.

For reasons explained below, the industry will be 'regulated' after privatization by the Director General of Electricity Supply who will supervise most of its activities. Price regulation will take a similar form to that for other recently privatized industries, using an $RPI - X + Y$ price formula for prices charged to smaller consumers (where RPI is the change in the retail price index, X is a percentage deduction from that change designed to squeeze the industry's costs and Y is a percentage addition for costs which can automatically be passed on).

Economic Issues in Privatizing Electricity Supply

The brief outline of the electricity privatization proposals above cannot do justice to all the complexities of what is probably the most complicated piece of privatization the government has yet attempted.[5] From an economist's point of view the principal complications arise from the 'natural monopoly' characteristics of parts of the industry. The nationalized esi was an umbrella for a number of different activities, some of which for efficiency reasons should be organized competitively, whereas others have natural monopoly elements which make them more suited to a sole supplier.

Generation is by far the biggest activity, accounting for around 80 per cent of the present industry's costs. Though it was a monopoly under nationalization there appear to be no economic reasons why that should be so. By turning it into a competitive activity it is, in principle, possible to achieve gains in productive efficiency (lower total costs) and in allocative efficiency (prices which are in closer alignment with those lower costs than they are now). One of the government's main aims in privatizing electricity supply is to inject competition into generation, in an attempt to realize these potential gains.

The other principal activity of the nationalized esi, apart from appliance sales and electrical contracting where it already worked in competition with the private sector, was the transportation of electricity to where it was needed, both over long distances (transmission) and over shorter distances (distribution). Since there appear to be efficiency advantages in having only one network of wires, transmission and distribution have natural monopoly characteristics. Although the retailing of electricity is not itself a natural monopoly activity, ownership of the national transmission system or a local distribution network places substantial monopoly power in the hands of the owner. Consequently, there is need for a means of consumer protection against monopolistic exploitation.

State ownership is one option; even though it is not in favour because of British experience with nationalization, it would have been possible to leave the natural monopoly elements of the esi in the hands of public corporations. The alternative, which the present government has adopted, is to privatize the natural monopolies but to regulate them. The National Grid Company and the electricity distributors will be obliged to allow use of their wires by third parties, their charges will be regulated and, as explained above, there will also be price regulation to protect consumers. Instead of the supervision by Ministers and civil servants which occurs under nationalization – which is exercised by such 'back door' methods as placing pressure on senior executives of the industry – the intention is to have more open and explicit regulation in which the rules of the game will presumably be clearer and operated much more in public.

Gains from Privatization

As explained above, governments have many different aims in privatizing public corporations. Revenue-raising appears to have dominated some past privatization schemes (such as British Gas) and encouraging wider share ownership is another popular political objective. Most economists, however, would argue that, whatever the political calculus may dictate, the prime aim of privatization should be to liberalize markets so as to realize the social benefits which greater competition can bring. The argument is that the generic problems of the nationalized industries result not so much from their being state-owned as from most of them being monopolies; consequently, they exhibit such characteristics as unresponsiveness to consumers' needs, lack of entrepreneurship and slowness to innovate. The way to cure these failings, it is argued, is to introduce competition. Privatization is not always necessary to inject competition: sometimes freeing entry to an industry is sufficient. But there are cases in which only by privatization can significant competition be introduced; that is probably true of the esi where the incumbent generator was so strong that past efforts to free entry did not produce any entrants.

Judging whether or not the government's electricity privatization scheme will be socially beneficial is extremely difficult at this early stage. The structure of the esi will change radically and it will take some years for the effects to become apparent. Some features of the scheme are welcome to liberal economists. For example, the attempt to introduce competition into generation; the separation of long distance transmission from generation so that the same organization does not control both; the open access provisions to the transmission and distribution systems; the more open method of regulation planned for the natural monopoly sectors; the greater power given to distributors (who are closer to consumers than electricity generators); the provision that distributors will be able to compete for customers in the areas of other distributors; and the penalties for poor service which distributors will have to pay in future.

However, whether the new arrangements provide net social benefits or not will depend, above all, on whether they actually do bring about competition. At the level of most consumers, competition is unlikely to appear. Most will still depend on their local distributor of electricity, though there may be some sales of electricity across boundaries by neighbouring distributors and larger consumers may be more inclined to shop around for power supplies from distributors or to contact direct with generators. If competition does appear, there will be downward pressure on costs and the price structure should be more reflective of those costs, providing better signals to consumers than in the past. Furthermore, regulating the industry should be a manageable problem because competition will provide much of the protection consumers need.

The emergence of genuine competition will be a function primarily of whether there is competition in generation to provide efficiency pressures in the sector of the industry where most costs are incurred and where there is most scope for competitive activity. If significant competition in generation does not appear, distributors and larger consumers will have only a limited choice of sources of supply and the new electricity supply industry could become little more than a different version of the cost-plus industry which existed under nationalization. The regulator would then have the near-impossible problem of trying to supervise all the activities of a very complex industry in an effort to protect consumers.

Competing Generators?

A number of commentators suggested before the privatization scheme was announced that the CEGB would need to be divided from the beginning into five or six generators if there was to be genuine competition in generation.[6] Instead, the government is initially to establish a duopoly (National Power and PowerGen) in generation in England and Wales but to provide conditions which, it hopes, will encourage other generators subsequently to enter the market. Presumably it also hopes that electricity imports, from Scotland and France, will increase.

There are reasons for doubting whether the government's scheme is capable of injecting significant competition in the foreseeable future. First, there is always a strong incentive to collude (either explicitly or implicitly) in duopoly since, by suppressing competition, both companies can gain at the consumers' expense. Because the market demand for electricity is highly inelastic with respect to price (in almost two-thirds of its uses there is no close substitute), two very large generators acting in concert can each be much better off than if they indulge in price competition. Of course, they may well choose not to make large profits because to do so would make them conspicuous; a quiet life at the consumers' expense is a more likely outcome. The danger of collusion is clearly increased by the common managerial origins of National Power and PowerGen – they are not companies that have grown up separately in competition one with another. Nor will one of them be, like Mercury in telecommunications, a new company formed with the specific aim of competing with an established monopolist. Second, entry into the industry will be difficult. The government seems to envisage competition growing over time. It may be that imports from Scotland (where surplus capacity will increase) and

France will rise, though it was not necessary to privatize in order to achieve that; the government could have insisted on increased electricity imports whilst keeping the industry nationalized. Whether any serious competition for National Power and PowerGen will develop from new private generators is more doubtful. Some new entrants have appeared but they are at a disadvantage because they have to find sites and raise finance at the same time as trying to negotiate with customers. The two big generators already have systems comprising a mix of power stations and they can much more readily raise finance. When the new regime has been established it will be extremely difficult by regulation to prevent the two generators (which will almost certainly obtain their assets at a discount to replacement cost when the industry is floated) from predatory pricing. They may be able to cross-subsidize when quoting for power supplies from existing stations or from plant to be constructed. Moreover, as argued above, they may well not compete vigorously with each other. In the circumstances, competitors may be very wary of entering the industry. No doubt some electricity distributors will use their new-found power to build and operate generating plant, though it is less clear whether that will benefit consumers. The distributors will have local monopolies and, despite the regulator, it will be hard to establish whether any plant they build is genuinely competitive or whether it is designed to satisfy managerial objectives such as expanding the size and the scope of their activities.

Thus, although the government deserves credit for deciding to split the CEGB, the division it is making may be insufficient to establish a genuinely competitive generation industry. Yet implementing its proposals will cause a great deal of disruption, bringing about all the *costs* of a more thorough-going structural change which established workable competition from the beginning – such as one which broke the CEGB into five or six competing generators. But a scheme which splits a monopoly into a duopoly and then relies on new entrants being able to fight their way into the market against these strong incumbents, may well be incapable of realizing any significant proportion of the *benefits* which one would expect a competitive market to provide.

Nuclear Power and Security of Supply

Nuclear power became a major issue in the government's privatization scheme. From the time of the 1987 Conservative Election Manifesto, it was clear that there was a likely inconsistency between two statements therein – one which said that electricity supply would be privatized and another which said the government wish to develop 'abundant, low-cost supplies of nuclear electricity'. The government tried to include nuclear power stations (existing and planned) in its privatization scheme by incorporating them in National Power. However, by November 1989 it was clear that there would be serious problems in selling shares in a generator which had a large amount of nuclear capacity. Consequently, it was decided not to include nuclear stations in the flotation of the electricity supply industry: instead existing nuclear stations and one which is under construction (Sizewell 'B') are, as explained above, to remain in the state sector in two new companies (Nuclear Electric and Scottish Nuclear). To ensure that there is a demand for the output of existing nuclear plant, the government is imposing on the electricity distributors a requirement (the 'non-fossil fuel obligation' or NFFO) to take a proportion of their electricity from nuclear and other non-fossil fuel power stations. Although it is no longer insisting on the building of more nuclear plant, the government is, in effect, over-riding the market by imposing the NFFO which, since nearly all present non-fossil generating capacity is nuclear, is mainly a protective device for nuclear power.

Circumstances in which, in principle, social gains can be made by over-riding market decision-making are quite common, although in practice there is no guarantee that action by real-world politicians and bureaucrats will realize those potential gains. In the case of nuclear power, however, it is not even clear that there are prima facie arguments for displacing the market since the government has not offered a clear statement of why it believes protection for nuclear power is justified. Instead, in the White Paper on electricity privatization and elsewhere, it relies on rather vague 'security' arguments which are uncomfortably reminiscent of the case which used to be made for protecting the British coal industry from competition.

There is a public interest in security of energy supply. Energy security has some aspects of a 'public good' – which because the provider cannot appropriate some or all of the benefits will not be provided in the 'correct' quantity by market forces – but that does not of course justify any action taken by a government in the name of security enhancement. Many people are doubtful of the case for promoting nuclear power as a means of security provision. It is not obvious that nuclear power is a secure form of energy supply compared with the alternatives: it has a history of long construction delays, unexpected shutdowns or derating of plant, and accidents which, rightly or wrongly, have caused serious public concern and have led in turn to more stringent safety requirements and higher costs. Though the government seems to see nuclear power as a means of diversifying energy sources (and diversification in itself is a justifiable means of security provision) in practice it is likely to constrain the electricity distributors, hampering the diversification which would otherwise naturally take place. They will, in effect, be forced to depend for a substantial part of their electricity supplies on one generator using a particular technology.[7]

Conclusions

This chapter has only touched on a few of the issues which arise from electricity privatization. Other important matters concern the problems which are likely to arise in flotation of the industry and whether it can be regulated satisfactorily. The two are interdependent since potential investors will examine the regulatory regime to determine to what extent the industry is likely to be profitable. Another very significant issue is the impact which electricity privatization will have on the British coal industry. The government intends to privatize coal, if it is returned to office in the early 1990s, but the presence of two dominant electricity generators, taking the bulk of the output of the coal industry, will most probably severely limit the government's options for coal privatization. Because of the duopsony power of the generators, investors may be reluctant to invest in a broken-up British Coal; the government may therefore have no alternative but to sell British Coal whole, even though coal is the one British energy industry with no natural monopoly elements.

To most economists the electricity privatization plan, though full of good intentions, appears to have many deficiencies, of which the most serious is the failure to establish a structure for the generating industry which maximizes the chances of genuine competition in the early years of privatization. It may be that potential entrants to the industry are sufficiently ingenious that they will be able to circumvent the various obstacles which have been placed in their way so that in the course of time competition will develop. But it seems a pity that life should be made so difficult for the many organizations that seem to want to enter electricity generation and that we should all have to wait to realize the benefits which competition could bring.

NOTES

1. This chapter is adapted from 'A Memorandum', by Colin Robinson and Eileen Marshall, submitted to the House of Commons Select Committee on Energy in October 1985, and from 'The Economics of Electricity Privatisation' in *Economics*, Autumn 1989.
2. Most notably, in the report of the Plowden Committee, 'The Structure of the Electricity Supply in England and Wales', Cmnd 6388, HMSO, 1976.
3. 'Privatising Electricity', Cm 322, HMSO, February 1988.
4. 'Privatisation of the Scottish Electricity Industry', Cm 327, HMSO, March 1988.

5. More detailed comments on the privatization proposals are in Colin Robinson, 'Competition in Electricity?', IEA Inquiry Number 2, Institute of Economic Affairs, March 1988; in Robinson, 'Privatising the Energy Industries', in C Veljanovski (ed), *Privatisation and Competition*, Institute of Economic Affairs, 1989; and in Robinson, 'Liberalizing the Energy Market', Manchester Statistical Society, 1990.
6. Alex Henney, 'Privatise Power', Centre for Policy Studies, 1987 and Allen Sykes and Colin Robinson, 'Current Choices', Centre for Policy Studies, 1987.
7. Colin Robinson and Eileen Marshall, 'The Security of Britain's Energy Supply, Government Policy and the Proposed Hinkley Point "C" ', Surrey Discussion Papers in Energy Economics, No 42, January 1989.

QUESTIONS FOR DISCUSSION

1. Why is it that while some economists favour privatization, others favour much tighter Government control of nationalized industries? Of the potential benefits of privatization, which, in your view, is likely to be the most significant? Give reasons for your answer.
2. In which sense are the principal complications associated with electricity privatization connected to the 'natural monopoly' characteristics of parts of the industry?
3. Explain why judging whether or not the government's electricity privatization scheme will be socially beneficial is extremely difficult.
4. How have the Government sought to protect the interests of consumers during its programme of privatization? What alternative ways might have been used?
5. Explain the implications of electricity privatization for the British coal industry.
6. Should nuclear power be protected on 'security' grounds?

5. Mergers and Merger Policy in the UK

Michael Utton

INTRODUCTION

The title of Competition Policy or (In the USA) Antitrust Policy is usually given to those measures designed to control abuses of a market position that may occur in the private sector. There are three broad cases to which the policy measures usually apply – monopoly by a single enterprise; monopoly by a group of enterprises acting together to control prices and other terms of trading (a cartel); and mergers between two (or more) sizeable enterprises which may create a monopoly. Although these cases are quite distinct and may require different institutions to deal with them (as in the UK where monopolies and mergers are investigated by the Monopolies and Mergers Commission, whereas cartels are examined by the Restrictive Practices Court) they are all concerned essentially with the same issue – market power.

Market power is the ability of one enterprise (or a group of enterprises acting together) to maintain prices persistently above long-run average costs. In the short-run prices may rise above costs for a number of reasons but in the absence of market power the divergence will be eroded by competition. If, however, prices persistently remain above costs into the long-run this implies that existing firms are able to exclude new competition from the market. Thus the ability of cartels to exclude new competition has long been regarded in the vast majority of cases as producing consequences both for consumers, through unduly high prices, and to producers by weakening incentives to efficiency. As a result most have been found to be illegal. In cases of monopoly or market dominance (since in practice few firms are in the fortunate position of having the whole market to themselves) the policy body has to decide whether the existing firm has been abusing its position by deliberately trying to exclude the entry or growth of new competition (which may, of course, come from enterprises already established in other markets). Perhaps the most extreme form of such behaviour is *predatory pricing* where the monopolist deliberately prices in selected regions or for selected products at a very low level in order to undermine a new entrant.

Merger policy is in some ways the most difficult and certainly the most topical of the three cases distinguished. Many mergers between small or medium sized enterprises have little or nothing to do with market power: an owner-founder may wish to sell out in order to sail single-handed round the world, start a rock group or merely reduce his/her golf handicap; growing companies with complementary assets may see merger as a logical next step in their development. In terms of numbers of mergers in any year these will be by far the greater category. However those of concern to the competition policy authorities will usually be of considerable size and involve the possible creation of, or increase in market power. One reason why the analysis of mergers is difficult is because it involves projecting forward the likely effects once the amalgamation has taken place. In particular, will the merged concern be able to exclude entry more effectively than was previously possible? In contrast with monopoly and cartel cases there is no past behaviour to use in the analysis. Statements of good intent made by the parties at the time of merger, even if entirely sincere, may subsequently be undermined by dramatic changes in market conditions such as unanticipated shifts in demand or a chain reaction amongst rival firms sparked off by the initial merger.

Rather than attempting to deal with all aspects of competition policy, this chapter focuses specifically on mergers. First, three main types of merger are distinguished, and the market power issue in large merger cases is examined in more detail. Second, the scope of the problem in the UK is investigated, by examining the recent trend of mergers as well as their effect on the level of industrial concentration and the controversy surrounding the subsequent performance of merged companies. Third, consideration is given to how merger policy has actually worked in the UK since its introduction in 1965, and some proposals are made for its reform.

TYPES OF MERGER AND THE ISSUE OF MARKET POWER

It is convenient to distinguish between three main types of merger: horizontal, vertical and conglomerate. Horizontal mergers occur between enterprises which sell into the same market. The merger for example between two enterprises selling confectionery in the UK can be classed as horizontal. A vertical merger involves enterprises which were previously in a supplier–customer relationship – a confectionery manufacturer merging with a chain of retail confectioners would be an example of a vertical merger. The final category involves all the remainder, that is, mergers between enterprises which previously had no markets in common and were not vertically related. If a confectionery firm decided to merge with a machine tool manufacturer, for example, this would fall clearly into the 'conglomerate' category.

Two important points should be noted about this classification. First, market power effects are most likely to flow from *horizontal* mergers simply because the firms are operating in the same market. This is not to say, of course, that *all* horizontal mergers, even those involving large companies, will necessarily lead to an increase in market power. Second, although the clear distinction between the different types is useful for analytical purposes, in practice most companies of any size operate in a number of different markets and have many subsidiaries. As a consequence the large mergers with which policy is concerned are likely to involve elements of more than one type. Thus the *main* characteristic of a particular merger may be horizontal but there may also be vertical or conglomerate aspects as well.

How is market power created or enhanced by merger? As we have already mentioned the most straightforward cases occur with horizontal mergers. If two firms, each with 50 per cent of the sales in a particular market agree to merge and if entry to the market is difficult for other firms, then a duopoly will be replaced by a monopoly and we may expect that the ability of the enterprise to control prices will be increased. Note however, the second part of the condition: entry to the market is difficult. The signifiance of this is as follows. If entry to the market is very easy, then although the merger may, in the short-run, create a firm with a market share of 100 per cent, the ability of the firm successfully to raise prices above costs will be constrained by the threat of new entry. Short-term excess profits resulting from monopoly prices will, with easy entry conditions, be short-lived because other firms will be attracted to the market and begin to erode the share of the merged firm. (Note the entrant firms do not have to be newly founded. Frequently they will be well established in other markets.) Most significant mergers will not, of course, involve a complete monopolization. In cases, however, where a sizeable increase in market share would occur if a merger was allowed there is a strong presumption that market power would increase. The dual condition, therefore, of a substantial increase in market share plus difficult entry conditions for other firms is likely to yield an increase in market power, and is likely to be challenged by the competition policy authorities.

Entry conditions are also significant in the case of vertical mergers. Even though very large firms may be involved, no market shares are increased by vertical mergers. The market power effect in such cases is most likely to arise where one of the firms involved already has a substantial market share at some stage of the production process and where entry is also difficult at that stage. Suppose, for example, a raw material supplier owns practically all of the known high grade deposits of an ore used in the subsequent manufacturing process. All manufacturers have to buy their supplies from this source. If the raw material supplier proposed a merger with a firm at the manufacturing stage, this would allow the integrated firm gradually to win control of manufacture by selling the ore at a differentially higher price to its manufacturing competitors. The market power that it already has at one stage of production may thus be gradually transmitted to the subsequent, manufacturing stage. Note, however, that this effect occurs only because of the impossibility of entry at the raw material stage. If the manufacturers had available plentiful alternative supplies of high grade raw materials, the market power effect of the vertical merger would disappear. Generally therefore a vertical merger will only cause a significant increase in market power if one stage of the production process is already dominated by one enterprise (or a small group of enterprises) and existing entry conditions are difficult.

The most controversial case involves the market power effects of conglomerate mergers. Not only do the firms have no markets in common, but they also do not stand in a supplier–customer relationship. How then is it possible for such mergers to create or increase market power, as defined? The answer usually given to this question is in terms of *indirect* effects. Thus a specialist firm which merges with another, already active in a number of other markets, may subsequently have its position strengthened by cross-subsidization. Resources earned in other markets by the conglomerate may be used to finance price cuts and temporary losses of the newly acquired specialist firm, in the expectation that this will weaken its rivals so that in the long-run its market power is increased. Such a policy is clearly very risky and also depends on the merged firm being able to prevent entry in the long-term once prices are increased again. Many observers are sceptical of the plausibility of the above argument and also point out that if merger policy prevents conglomerate mergers it may remove a useful incentive to management efficiency. In mergers effected through a takeover bid, amongst the first casualties are often the previous senior executives. To minimize the risk of a bid, the management has a strong incentive to maintain the internal efficiency and profitability of the company so that shareholders are loath to sell out. However, if the threat of takeover is removed because of a tough merger policy towards conglomerate mergers, managements may over time become correspondingly slack.

For these and similar reasons it is now probably true to say that competition policy authorities are much more ready to scrutinize and control horizontal and vertical mergers than conglomerate mergers, although the sheer size of some recent bids and in a number of cases the rather unconventional form of the type of finance involved (with a heavy reliance on debt) has convinced a number of observers that the emphasis of merger policy should change.

In the analysis that follows it is assumed that the mergers involve a market power effect. It is possible to use simple market analysis to highlight the dilemma that may confront an antitrust agency asked to assess the economic effects of a proposed merger. If the creation of market power is the issue, the task of merger policy may appear deceptively simple – all mergers that lead to an increase in market power should be prevented. The problem is that many mergers of size may simultaneously enhance market power but also promise economies. In fact often an important incentive for merger may be the savings in cost that may be made following reorganization through merger. Product lines and distribution networks may be rationalized; savings in standby capacity and inventory levels may be made; central administration and research and development costs may be reduced, relative to output. In short, it is often argued, especially prior to the event, that the whole is greater than the sum of the parts.

The problem in such cases can be illustrated with the help of Figure 5.1. The market demand curve is shown by D, the line AC_1 shows the average costs of the two (or more) firms involved, prior to the merger. (Note the average cost curves are drawn as horizontal rather than U- or L-shaped, for the sake of clarity.) Assuming competition in the market, a pre-merger price of P_1 is charged for a total output of Q_1. If the merger proceeds, cost savings may be made which would reduce average costs of the combined firm to AC_2. However, the increase in market power created by the merger would allow the enterprise to charge a higher price, P_2, by restricting output to Q_2. The saving in cost that occurs (for the smaller output) is shown by the rectangle marked G. The triangle marked L represents the loss in consumer surplus that results from the creation of market power. (It is exactly the type of loss that occurs when a previously competitive industry is monopolized.) The problem for the policy body is to determine whether the cost savings, G, are greater than the consumer surplus loss, L. A simple decision rule might then be, if the cost savings outweigh the consumer surplus losses then the merger could be allowed to proceed, otherwise it would be blocked.

The importance of this simple analysis lies in the emphasis placed on the *trade-off*. Sizeable mergers may bring gains as well as losses, and a rational policy should take this into account. It must be emphasized, however, that the simple trade-off is really only the beginning of what may have to be a

Figure 5.1   The trade-offs in a merger case

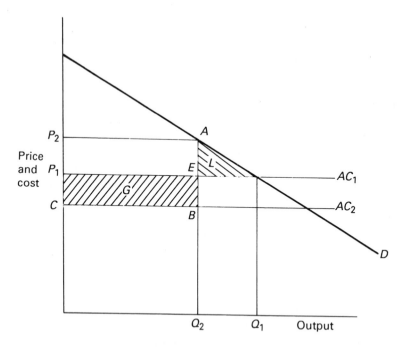

much more complex analysis. There are at least three further factors that need to be considered. First, it may be necessary for the policy body to decide whether the merger under review is likely to spark off other mergers in the market. It is quite possible that other competitors will feel their own position threatened should the initial merger proceed. As a defence, therefore, they may themselves seek a partner and attempt to merge. In other words the original merger may set off a chain reaction and the eventual increase in concentration in the market may be much greater than would have resulted from a simple case. The greater the danger of this happening the more inclined the policy body may be to block the merger.

Second, the comparative static analysis illustrated in Figure 5.1 tends to obscure the importance of the timing of the cost savings. Thus while the market power may be achieved almost as soon as the merger is completed, it may take some time to realize the cost savings. Furthermore, it might also be possible to achieve the cost reductions by internal reorganization and growth. Although the savings may take longer if gained in this way there may be little or no effect on market power. In this case the gains would be made without any countervailing losses. The policy body may thus have to decide whether the *net* gains from the merger are greater than the somewhat later gains from the internal reorganization. Clearly if there was no difference in the timing and size of the cost savings achieved by merger or internal growth then there would be no case for allowing the merger.

Thirdly, it is clear from Figure 5.1 that there is an important income re-distribution effect as a result of the merger. Prior to the merger prices were, by assumption, equal to average cost and therefore no supernormal profits were earned. Following the merger and the consequent rise in prices a supernormal profit of P_2ABC is earned by the combined enter-prise. The lower portion (G), as we have seen, represents the reduction in costs following the merger, but the higher portion, P_1P_2AE, represents a transfer from consumers to the producer. In the trade-off it is therefore formally treated as neutral. Such treatment may be justified, for example, on the ground that income redistribution is the concern of fiscal rather than competition or antitrust policy. On the other hand it might be argued that in merger cases such transfers of income should not be treated as neutral since they may, for example, cause unrest amongst the labour force and this may delay the achievement of the cost savings. In that case part, at least, of the income transfer may be treated negatively. When added to the welfare loss L the result may be that some mergers which on a simple trade-off might have been allowed, may be prevented when other factors are taken into account.

The trade-off framework discussed above is a useful tool in the prelimi-nary analysis of significant mergers. It forces our attention on to the main issues. However, it is very important not to let the apparent simplicity of the approach obscure the important extensions and modifications that have also been sketched.

THE SCALE OF THE PROBLEM: THE RECENT TREND OF MERGERS IN THE UK

It has long been observed that the aggregate level of merger activity in an economy such as the UK is cyclical and frequently follows quite closely the volume of trading on the stock exchange. Concern at the growing volume of post-war merger activity observed in the 1960s, when mergers were first brought within the scope of UK competition policy (see below) has led to a great deal of official and academic interest. One effect of this has been a much fuller record of the level and direction of merger activity. Thus Table 5.1 shows the total number of mergers in the UK (column 1) and their cost in terms of current expenditure (column 2) over the period 1969 to 1987. Since *current* expenditures will obviously be affected by

Table 5.1   *Mergers by industrial and commercial companies within the UK*
             1969–87

| | Number of companies Acquired | Expenditure | | |
| | | Current prices (£m) | Constant (1986) Prices (£bn) | Average (1986) Price (£m) |
Year	(1)	(2)	(3)	(4)
1969	846	1069	6.1	7.2
1970	793	1122	5.9	7.4
1971	884	911	4.4	5.0
1972	1210	2532	11.4	9.4
1973	1205	1304	5.4	4.5
1974	504	508	1.7	3.4
1975	315	291	0.8	2.5
1976	353	448	1.1	3.1
1977	481	824	1.7	3.5
1978	567	1140	2.2	3.9
1979	534	1656	2.8	5.2
1980	469	1475	2.1	4.5
1981	452	1144	1.5	3.3
1982	463	2206	2.6	5.6
1983	447	2343	2.7	6.0
1984	568	5474	5.9	10.4
1985	474	7090	7.2	15.2
1986	696	14935	14.9	21.4
1987	1125	15363	14.8	13.2

Source: Mergers Policy, Department of Trade and Industry, HMSO, 1988.

inflation which was especially acute in the mid 1970s an attempt is made to remove this effect by deflating the current series by a price index. Column 3 therefore gives that expenditure on mergers at constant (1986) prices. Over the entire period shown nearly 12 500 enterprises disappeared in mergers at a cost of more than £80 billions (in 1986 prices). In the earlier part of the period the cyclical pattern shows up fairly clearly. A peak was reached, for example in 1972–73. In fact the *average* size of acquisitions in 1972 was £9.4 millions (in constant price terms) and this figure was only exceeded in 1984 and the succeeding years (column 4). In the wake of the secondary banking crisis and declines on the stock exchange the volume of activity declined dramatically, reaching a low point in 1975. A second peak can be distinguished in the years 1978–79 but in terms of *real* expenditure this was far below the level of 1972. An important feature since 1982 is that the volume of expenditure in real terms has increased in each successive year (with a marginal decline in 1987). In 1986 the *average* expenditure on each acquisition was more than £21 millions, well over twice as much (in real terms) as the previous peak year in 1972. Whereas the previous merger booms of 1972–3 and 1978–79 were short-lived, the current phase of very high expenditure has been maintained for at least four years and there is little sign at present of it coming to an end.

Given this high volume of merger activity two questions having an important general bearing on policy suggest themselves. First, what has been the impact of mergers on the level of concentration in industry; and second, do mergers tend on the whole, to improve the performance of the enterprises involved? Both questions raise a large number of complex statistical and measurement problems. For these and other reasons neither question has yet received a definitive answer. In particular, considerable controversy still surrounds the issue of what effect mergers have on the performance of the participating firms. Some of the main conclusions on these questions are summarized below, but any reader who wishes to examine the evidence in more detail should consult the recent paper by Hughes in the study edited by Fairburn and Kay, see References.

As far as concentration is concerned, a number of studies using a variety of methods and covering different time periods have concluded that mergers have played an important part in the changing structure of UK industry. For example, estimates of the extent to which mergers have contributed to increases in concentration in the manufacturing sector have varied from about one-third to more than 100 per cent, that is, in the absence of merger, concentration would actually have fallen. Naturally there is considerable variation between sectors and markets of the precise effect of mergers but usually where one firm has retained a position of dominance for a long period and in the presence of substantial market growth, mergers have played an important part. However, we should also note that the *internal* growth of firms, as well as changes in the relative growth rates of firms of different sizes and the emergence of new and rapidly growing firms may tend to mitigate over time the immediate effects of mergers on the concentration of industry.

When we were discussing the policy trade-offs in the previous section, a central role was assigned to the possible cost savings that may result from merger. In fact if the post-merger performance of merged companies is often greatly superior to the (anticipated) performance had the companies remained separate, then there is more reason to adopt a fairly tolerant policy towards large mergers. Investigators who have tried to get a clear answer to this question, however, have had great difficulty in obtaining a suitable measure of performance. In practice, changes in costs following merger may be very difficult to measure. Although many have relied on profitability as a performance indicator we need to recognize that this may actually obscure the *policy* question with which we are mainly concerned.

Improved profitability following merger *may* reflect cost savings but it may equally be due to the exploitation of increased market power (some of which was unappreciated by the stock exchange at the time of the merger). A large number of studies have now been carried out into the profitability effects of mergers, and on the whole the weight of the evidence seems, if anything, to suggest that profitability either deteriorates or at best remains unchanged after merger. The longer the period observed after merger the less favourable, on average, the results. Putting this in a slightly different way, there is little positive evidence that on the whole merger leads to a sustained improvement in profits.

Other researchers have used a rather different approach to the gains and losses from mergers. Proponents of this alternative view have argued that the stock exchange can assimilate and respond to all the information relevant to a particular merger, including potential cost changes and market power effects. As a result, when the merger is announced the share prices of the firms involved will be adjusted to reflect this assessment. The difference between the share prices before and after the merger announcement is thus a measure of the gains (or losses) that can be expected if the merger proceeds. Using this approach, studies of samples of companies involved in recent mergers have concluded that, on average, shareholders in acquired companies have definitely benefited from an appreciation in the price of their holdings in the period immediately before and after the completion of the merger. For shareholders in the acquiring companies the gain was either marginally positive or negligible over the same period. To this extent, therefore, we may conclude that if the stock exchange generally responds correctly to the underlying real effects that mergers involve, then on average, there is a net gain in the short run. Unfortunately the sting is in the tail, because if the analysis is extended beyond the immediate period of the merger, the conclusions are rather different. Instead of the apparent gains increasing as the immediate problems of reorganization following merger are sorted out, the reverse appears to happen. The longer the period studied after the completion of merger, the smaller the gains appear to be, on average.

Thus, while there is quite strong evidence that merger activity has recently been running at very high levels and that this has had an important impact on the concentration of industry, the evidence on the subsequent performance of merged companies is much more ambiguous. Short-run gains may be made by promoters and shareholders, but longer term cost reductions may be comparatively rare. These results thus indicate that merger policy has a central role to play in the maintenance of a competitive economy.

MERGER POLICY IN THE UK

Machinery for the investigation and control of larger mergers in the UK dates from 1965 when the first post-war increase in merger activity was taking place. Although the details of the policy have changed somewhat since then, the essentials remain largely the same. The remarks that follow refer to the current position.

Overall responsibility for UK competition policy rests with the Director General of Fair Trading (DGFT) whose office (OFT) is responsible amongst other things for collecting information, assessing complaints from customers, advising the Secretary of State (for Trade and Industry) and in some instances initiating action. (Although not discussed further here, his responsibility also covers market dominance, cartels and issues of consumer protection.) Under the relevant legislation certain mergers (we discuss the criteria in more detail below) may be referred by the Secretary of State to the Monopolies and Mergers Commission (MMC). Before any reference is made two preliminary stages are completed. First, an informal 'merger panel' made up of officials in the DTI and the OFT, including the Director General, carries out a preliminary review of the proposed merger to determine whether there is a case for recommending a reference to the MMC. If the panel feels that there is such a case, the Director General prepares a detailed recommendation for the Secretary of State who then has to decide whether or not to make the reference to the MMC.

If a reference is made, the MMC then has to determine whether or not the merger is likely to operate against the public interest. Its report can be made in six months but in recent cases the Minister has often directed the MMC to report in three months. Under the rules of the Stock Exchange, if a reference is made then any outstanding bid for the companies involved lapses. If the MMC finds that a proposed merger is not likely to operate against the public interest then the Secretary of State must accept this recommendation and the merger can proceed, if the companies so wish. On the other hand, if the MMC finds that the merger *is* likely to operate against the public interest, the Secretary of State can either accept that recommendation and effectively block the merger, or reject it and allow the merger to proceed, possibly subject to conditions. In practice the Secretary of State nearly always does accept the conclusions of the MMC, although there is a precedent where he did not.

As mentioned above, the vast majority of mergers have nothing to do with market power and these proceed without policy interference. To be the subject of a possible reference to the MMC, proposed mergers must meet at least one of two criteria laid down in the legislation. The merger must *either* create or increase a market share of 25 per cent or more, *or* involve the acquisition of assets valued at £30 millions or more. There is no restriction under which criterion a particular reference is made to the MMC. Clearly the asset criterion is general enough to encompass *any* merger of size, whether horizontal, vertical or conglomerate. (In fact the threshold size has twice been revised upwards because of inflation. Originally it was £5 millions but in 1980 it was raised to £15 millions and to the present figure in 1984.) The market share criterion which is less frequently used, applies particularly to horizontal mergers and the threshold is sufficiently low to ensure that any proposed merger likely to affect the public interest can, if necessary, be investigated.

But what in merger cases is 'the public interest'? It is a phrase frequently used by politicians wishing to justify policies that seem unpopular. In fact the MMC has a very wide discretion in interpreting the public interest in a particular case. They are allowed to take account of any factors that they feel are relevant but from 1973 onwards (following the passage of the Fair Trading Act) have been asked to place special emphasis on the competitive effects of a proposed merger.

It is very important to note that even though the MMC only receives references after they have been examined by the merger panel and the Secretary of State, there is *no* presumption that the mergers are likely to operate against the public interest. The MMC starts each enquiry from a position of neutrality. Over the years this stance has been strongly criticized by a number of observers who feel that it tends in practice to work in favour of the proposed mergers and, as we shall see below, has led to calls for the initial presumption of the MMC to be revised.

Before commenting on the performance of the MMC in merger cases we can look briefly at the size of its task. Tables 5.2 and 5.3 show the number of mergers falling within the scope of the legislation, and give a breakdown by type of those proposed mergers referred to the MMC. Since the legislation was introduced in the mid 1960s the proportion of mergers referred has remained remarkably constant at between 2 and 3 per cent of all those passing one or other of the criteria referred to above (see Table 5.2). This occurred despite the considerable increase in the total number falling within the legislation since 1975. Growing concern about the increase in size of the largest mergers and the effect on the structure and performance of industry led, however, to an increase in the total *number* of mergers referred. In the five-year period 1980–84, 31 mergers were referred compared with 38 in the previous fifteen years. For the most recent years (1985–87), after falling somewhat in 1985, the pace of merger activity has accelerated and a peak of 321 cases were reported as falling within the legislation in 1987.

In the wake of all this activity what has been the direct impact of the

Table 5.2   Merger activity and referrals to the Monopolies and Mergers Commission, 1965–87

Period	Within the legislation	Referred to the MMC	
		Number	%
1965–9	466	10	2.1
1970–4	579	19	3.3
1975–9	903	19	2.1
1980–4	987	31	3.1
1985	192	6	3.1
1986	313	13	4.2
1987	321	6	1.9

Source: Annual Reports of the Board of Trade and the Director General of Fair Trading.

Table 5.3   Mergers referred to the Monopolies and Mergers Commission, 1965–87

Merger type	Referred	Abandoned before MMC report issued	Public interest conclusion	
			Against	Not against
Horizontal	72	19	23	30
Vertical	7	1	1	5
Conglomerate	25	11	5	9
Total	104	31	29	44

Source: Review of Monopolies and Merger Policy, HMSO, 1978 and Reports of the Director General of Fair Trading.

machinery of merger control in the UK? Some indication of this is given in Table 5.3 which shows both the type of proposed mergers referred (according to the classification discussed above) and the outcome of the MMC enquiries. Not surprisingly, by far the largest category of mergers referred have been horizontal, where the impact on market power may be greatest. Out of 104 referrals up to 1987, 72 (or 69 per cent) have been horizontal, 7 have been vertical and 25 conglomerate. It should be noted, however, that in recent years there has been much less inclination on the part of the Secretary of State to refer conglomerate mergers. Current policy lays much greater emphasis on sizeable mergers where a direct and substantial impact on competition might be expected. Altogether the MMC has concluded that some 29 merger proposals would be likely to operate against the public interest, and in all but one of these cases the

Secretary of State has accepted this recommendation and the mergers have not proceeded. To these we should add the other 31 proposals which were abandoned before the MMC had submitted its report. Thus a total of 60 mergers have been stopped as a result of referral to the MMC. As a proportion of *all* mergers falling within the legislation, this represents less than 2 per cent. The remaining 44 cases shown in the table were found by the MMC as *not* likely to operate against the public interest and therefore could proceed. The figures in the table, of course, understate the impact of merger policy on the total number of mergers occuring in the period shown. The very fact that the policy is in place will have deterred an unknown number of possible mergers. The likelihood of a reference to the MCC of any horizontal merger which significantly increases market share is now quite high. The period leading up to and during a reference is one of considerable uncertainty for the companies involved and quite costly in terms of executive time in preparing evidence and appearing at the MMC enquiry. Thus mergers which might have gone ahead without hindrance prior to 1965 may now be rejected by the top management at an early stage of consideration, simply because they believe they would eventually be blocked.

It is not possible to discuss here in detail the kinds of economic argument that the MMC has used in the many cases before arriving at its final recommendations. The best way to find out the type of analysis used and how it has been assessed is to consult one or two recent merger reports of the MMC. Not surprisingly over the 25 years or so during which it has been reporting on mergers the quality of the reports has varied, and observers have been quick to pinpoint what they see as shortcomings in the economic analysis. We set out below some of the more general criticisms that have been made of UK mergers policy, most of which have also been discussed in the two official reviews that have taken place (in 1978 and 1988 – see list of References).

First, a point of continuing controversy has been the neutral presumption from which the MMC starts all of its enquiries. In fact the MMC has to decide whether or not the merger is likely to operate *against* the public interest. It has been argued that this tends to work in favour of those merger proposals which it has to consider. There is no onus on the companies concerned to demonstrate that the merger could, for example, produce cost reductions (of the kind discussed above) even though in some cases they may feel it would benefit their case to do so. Many observers have argued that, given the importance of those mergers that are actually referred to the MMC (after the preliminary screening procedure and assessment), the initial presumption should change so that companies wishing to merge would have to demonstate that the merger would be positively in the public interest. In terms of the Williamson trade-off (Williamson, 1987) this would force the companies to quantify systematically the cost savings that they envisaged and the MMC would then be in a stronger position to weigh up these advantages against the detriments caused by the increase in market share. So far, however, this seemingly modest reform has been resisted.

Second, there has been increasing concern about lobbying and political pressures that can be brought to bear with the present system. Thus although the DGFT has overall responsibility for competition policy including the power to make references to the MMC in monopoly cases, the Secretary of State has sole responsibility for making merger references. There is a strong case for removing responsibility on such a sensitive matter from the political arena altogether and giving it to the DGFT. Equally important recently have been the pressures placed on the screening panel by lobbying from the interested parties. With so much at stake and currently no sanctions available against those who try to influence the panel one way or the other, the growth of lobbying is hardly surprising even if it is regarded as undesirable. Short of giving the mergers panel a more official status underpinned by severe penalties against lobbying, it is difficult at present to see how the situation can be improved.

The recent official review has however, made some interesting and important proposals which are likely to be incorporated into future procedures for merger control. Companies have often complained in the past that MMC reports cannot be used as a guide to whether a merger they are presently considering will be referred, nor if it is referred, to whether it is likely to be cleared or not. The difficulties of arranging a merger are thus increased by the uncertainty surrounding the procedure on merger references. The recent review has therefore proposed that parties to a proposed merger could voluntarily pre-notify in confidence the Office of Fair Trading of their intentions. Within a very short time (possibly four weeks) the companies would then either be given clearance for the merger to proceed without a reference to the MMC or be told that there was a strong possibility that a reference would be made. The mechanism would thus ensure at a very early stage that in the majority of cases merger proposals were cleared.

A second proposal would also help to remove uncertainty and speed up the overall procedure. Firms could give a binding undertaking to the Office of Fair Trading that prior to the completion of a merger they would divest themselves of certain assets. Thus, for example, if a proposed merger would considerably increase the joint market share and therefore be the subject of a reference, the acquiring company could sell off the relevant productive capacity so as to minimize or eliminate altogether the market share effect. Having given such an undertaking the merger could then be cleared without a reference to the MMC, thus avoiding the delay that referral would inevitably entail.

The current proposals when implemented will undoubtedly help to streamline the procedure of merger policy without, however, making any fundamental change of emphasis. In particular there is still no onus on the companies involved to demonstrate that their merger would be positively in the public interest.

CONCLUSIONS

In recent years, merger policy has assumed increasing importance as the volume of mergers has continued to rise and some individual bids break new records for their size. Amid the great controversy that very often surrounds such activity, especially if the bidding firm is foreign or if the bid is treated with hostility by the target firm, it is easy to lose sight of the main issue, so far as policy is concerned. We have argued that the focus of that policy should be whether or not a proposed merger would enhance market power. If the answer to this question is positive then the merger might still be allowed if there are sufficient offsetting advantages in the form of reductions in cost. We also noted, however, that the simple trade-off might in many cases be complicated by other factors.

Once proposed mergers are referred to the MMC in the UK it can take into account any factors that it regards relevant in deciding the public interest. There has been a growing feeling, however, that the neutral position from which it has to start the enquiries has probably worked in favour of the companies wishing to merge. Certainly the number of mergers directly halted as a result of the policy has been comparatively small. As yet, however, the suggestion that large companies wishing to merge should have to demonstrate to the MMC that they would bring substantial benefits to the public, has been resisted.

REFERENCES

Department of Trade and Industry (1988), *Mergers Policy*, HMSO.

Fairburn, J. and Kay, J. (1989), *Mergers and Merger Policy*, Oxford University Press.

Green Paper (1978), *A Review of Monopolies and Mergers Policy*, Cmnd7198, HMSO.

Hay, D. and Vickers, J. (1988), 'The Reform of UK Competition Policy', *National Institute Economic Review*, August.

Williamson, O. E., (1987), *Antitrust Economics*, Chapter 1, Blackwells.

QUESTIONS FOR DISCUSSION

1. What do you understand by the concepts of 'market power' and 'predatory pricing'?
2. Using examples, distinguish carefully between horizontal, vertical and conglomerate mergers. Which type of merger is most likely to affect market power?
3. In what way may a tough policy towards conglomerate mergers encourage slack management?
4. Analyse the statement that 'sizeable mergers may bring gains as well as losses and a national policy should take this into account'.
5. Outline and account for the recent trend of mergers in the UK.
6. Provide a critical assessment of merger policy in the UK.

6. The Role of the State: Retreat and Rehabilitation

Tony Killick[1]

THE STATE IN RETREAT

That the 1980s witnessed a major disillusionment with the state as an economic agent − by economists scarcely less than politicians − is an assertion that scarcely needs elaboration. Fiscal policies have come to be seen as creating major disincentives; attempts at macroeconomic management as destabilizing or doomed to impotence; state attempts to plan, regulate and control as distorting the economy and spawning parallel markets; publicly-owned enterprises as inefficient and incapable of adequate self-improvement. However, it is important for present purposes to trace the developments within the economic theory which led to this turning-away of the discipline from the *dirigisme* of earlier decades.

A very important contributor to this shift, of course, was the breakdown of the Keynesian consensus and the associated rise of the monetarist and rational expectations schools. With its commitment to full employment, orthodox Keynesianism proved unable to cope with the inflation that became increasingly rapid during the 1970s. The postulated Phillips curve relationship between unemployment and inflation seemed increasingly to break down, with accelerating inflation becoming associated with a slow-down in economic growth and actual increases in the trend rate of unemployment − a situation of 'stagflation' with which most incomes policies could not deal and to which received macro theory seemed to have little response. It became increasingly apparent that wage negotiators were beginning to anticipate both future inflation and government policies, destroying the stability [and thus the usefulness] of the Phillips curve relationship and introducing the distinction between anticipated and unanticipated policy actions which became one of the pillars of rational expectations theory. While it may be justified to ignore the influence of expectations in the short run, it is not so over the longer term, as people have time to adjust to − and begin to anticipate − government actions, so

62

part of the criticism of Keynesianism was, in effect, that its orientation was too short-term.

Keynesian treatment of time came to be further criticized on the additional ground that it tended to overlook the complications for policy of introducing time lags, as well as the complex interactions between policy instruments and the economic variables they are seeking to influence. Introducing these interactions and lead times (a) between the occurrence of a change in economic conditions and information about it, (b) between receipt of that information and the introduction of policy actions to correct for that change, and (c) between the introduction of a policy and its effect on the economy, can easily mean that measures intended to be stabilizing turn out to have the opposite result.

Its emphasis on demand management and relative neglect of supply-side conditions provided a further stick with which the Keynesian consensus could be beaten, not the least because of the large supply shocks that were experienced in the 1970s, particularly via petroleum prices. There is today wide agreement on the importance of the supply side for the macroeconomic performance of an economy, and much contemporary policy is intended to influence supply variables through the manipulation of pecuniary incentives.

First monetarism, then rational expectations (RE), then the 'new classical' macroeconomics (NCM) came forward to fill the vacuum left by the attack on Keynesianism. The monetarist position is summarized by Friedman's famous dictum that 'Inflation is always and everywhere a monetary phenomenon ... and can be produced only by a more rapid increase in the quantity of money than in output', and by his associated denial that monetary expansion can result in any sustained increase in real output. It sees fiscal expansion as merely 'crowding out' private sector expenditures, with reduction in the latter tending to negate the intended effects of a fiscal stimulus. It does not, however, completely deny the possibility of deflationary unemployment, and in advocating a policy of expanding money supply at a steady rate it envisages a benign influence of government policies on economic stability.

The RE school takes the analysis further and one of its attractions is that it applies to macroeconomic issues the same assumptions of rational maximizing behaviour which underlie standard micro theory. In particular, it applies them to the acquisition and processing of information and to the formation of expectations. It argues, for example in its critique of Phillips curve analysis, that economic agents will learn from past mistakes and come to anticipate systematic government policies, thus rendering them impotent. Only unexpected policies are able to influence real variables.

The NCM school takes the analysis a step further, combining rational expectations with 'natural rate' theories of unemployment. In fact, disagreements about the nature of unemployment and the extent, or possibility, of deflationary unemployment have been a sub-plot in the macroeconomic controversies described here. The disagreement is largely about whether the labour market clears or not and, if so, how quickly. Natural-rate unemployment is essentially voluntary, although it also includes unemployment arising from frictional and structural causes. The NCM school sees the labour market as clearing almost instantly through the movement of wages and prices. Since, therefore, it is in equilibrium, any remaining unemployment must be voluntary, at least for the labour force considered collectively. A policy implication of this view is that, contrary to the Keynesian position, unemployment cannot be reduced by demand expansion. This conclusion is in line with a general denial by the NCM school of any possible influence on the economy of demand management policies, emphasizing instead the importance of tax incentives and other measures to improve the efficiency of the labour market.

These more recent contributions to macro theory are nevertheless deeply pessimistic about the feasibility of effective macroeconomic management and in this way have contributed importantly to a generally more jaundiced view of the effects of government policy interventions. By analogy with the concept of 'market failure' (discussed shortly) there is now far greater emphasis on the extent of 'government failure', and the existence of a market failure is no longer accepted as constituting a case for intervention. The reasons can be summarized as follows:

1. The government is not necessarily well informed about the nature of a given problem, nor about the complex consequences of its own policy actions, which may produce perverse or unwanted effects. National planning magnifies any mistakes or unwanted results, as compared with the more limited effects of mistakes by individual economic agents in the marketplace.
2. Governments, in any case, have only partial control over the consequences of their actions.
3. There are often large differences between policy measures on the drawing board and the way they are implemented. There are large intrinsic difficulties in improving the accountability and control of bureaucracies, and the problem is worsened both by the existence of corruption, nepotism and other malpractices and by the tendency for state agencies to be 'captured' by special interest groups.
4. Since lump-sum taxes, which do not affect incentives at the margin, are invariably not available to governments, any increase in taxation

necessitated as a result of a policy intervention will itself introduce new 'distortions' by affecting relative prices and incentives.

Theories of rent-seeking and directly unproductive profit-seeking activities (DUPs) have added further strings to this bow. Common examples include efforts by businessmen to secure allocations of import licences, and the scarcity premia they will earn, and to persuade governments to provide protection against competition, or a budgetary subsidy. The essential quality of these activites is that, although they consume real resources and may well be highly profitable, they contribute nothing to output. DUPs are thus seen as an *additional* cost of actual or potential policy interventions and a further reason, therefore, why an intervention in the face of a market failure may worsen rather than improve the situation. This theoretical insight has been particularly prominent in the literature on international trade policy.

Changing views on the efficiency effects of measures to reduce poverty and/or inequality have added to the growing scepticism about state interventions. This is chiefly an application of the final point listed above. In formal terms, in the absence of costless distortion-free taxes and subsidies, policies which redistribute incomes will necessitate departures from Pareto optimality and thus create a trade-off between efficiency and equality. Less formally, policy in the 1980s has been concerned to improve economic incentives but the incentive problem is seen as the inverse of the income redistribution problem. This is an issue that is crystallized in debates about the desirable progressivity of income taxes.

Developments in the literature on market structures have also made a contribution to the retreat from interventionism, in the form of the theory of 'contestable' markets. This introduces the idea that while there may not be competition *within* a given product market there may be competition *for* that market, and that the possibility of new entrants is itself a constraint on the exercise of monopoly power. The key condition is that the industry should be characterized by freedom of entry and exit. A firm can thus only be said to be a monopolist if it can discount the possibility of entry by a competitor. The relevance of this to the discussion in hand is that it apparently reduces the scope, or need, for state anti-monopoly measures. Even for 'natural' monopolies, the mere absence of actual competition within a market ceases to be a sufficient indicator of monopoly power.

These and other influences, in combination with the elaboration of the 'public choice' theory of government, help to explain a change of attitudes by many economists towards the nature of the state itself as an economic agent. Previously the general presumption was that the state was benign in

Table 6.1   Size of public sector in OECD countries, 1960–86

	Total government expenditure (% GDP)	Current government receipts (% GDP)
1960	28.5	28.3
1970	32.4	31.2
1980	39.3	35.7
1981	40.0	36.0
1982	41.4	36.1
1983	41.5	35.8
1984	40.5	35.6
1985	40.7	36.0
1986	40.2	35.7

Source: OECD Economic Outlook, December 1982 Tables R8 and R9, and June, 1988, Tables R14 and R15.

its intentions, with the theory of policy centred around the question of how best the state could maximize social welfare. There is nowadays far less readiness to assume that the state is benign, acting on behalf of the public interest to maximize social welfare.

Public choice theory, which has fruitfully applied the methods of economics to the analysis of politics, makes a contrary assumption: that the state as an institution, the government as a collectivity and politicians, bureaucrats and other individual actors in political processes each act to serve their own interests. Within this model of politics the voter is analogous to the consumer in economic life, and democracy to consumers' sovereignty. The absence of democracy leads to maximization of producers' (that is, politicians, bureaucrats) surplus, rather than social welfare, and is thus analogous to monopoly.

A view of the state as an agent, exerting monopoly power to maximize its own revenues, was consistent with the seemingly inexorable rise during the 1960s and especially, the 1970s in the size of the public sector and relative to total economic activity. Table 6.1 shows trends for all OECD countries taken together, expressed as percentages of GDP. Tax burdens were rising relative to incomes and the late 1970s saw the emergence of symptoms of a 'tax revolt' in various industrial countries. There was a growing belief, exacerbated by a slow-down in growth, that this trend could not continue indefinitely but that it would take a determined effort to halt the trend, let alone to reverse it. Such concerns, and doubts about the marginal benefits derived from additional expansions of state activity, contributed further to the shift in opinion away from interventionism. (In the event, it appears from these statistics that both expenditures and revenues, relative to GDP, peaked in the early 1980s, although the failure of either proportion to show much diminution since reinforces the view that actually reversing the trend will be a difficult task.)

This catalogue of influences on the retreat from *dirigisme* adds up to a rather formidable set of arguments. It has been derived, for the most part, from writers within the mainstream of economics. What should be added – and what makes the case all the stronger – is that the scepticism is by no means confined to those of a conservative disposition. Radical writers are scarcely less dismissive of interventionism. Moreover, economic reforms under way in China, the Soviet Union and other socialist countries are based on a recognition that central planning approaches are not working well, and there is a desire to make more, albeit carefully circumscribed, use of material incentives and market forces. We should also mention seemingly leftist governments in Western Europe, for example in France and Spain, which have undertaken policies more often associated with conservative governments, and the various other democratic socialist parties which have re-thought, or are attempting to re-think, their policies to make them less *dirigiste*, more accepting of market mechanisms. It would not be correct to characterize this situation as a disillusionment, for Marxian writers have always viewed governments as representative of specific class interest, usually opposed to the interests of the mass of the population. They thus have a good deal in common with more conservative authors in the public choice tradition in seeing the state as predatory rather than benign. What to a less sceptical economist might look like policy 'mistakes' may appear an entirely rational promotion of special interests to those – left or right – who see the state as acting on behalf of privileged interest groups.

To sum up, it is evident that these intellectual strands are responses to genuine felt deficiencies, by no means just a matter of fashion or fad. There is no case for trying to turn back the clock and reverting to the approaches of earlier decades, nor would there be intellectual support for such a regression. But with any human response to a stimulus there is a danger of over-reaction, and there is evidence of a realization of this in economics. It is to this that we turn next.

THE PARTIAL REHABILITATION OF THE STATE

By no means all the brave promise of post-Keynesian macro theorizing to banish the state from the tasks of economic stabilization has been fulfilled. There has, in fact, been a substantial decline in enthusiasm for monetarist, RE and NCM theory. The research from which Friedman derived many of his policy conclusions has been subjected to severe methodological criticism to which no response has been forthcoming. The monetarist approach to policy has also been undermined by large and rapid shifts in the demand-for-money function which the theory assumes to be stable. Private sector behaviour is not now regarded as stabilizing in the way postulated by monetary theory, and that theory is now seen as glossing over the large difficulties of defining and controlling money supply, given greater force as a result of recent innovations in financial instruments.

'Natural rate' theories of unemployment are also now being regarded with more scepticism. Such theories differentiate sharply between structural and cyclical unemployment but recent research indicates that the two in fact tend to move together, raising questions about whether they are separate, independent and identifiable components of total unemployment, as 'natural rate' theory requires.

There have been retreats too on the RE and NCM fronts. Rational expectations theory is particularly criticized for the unrealistic claims it makes for individuals' ability and willingness to absorb and process information, and to act upon the results. RE models assume that agents behave as if they know as much about the structure of the economy as the policy-makers, even though the structure and underlying relationships are constantly changing. There are also criticisms of the extreme assumptions of the NCM approach, of its difficulty in explaining unemployment in a market-clearing context and its inability to explain observed real effects of monetary policy.

Perhaps most pertinent to our present purposes, none of the successive attempts in the new macroeconomics to 'prove' the inevitable impotence of government attempts at macro management is regarded as having succeeded, mainly because of the extreme assumptions that have to be made for the proofs to hold. Thus, Friedman's 'proof' that active monetary policies will be entirely ineffective rests on *simultaneous* stabilizing actions by the private sector. We have referred already to the extreme assumptions of the RE model; the NCM school is vulnerable to the same attack, not only because it takes over the assumptions of rational expectations theory, but also because the NCM model is one in which all markets clear instantaneously (thus making all unemployment voluntary). Attempts to show the inevitable impotence of government policy because of completely offsetting behaviour by private agents (complete crowding out) are no longer regarded as successful, or even helpful. Models which modify the RE and NCM assumptions, while retaining many other features, suggest there is scope for active government macro management. Indeed, by also drawing attention to the importance of the supply side in macroeconomic performance, the new theories may actually point to the need for a wider range of policy interventions.

At a practical policy-making level there is also evidence of a retreat from the more *laissez-faire* approaches of the earlier 1980s. There are similarities between the 'New Cambridge' doctrines that were severely criticized by monetarist and RE writers a few years ago and the received wisdom of the present time that sees a strong link between the budgetary and balance of payments deficits of the USA; and an apparent reversion to Keynesian orthodoxy in solutions advocated by the Group of Seven. The recognition by the finance ministers of the G7 countries, of the costs of freely floating market-determined exchange rates, and their conversion to the merits of managed rates provides a further example. There has also been a substantial retreat from the prescriptions of strict monetarism, which have proved politically and technically unfeasible.

None of the above should be read as implying that the new theories have been wholly rejected. Far from it, for instance, the recommendation that government policies should be targeted to achieve some given and stable rate of growth of *nominal* GDP has become orthodoxy. (This rule does seem curious, though, for neither governments nor their citizenry are likely to be indifferent about the shares of real growth and inflation in any increase in nominal GDP, in which case it might be better to have separate targets for each.) There is similar acceptance of the main thrust of the RE school: that policy-makers must in designing policies take the expectations of the public more fully into account, a requirement which considerably adds to the complexities of policy formation and which probably reduces the probability that a given policy will achieve the desired result. However, the more extreme anti-intervention claims of some advocates of the new theories are rejected.

There is a similar story to tell when it comes to the policy implications of the theory of contestable markets. There has been developed a theory of perfectly contestable markets, analogous to perfect competition, from which a case can be derived for reduced state anti-monopoly interventions. Here too, however, extremely demanding conditions must be satisfied for a market to be perfectly contestable. There must be no legal cost (including sunken cost) or other constraints whatsoever on entry and exit from the market, and only when these conditions are satisfied will 'hit and run' competition of the type that would constrain an incumbent monopolist be possible. Clearly such conditions are unlikely to be satisfied in the real world, particularly in 'natural monopoly' industries, so that the potential scope for anti-monopoly interventions is, in practice, not much reduced. What the theory does do, however, is to remind us of the importance of entry conditions in conditioning the scope for monopoly rents and as a variable for policy to influence.

In other areas too there are trends in the literature that reassert the potential value of government interventions, and which disagree with the view that most economic distortions are the result of such interventions. Thus, the concept of 'market failures' has proved quite robust against the criticisms of pro-market writers. Market failures include:

1. Failures of competition, existence of monopoly power.
2. The existence of certain desirable goods and services that would not be supplied (or not efficiently) by private markets because they could not be made profitable – public goods.
3. Externalities: disbenefits which are not reflected in producer's costs; benefits which are not reflected in their revenues.
4. Incomplete markets, where markets fail to produce items which people desire even though they would be willing to pay more than the cost of production for them. Various kinds of insurance are a common example, as are forward markets. Also covered here is the case of inadequate co-ordination of complementary producers.
5. Information failures, most notably a tendency to under-produce information to which access cannot be limited. Other examples include possible creation of *mis*information, necessitating regulations to secure truthfulness in advertising.
6. Macroeconomic disequilibria, including inflation and cyclical unemployment.
7. Poverty and inequality: market solutions may result in conditions which are inconsistent with societal preferences on such matters.
8. The need for governments to promote or produce 'merit goods' because individuals do not always act in what is regarded by the state as their own best interests. Laws requiring seat belts to be worn in cars are an example; health warnings against cigarettes are a negative illustration.

In addition to these largely 'allocative' failures, there is also an important set of what has been described as *dynamic*, or 'creative', market failures. This refers to failures to expand the production frontier at an optimal rate. This might result, for example, from suboptimal levels of investment and innovation, perhaps due to scale economies, or from inadequate supplies of entrepreneurial abilities to exploit economic opportunities and propel the economy forward.

Relatedly, there has in recent years been particular interest in the issues thrown up by various kinds of 'Prisoner's Dilemma' and by the existence of common property rights. A 'new political economy' school has grown up which is principally interested in situations – such as those described by the Prisoner's Dilemma' – in which co-operative solutions, which may conflict with the outcomes resulting from atomistic maximizing behaviour, produce superior results. Their conclusion is that co-operative behaviour cannot be secured voluntarily, leaving the state as a probable agency for enforcing a co-operative solution.

Both in the literature and in politics, there has also been growing concern with environmental issues. In their economic aspects, these largely concern the existence of important external diseconomies – side-effects of industrial and agricultural production which are harmful to society but are not fully reflected in production costs and are thus overproduced.

Mention was made earlier of the theory of directly unproductive profit-seeking (DUP) activities as giving increasing weight to the costs of policy-induced economic distortion. Here too, however, the theory is not unambiguously anti-interventionist, for many DUPs result from the existence of monopoly power and the scarcity-premia it can create, which can just as well occur in the private as the public sector.

Finally, it should be said that debates about what the evidence shows concerning the relative efficiency of markets and state interventions are far from over. For example, the evidence comparing the performance of private and public enterprises is not uniformly in favour of the former; and the chief conclusion of analyses of the policy of privatization or divestiture is that the degree of competition in an industry is a more important determinant of the economic and social efficiency of an enterprise than the nature of its ownership. And it has not gone unnoticed that two of the most successful economies of the post-war period – Japan and South Korea – are scarcely exemplars of the free-market model. While there has, thus, been a partial rehabilitation in economics of the desirability of state interventions in the macroeconomic and microeconomic management of the economy, how extensive those interventions should be and what boundaries should be drawn round the role of the state remain the subjects of intense debate.

THE ROLE OF THE STATE: CLARIFICATIONS AND COMPLICATIONS

In considering the desirable role of the state there are essentially two different issues, which are sometimes confused, first, how large should the state be in relation to total economic activity; and second, what types of policy instrument should the state employ? To ask, 'Is it likely to be in the public interest for the state to intervene here?' is different from the question, 'If so, what would be the most effective type of measure for it to introduce?' A particularly common source of confusion is between arguments for a reduction in the role of the state and arguments for a shift from policies of planning and control to policies which work through markets. Suggestions, for example, for a change in government import policies from quantitative restrictions to tariffs are not, *per se*, about the extent to which government action is necessary to limit imports, but about the most efficient way of achieving that objective. Similarly, the liberalization of financial markets does not do away with the need for policy instruments to influence the volume of credit and may well be associated with the creation of new regulatory bodies to safeguard the interests of depositors and investors.

As has already been suggested, the balance of the arguments about 'controls versus markets' has shifted against controls, with major implications for the design of policy strategies. While there is a tendency in that direction, shifting policies in more market-orientated directions is not synonymous with reducing the relative role of the state. For one thing, it is entirely open to governments to make the judgement that some prices are too important to be determined by markets alone. Interest, wage and exchange rates are obvious examples. At a more micro level, fuel and agricultural input prices are among those in which the government is likely to take a close interest, as are the prices charged by private monopolies.

The question of how large the state should be, asked generally, is often an unhelpful one. Ideological and other preferences and the policy objectives that arise from them, past practices, socio-economic structures, the supply of private entrepreneurship – as well as the capabilities of the state itself – are all factors which differ markedly between countries, which is why the relative importance of the public and private sectors varies so much across countries. Since the essence of the problem is one of balancing market failures against state failures, of calculating the costs of state inaction against the cost of state intervention, the solution which suggests itself is that the respective roles of the public and private sectors should be determined by the comparative advantage of each. There are, of course, intractable measurement problems involved in such an application of a cost-benefit approach. Another difficulty is that evaluators' objectives differ, some placing more importance, say, on personal liberty, others on the satisfaction of basic wants. As a result, there would be disagreement about the 'shadow prices' that should be employed in such an evaluation. Nevertheless, the comparative advantage approach has merits as a way of thinking about this subject, particularly for those of a pragmatic bent.

Having made the basic point, it is, however, necessary to add some qualifications. First, while it is often over-stressed, the question of the absolute size of the state *is* significant in terms of its implications for liberty and for the incentive effects of the resulting levels of taxation and state provision. Since many interventions are revenue-using they imply greater taxation, and since neutral taxes are unavailable this taxation tends to have adverse effects on economic incentives that must be set against any positive effects resulting from the interventions themselves.

Second, we should note that the clear distinction we have so far been drawing between the public and private sectors is in practice often absent. This is clearly the case in the productive system where between the 'pure' cases of public and private enterprises there are likely to be jointly-owned ventures, public concerns with hired-in private sector managements, private concerns operating publicly-licensed franchises, co-operatives, and so on. In the use of resources too, the distinction between public and private consumption may be blurred, for example, through the use of public subsidies for basic necessities, or 'privately-provided' education, health and housing.

A more general – and important – point, however, is that state–private relationships are generally symbiotic. The returns to a new factory, for example, may depend crucially on investment by the state in a new road, and the economic viability of that road may depend no less crucially on its use by the factory. In terms of personnel too, it can be hard to know private from public agents, as in governments and public administrations many of whose members are actively engaged in business; or where private agents are so beholden to the state for their incomes as to effectively eliminate their independence. A further illustration is in the realm of taxation, where government revenues from a given tax system are highly sensitive to the level of activity in the private sector, just as the performance of the private sector will be influenced by the structure of the tax system. It is also possible that the abandonment by the state of a policy that was having adverse economic effects would strengthen its capacities to act effectively elsewhere in the economy, for example, by permitting it to concentrate its resources on a narrower range of tasks, or by raising its credibility with the general public. To return to the examples of Japan and South Korea, the lesson to be learned from their success is not that they left markets free – for they did not – but that in both cases the relationships established between their governments and private sectors were highly supportive and non-antagonistic.

A closely related difficulty about delineating the desirable role of the state concerns the fuller appreciation economists now have of the complex interrelations that commonly exist between a policy intervention and the economic system. It was, for example, growing understanding of the complex interactions between target and instrument variables that contributed to the erosion of Keynesian orthodoxy and awareness that well-intended policies could easily be dysfunctional, especially when time lags were introduced.

The recent literature on fiscal stance and on the economic effects of budgetary deficits is similarly much concerned with the feedbacks between fiscal and other economic variables, since much of government revenue and some expenditures are partially determined by the level of economic activity as a whole – a factor which makes it difficult to ensure that fiscal policy moves the economy in the way intended. For related reasons the concept of the 'structural' budget deficit is employed, which relates to the deficit that would result from a given set of fiscal decisions *and* some trend value of GDP. A second example of feedbacks can be drawn from recent writings on trade policy in conditions of imperfect competition. This draws attention to the dependence of the effects of trade policies on the precise nature of the structure of the industry in question. Thus, even though familiar principles of trade policy apply, no universal prescriptions emerge.

A SUMMARY

Intellectual developments in the 1970s and 1980s raising questions about the effectiveness and desirability of state interventions in various aspects of economic life were a fruitful response to real problems. There is no question of reverting to the *status quo ante*. At the same time, there was a tendency for the reaction against *dirigisme* to go too far, with the more extreme theoretical attempts to 'prove' the impossibility of effective government action having been unsuccessful. There has thus occurred a partial rehabilitation of the state – but one which has left much scope for debate about the desirable extent of its involvement in the economy.

In approaching this question a comparative advantage approach can be useful, at least when there is a consensus about goals, leaving the resulting relative importance of public and private sectors to be determined as an outcome of the relative efficiencies of each sector. In any case, the dividing line between the 'public' and 'private' sectors is often cloudy. It has been suggested that there is increased support for the view that policies operating through market forces are more likely to succeed than policies of control and command. The effect of this is likely to limit the scope for state interventions to some extent; greater awareness of the complexity of policy–economy interactions also provides a reason for caution in urging policy interventions.

NOTE

This chapter is abridged from Killick, A. (1989), 'A Reaction Too Far: Economic Theory and the Role of the State in Developing Countries', London: Overseas Development Institute. Students can consult the original version for a comprehensive list of references.

QUESTIONS FOR DISCUSSION

1. Distinguish between the 'Keynesian', 'monetarist', 'rational expectations' and 'new classical' schools of thought concerning the role of macroeconomic policy.
2. In what ways have developments in the literature on market structures contributed to the retreat from interventionism?
3. In what sense do Marxian writers have a good deal in common with more conservative authors in the public choice tradition?
4. In what ways has the 'brave promise' of post Keynesian theorizing failed to be fulfilled?
5. Can the 'new theories' be wholly rejected? If not, why not?
6. Discuss the view that 'shifting policies in more market-oriented directions is not synonymous with reducing the relative role of the state'.

7. The Economics of Defence Spending

Michael Asteris and Heather Bird

INTRODUCTION

The defence of the realm is the first duty of any UK government. It is, however, a very expensive activity, accounting for public expenditure of more than £20 billion in the financial year 1989–90. In peacetime defence spending is an insurance premium incurred to prevent war. In other words, deterrence constitutes defence 'output'. This output can be achieved by various blends of personnel and equipment, nuclear and conventional forces, or land, sea and air units. The task of defence planners is to select the mix of inputs which will produce the maximum defence output for a specified level of expenditure.

This chapter has the following objectives. First, it sets out to establish the 'public good' nature of national defence. Second, the problems of determining the appropriate quantity of resources to be devoted to defence as a whole, and the distribution of that total within the sector, are discussed from the point of view of economic efficiency. Having explored some of the more general theoretical issues, the practical considerations that determine actual UK defence spending and policy are examined in greater detail. This involves an outline of Britain's defence roles, and their costs, an explanation of the economic pressures on the defence programme, and an assessment of the measures which the Government is taking to alleviate these pressures. Finally the options for the 1990s are considered, although in the light of the momentous political changes in Central and Eastern Europe in late 1989, there must be considerable uncertainty about future developments.

DEFENCE AS A PUBLIC GOOD

National defence is usually cited as the classic example of a good or service that will not be efficiently supplied in a private market, and which requires public provision if the good is to be provided at all. Public goods, together with externalities, increasing returns to scale and inequalities in the distribution of income, constitute market failures that reduce the efficiency of the price system and justify government involvement of some type in the economy. Whilst these other market failures may be dealt with by various combinations of market-improving methods, (including regulations, and taxes or subsidies on prices and incomes), it is argued that the particular characteristics of public goods mean that the market has to be replaced, and the goods publicly produced.

Public goods are characterized by non-rivalry in consumption, non-exclusion and non-rejectability. Non-rivalry in consumption means that one individual can consume a unit of a good or service without reducing the amount available for others. Although the marginal cost of producing an extra unit of output is likely to be positive, the marginal cost associated with an extra user is zero. In a private market this would mean that, for efficiency, users should be charged according to their marginal valuations, which in all probability would vary widely. This is clearly impractical and the outcome would be an inefficient level of private output. The non-rivalry characteristic can be applied to national defence, although not to other privately marketed goods, such as butter, nor even to certain other publicly provided goods like health care, education and roads.

Non-exclusion means that the consumption of a good or service by one individual does not preclude anyone else from benefiting from that good or service. Once the good or service is produced, there is therefore a 'free rider' problem. This reduces the incentive for any individual to provide the good and makes it impossible to charge for the product; the market fails entirely, and public provision is required if there is to be any supply at all. The non-exclusion characteristic can also be applied to national defence, but not to privately marketed goods like butter, nor indeed to health care, education or roads.

The non-rejectability characteristic requires that an individual cannot reject the good or service, even if they do not want it. Again, there is little the individual can do directly about the defence programme implemented by a democratically elected government, even if he or she disapproves of it. Ultimately, with sufficient support, the government could be voted out of office. Economists have become increasingly interested in voting behaviour, and the extent to which government decision-making reflects the preferences of voters. Arrow's paradox of voting and the practice of log-rolling, whereby politicians trade support for issues amongst themselves, mean that decisions may in fact reflect minority rather than majority views. Individuals can, however, reject butter (for low cholesterol margarines), and even health care, certain levels or types of education and road use can be avoided if so desired.

National defence meets basically all three criteria for something to be classified as a public good, although other goods and services that are traditionally provided collectively in the UK, like health care, education and roads, do not. The non-exclusion criterion in particular means that, in the absence of collective provision by government on behalf of society, national defence would not be supplied. Health care, education and roads can be (and indeed in some circumstances are) privately produced and they are not, therefore, classed as pure public goods. However, various other market failures, (typically externalities) mean that private market provision of these goods is likely to be inefficient, and probably unjust as well. Governments may therefore deem it meritorious to supply such goods and services, and they are known as 'merit goods' because they are goods that society thinks all people should have access to, irrespective of their level of income.

Of course, it is not necessarily the case that goods and services produced by the government are financed by tax revenue or borrowing. A distinction needs to be drawn between public production and public financing. Some goods and services can be publicly supplied but privately financed, through the sale of the product to consumers. (In the UK this still applies to coal, railways and the postal service.) Relatively small amounts of revenue are also collected through charges levied on the NHS, education and road use, but defence is funded completely from the public purse. It must, however, be remembered that some 40 per cent of defence spending is on equipment that is produced by the private sector, even though the quantity purchased is determined by the Government and public funds are used to pay for it. In theory there is no reason why other elements of defence have to be produced by the Government. Private armies existed in previous centuries, and it might still be possible for governments to specify the amount of manpower required and use tax revenues to purchase from private contractors. Indeed private security firms are employed to guard some military establishments in the UK. This illustrates that defence may not have to be produced in the public sector, even though an economic case can be made for collective finance. In fact the evidence suggests that competitive private tendering brings efficiency gains in certain areas.

The next question to ask is how the government determines the optimal amount of a public good to supply. Economic theory suggests that society should produce up to the point where the marginal cost of extra production to society equals the marginal social benefit of higher output (MSC = MSB). The MSB derives from the demand for the public good. Society's benefit (demand) will be the sum of all individual benefits (demands). In the case of a private good, the market demand curve is the horizontal sum

Figure 7.1   Market demand for a public good

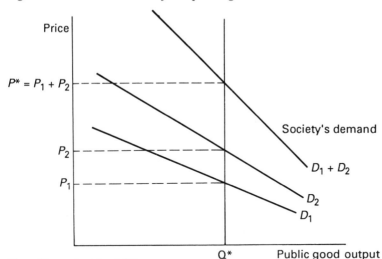

Note: For output level Q*,
Individual 1 would be prepared to pay P_1
Individual 2 would be prepared to pay P_2
Society, composed of individuals *1* and *2*, would be prepared to pay
$P^* = P_1 + P_2$

of individual demands, because purchase by one individual precludes others from buying the good. But with public goods, because of non-excludability, the market demand is the vertical sum of individual demands. Figure 7.1 illustrates this point, assuming society comprises two individuals, 1 and 2.

Assuming increasing and then decreasing returns to scale in the supply of the public good, society's MC curve will fall at first and then rise. Society's demand curve reflects its marginal valuation of each unit. So Figure 7.2 shows the socially optimal quantity of the public good at the intersection of the MSC and MSB curve, that is, at E.

In practice, the problem is to ascertain people's willingness to pay so that MSB can be derived. The free-rider problem may cause individuals to understate their true valuations. So output decisions are made through the political process. Cost–benefit analysis can be used by governments to decide whether a project is worthwhile from an economic point of view. Wider social considerations beyond the purely financial ones may be significant.

Some studies attempt to measure the redistributional implications of publicly funded and produced goods and services[1]. Despite problems, it may be possible to distribute the benefits from government health, educa-

Figure 7.2   Marginal social costs and benefits of a public good

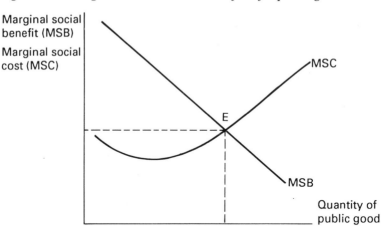

tion, housing and road expenditure across groups of households classified by income. But it is usually assumed that defence affects all citizens equally. The structure of the taxation system used to raise the finance for such expenditures also has equity effects. Changes in the structure of UK taxation recently, (particularly the removal of high marginal rates of income tax, the erosion of the income tax threshold, the increase in indirect tax and the introduction of the poll tax), have reduced the progressiveness in the system.

DETERMINING PUBLIC EXPENDITURE ON DEFENCE

Understandably, questions relating to the choice of the appropriate level and distribution of defence spending by government are of concern to economists. Since resources are limited it is not possible to achieve all desired ends, so a scale of priorities is needed. The cost of any objective can therefore be measured in terms of what has to be sacrificed in order to achieve it. This, of course, is known as opportunity cost. Defence provides an excellent example of this fundamental economic concept, because it involves both the choice between military and civilian expenditure and the necessity of selecting priorities within the defence budget.

To achieve an efficient allocation of scarce resources, economists would apply marginalist principles. In so far as the Government's choice between spending money on defence, as opposed to health, education, road building or other programmes is concerned, the efficient distribution of resources between sectors would be that which equalized the marginal rate of return to society from expenditure on each sector. This would ensure that every extra pound of tax payers' money spent on defence would yield the same extra utility to society as each extra pound spent on health, education or roads. Under these circumstances, public money could not be reallocated to increase society's welfare. It is, however, unlikely that such a rule could ever be applied except in a fairly loose fashion. But asking the relevant question may be helpful, even where it is difficult to give a precise answer.

The next tier in the decision-making process is to decide how to allocate resources within the defence budget. This would involve, for example, making choices between expenditure on nuclear as opposed to conventional weapons, the army as opposed to the navy or air force, a tank as opposed to a frigate or a Harrier jet aircraft. Which allocation of expenditure would generate the greatest security return? The same basic economic principles apply, and the same practical problems arise, not least the fact that many of the concepts used, such as the marginal security yield of different defence systems, are frequently intangible.

There are severe problems associated with the calculation of such rates of return, which essentially involve a comparison, in money terms, of the costs and benefits of alternative public sector investments. Many relevant benefits are difficult to measure objectively since no money value is immediately available. How can we value human life in the case of health investments, or the deterrent effect of defence expenditure, or the productivity gains from education expenditure or time savings from new roads? By using various techniques, economists elicit shadow prices for these and other non-marketable effects, but they are often little more than rough estimates, and they give rise to much uncertainty and debate about the outcomes of the analyses. The difficulties are made even more acute in that most forms of government expenditure involve externalities, such as the R & D spillover often associated with military programmes. Moreover, in calculating rates of return, the time dimension is significant. How do you compare the immediate benefits from reduced hospital waiting lists against greater national security in ten or more years' time? A great deal hinges on the choice of the social discount rate, which is itself somewhat imprecise.

Leaving aside the seemingly intractable problems of calculating such rates of return, this approach assumes that the government's objective is to allocate scarce resources as efficiently as possible, and indeed that this efficiency is synonymous with maximum social welfare. (The relevance of distributional equality to social welfare is ignored.) The public choice approach however – discussed in more detail by Tony Killick in Chapter 6

– argues that politicians and civil servants are in the business of maximizing their own utilities, which, for the politicians means maximizing the lengths of their political lives, and for civil servants, may mean maximizing their own salaries and power. In the long run, such activities are likely to increase the size of the public sector. Even so, social welfare considerations may act as a constraint on the utility maximizing behaviour of politicians and bureaucrats.

Public choice theory suggests that politicians may be tempted to move resources from high to low return sectors, if they perceive this as likely to result in a net increase in votes, or satisfy a powerful lobby group such as the domestic defence industry. In practice, of course, the decision about how much public money to allocate to different sectors is the result of an annual planning process involving revenue raising (taxation), macroeconomic stabilization and political considerations, as well as claims on resources by spending departments. The Government's spending proposals are set out annually in the public expenditure white paper, which is debated in Parliament. There has been much discussion about the planning and control of public expenditure in the light of its fast growth in the 1950s and 1960s. Attempts have been made to contain, and even reverse, this growth since the mid 1970s. The strategic importance of defence has resulted in periodic defence reviews, in which the future plans for the sector are outlined and from which the public expenditure implications are drawn each year. Recent developments in Eastern Europe are likely to prompt a major review of UK defence expenditure in the early 1990s. Moreover, accelerating inflation in the UK has served to reduce the real value of the defence budget and has forced the Government to consider where economies can be made.

DEFENCE ROLES AND COSTS

Effective defence of the UK in the late twentieth century is provided collectively through the North Atlantic Treaty Organization (NATO). Within this framework, Britain's armed forces have four distinct but complementary main roles:

1. The provision of an independent strategic nuclear deterrent. For two decades this ultimate guarantee of Britain's security has consisted of four submarines fitted with Polaris missiles. These vessels will be replaced by Trident-carrying missile submarines in the mid 1990s.
2. The direct defence of the United Kingdom. This involves all three services and is more than simply a matter of defending the homeland.

The UK serves as a forward operating base for maritime operations in the Atlantic and as a rear operating base for ground and air forces on the Continent.
3. A contribution to the defence of the European Mainland. This largely takes the form of British Forces Germany which has two components, the British Army of the Rhine (BAOR) and RAF Germany (RAF(G)). The total strength of BAOR is approximately 56 000, although when reinforced on mobilization by regular and Territorial units and by reservists this would increase to about 150 000. RAF(G) normally has about 10 000 personnel in Germany and forms part of NATOs Second Tactical Air Force.
4. A contribution to the defence of the Eastern Atlantic and Channel areas. The UK has the largest navy of any European NATO country and provides some 70 per cent of ships available in these areas. The scale of the contribution reflects the fact that the sea lines of communication across the Atlantic, English Channel and North Sea are vital to NATOs reinforcement and resupply plans.

In addition to the principal defence roles, there are a number of commitments beyond the NATO region, including the stationing of forces in the Falkland Islands, Hong Kong, Belize, Brunei and Cyprus. These 'out-of-area' responsibilities are, in essence, the scattered remnants of what once constituted an imperial defence commitment.

Programme Shares

Such an extensive military programme makes substantial demands on national resources. The defence budget for the financial year 1989–90 amounts to £20 143 million – more than 10 per cent of general government expenditure and about 4 per cent of gross domestic product (GDP). Some £9 000m of defence funding is allocated to support functions, for example, training and contingency stocks. This expenditure underpins front-line capabilities. As Table 7.1 demonstrates, the remaining £11 108m can be directly assigned to each of the nation's principal roles. The table also shows the approximate proportion of attributable costs absorbed by each of the major commitments.

Servicing such a spectrum of commitments implies that Britain must maintain a full range of modern forces. The requirement translates into an absence of specialization in terms of any one arm of the services. This balanced mix of forces necessitates a labour intensive army, together with an airforce and navy which are relatively capital intensive. Consequently,

Table 7.1   Estimated costs of defence commitments 1989–90[a]

Commitment		Cost (£m)	Percentage of total
Nuclear Strategic Force		1158	10
Defence of Home Base		2189	20
Defence of Central Front		4349	40
of which:	BAOR (incl reinforcement)	(3163)	
	RAF Germany (inc reinforcements)	(1123)	
	Berlin	(63)	
Maritime		2590	23
of which:	Eastern Atlantic	(2048)	
	Channel	(542)	
Other[b]		822	7
TOTAL		11,108	100

Source: Statement on the Defence Estimates 1989, Cm 675–1, London: HMSO, p 38.

Notes: a All the costs shown include directly attributable expenditure on capital works and equipment, and running costs for material and manpower. The costs of operational headquarters, bases and general operational support have been attributed *pro rata*.

b Includes the costs of amphibious capability, the Allied Command Europe Mobile Force, The United Kingdom Mobile Force, and out-of-area commitments.

ground, sea and air forces absorb roughly equal proportions of budget outlays.

International Comparisons

Maintaining a broad 'great power in miniature' capability through to the late 1980s has placed a comparatively heavy economic burden on the UK. This is apparent from Table 7.2, which reveals that of the NATO nations only the USA and Greece have devoted a greater proportion of GDP to military ends in recent years. Yet for many years prior to the 1980s, Britain's rate of economic growth was considerably lower than that of most other Alliance members. The outcome of this longer-run trend has been to place the UK among the less prosperous nations of the Atlantic Alliance. Compared with other leading members of NATO, Britain is therefore unique in having a high ratio of defence spending to GDP, together with a low per capita income.

Table 7.2   Defence expenditure of NATO members as a percentage of GDP at current prices

Country	1980	1984	1985	1986	1987	1988ᵃ
Belgium	3.4	3.1	3.1	3.0	3.0	2.9
Canada	1.9	2.2	2.2	2.2	2.1	2.1
Denmark	2.4	2.3	2.2	2.0	2.1	2.2
France	4.0	4.0	4.0	3.9	3.9	3.8
Germanyᵇ	3.3	3.3	3.2	3.1	3.1	3.0
Greece	5.7	7.1	7.0	6.1	6.2	6.6
Italy	2.1	2.3	2.3	2.2	2.4	2.4
Luxembourg	1.2	1.2	1.1	1.1	1.2	1.3
Netherlands	3.1	3.2	3.1	3.1	3.0	3.0
Norway	2.9	2.8	3.1	3.1	3.4	3.3
Portugal	3.5	3.3	3.2	3.2	3.1	3.1
Spain	2.3	2.4	2.4	2.2	2.4	2.2
Turkey	4.6	4.4	4.4	4.8	4.4	4.2
United Kingdom	5.0	5.5	5.2	5.0	4.7	4.5
United States	5.1	6.2	6.5	6.7	6.5	6.1

Source: NATO Review, **36**, (6), p 31.

Notes: a Estimate
b These percentages exclude expenditure on Berlin.

ECONOMIC PRESSURES

Having elucidated the UK's military roles and their cost it is appropriate to turn to an examination of the economic pressures on the defence programme, starting with an outline of trends since 1945.

Post-War Trends, 1945–89

In essence, British defence policy can be reduced to a simple equation. On the one side are military and political aspirations, which together determine the desired defence effort. On the other side are to be found the economic constraints, in the sense of the nation's ability or willingness to bear the cost. In the long term, military and political aspirations must be equal to or less than the level dictated by economic constraints. What one could term the central dilemma of post-war defence policy has been the almost perennial tendency for military and political aspirations to try and exceed this level. In short, successive governments have identified vital defence obligations which they have then been reluctant to fund adequately. Examples of this tendency to overstretch are provided by the experiences of the immediate post-war period, the early 1950s and the mid 1960s – hence, the resort to periodic cutbacks in obligations euphemistically referred to as defence reviews. From the mid 1940s to the mid 1970s these exercises in retrenchment accounting sought to realign aspirations and resources by reducing extra-European commitments.[2]

The importance of maintaining Britain's contribution to NATO was a focal theme of the 1974 defence review which temporarily brought force plans and expenditure plans into line. By the final years of the decade, however, the defence programme was once again displaying the clear characteristics of overstretching.

On entering office in 1979 the Conservative administration emphasized its determination to upgrade defence in the pattern of national spending. This increased priority was highlighted by the Government's early endorsement of the NATO aim (adopted in 1977) to increase defence spending, in real terms, at an annual rate of 3 per cent until the end of the financial year 1985/6. This rise notwithstanding, in 1981 it was decided to look again at the existing defence programme. However, the review was overtaken by the 1982 Falklands Conflict and many of its proposals were either amended or abandoned. More specifically, a number of the intended cuts in the surface fleet – including the scrapping of the Royal Navy's assault ships and the sale of an Invincible-class carrier – were not implemented.

By the mid-1980s financial provision for military purposes was more than one-fifth greater in real terms than in 1979, despite the Government's strong desire to restrain the growth of public expenditure. This substantial increase led to defence becoming the second largest spending programme after social security, whereas in the late 1970s it also trailed education and health.

Since then defence has been required to play a more positive role in containing government spending. In real terms, (excluding outlays attributable to the Falkland Islands, which between 1982 and 1989 were met from outside the defence budget), there has been a cumulative reduction in military expenditure during the latter years of the 1980s of about 4 per cent. This still leaves spending a good deal higher than in 1979, although as a percentage of total government expenditure, defence has slipped below health and education into fourth place. However, pressures on the defence budget have remained intense.

Rising Costs

The basic reason for this situation is that the cost of defence inputs – manpower, equipment and other items – tend to rise faster than prices in the economy as a whole. This Relative Price Effect (RPE) – which is expressed as an index of defence prices divided by the GDP (market prices) deflator – implies that the volume of military capability purchased by a given budget, at constant prices, tends to decline over time.

Manpower accounts for over 40 per cent of defence spending. This large slice of the total reflects the fact that the remuneration of regular forces and civilian staff must be set competitively in order to attract and retain the desired quantity and quality of personnel.[3] Unfortunately, maintaining adequate rates of pay increases the pressure on the Ministry of Defence (MoD) because the cost of awards above the level of GDP inflation must be met from elsewhere in the defence budget. The pay problem is accentuated by the shrinkage in the pool of potential military manpower. Between 1980 and 1995 the number of men in the 16–19 age group – from which the Services largely recruit – will fall by more than a third. This demographic trough is already leading to manpower shortages – hardly the sort of conditions in which to contemplate tight pay restraints.

Equipment absorbs a further 40 per cent or so of defence outlays. In part, rising procurement costs reflect the fact that competition in many sectors of the market for defence products has tended to be very limited, thereby reducing the incentive to give the greatest value for money.[4] However, the cost increases also reflect the increased sophistication of successive generations of weapons in response to rapid developments in technology, and changes in the perceived threat. For example, the Type 22 frigate cost four times the price of its predecessor, the Leander, and a Seawolf guided missile three and a quarter times that of Seacat. These generation-on-generation cost increases are not included in formal RPE statistics provided by the MoD. To a degree the extra cost of more sophisticated weapons constitutes greater output in the sense of permitting what Americans term 'more bangs for the bucks'. Yet national accounting conventions do not allow for the improved performance of newer equipment. In a purely defence context, there may, however, be considerable merit in this omission since the effectiveness of a weapon depends upon performance relative to that of an enemy. Hence, if the equipment of an opponent is improving at a similar rate, then output in terms of deterrence is unchanged.

Whatever the causes, rising procurement costs tend to be self-perpetuat-

Table 7.3   The relative price effect

	Total defence budget	Pay	Non-pay	Equipment only
1975/76	− 2.2	− 5.3	.2	− 1.7
1976/77	3.6	5.5	2.1	7.2
1977/78	− .8	− 4.6	1.8	3.1
1978/79	− .3	.6	− .8	1.1
1979/80	2.5	2.6	1.6	.0
1980/81	− .6	− 1.9	.1	.0
1981/82	1.3	.1	2.0	3.1
1982/83	.7	− 1.1	1.4	2.7
1983/84	1.3	2.1	.8	1.5
1984/85	1.4	.2	1.9	2.1
1985/86	− .5	.7	− 1.0	− .2
1986/87	1.4	3.8	.2	2.1
1987/88	.6	1.6	.0	− .6
1988/89	− 1.5	− .3	− 2.2	− 3.5

Source: Fourth Report from the Defence Committee, 'Statement on the Defence Estimates 1989', HC 383 (1988–89 Session) London: HMSO, p 46.

Notes: 1. Figures for 1988–89 are provisional.
2. A minus sign indicates a negative RPE, that is a net gain to the defence budget.
3. Pay relates to Service and civilian pay and Service pensions. Non-pay relates to equipment, works, fuel and material costs. The figures for RPE for non-pay are derived partly from price indices for inputs used by defence contractors, as well as from information on costs of equipment to the MoD. For this reason the estimates may not fully reflect changes in productivity in defence production and in output prices.

ing because fewer ships, planes and tanks can be afforded. The result is shorter production runs with a consequent loss of economies of scale and the spreading of heavy research and development costs over only a few units. In contrast to the civilian sector, technological change is thus unable to act as a cost-reducing force.

Table 7.3 shows the RPE, during the years 1975/76 to 1988/89, for the total defence budget, for the pay element of the budget, for the non-pay element of the budget, and for equipment only. It is clear from the figures presented that all four categories display significant fluctuations. For the period as a whole, the median RPE for the total defence budget was in the region of 0.7 per cent per annum. This constitutes a substantial sum of money when accumulated over the entire period. Moreover, it is a sum which considerably underestimates overall cost pressures because, as noted earlier, the factor by which the cost of a new generation of defence equipment exceeds the cost of its predecessor in real terms is not included in the calculation.

REMEDIAL MEASURES

In an attempt to avoid either a substantial increase in the resources devoted to defence, or a major reconsideration of defence policy, the Government is attempting to deal with the problem of cost escalation in the military sector by improving the efficiency with which resources are used. This policy is being pursued on a number of fronts, including providing support activities as cost-effectively as possible so as to release resources for the front line. Consequently, services such as catering, cleaning and maintenance are being put out to contract. The centrepiece of the efficiency initiative is, however, the introduction of a more commercial approach to procurement, in order to slow the trend of increasing equipment costs. Increased competition is at the heart of the new policy. Since the early 1980s, the MoD has raised the proportion of contracts awarded on the basis of competitive forces from around 30 per cent to half or more. Numerous measures have been taken to promote competition, including:

1. The early advertising of major tenders and contracts so as to encourage more firms to bid for defence contract and sub-contract work.
2. The launch of a small firms initiative aimed at helping UK companies to enter the defence market.
3. The ending of the arrangement under which design contractors could normally expect to obtain at least the first production order. The MoD now reserves the right to go to competition for production.

The more commercial approach has had a significant impact on the cost of a number of individual projects. For example, in a competition for the supply of the Tucano trainer aircraft simulator the winning tender was more than 40 per cent lower than originally estimated; and competition for the order to produce tank thermal-imaging systems produced 20 per cent savings against previous budgetary estimates.[5] The success of this approach may be reflected in the negative RPE values in 1988/9, shown in Table 7.3. Such illustrations not withstanding, the Government's desire for more extensive competition is greatly constrained by the fact that in many spheres of procurement the sheer research and development effort required to produce major weapons systems precludes the existence of more than one or two domestic suppliers of particular items. Indeed, even with a single supplier, the needs of the MoD may be insufficient to generate the economies of scale necessary to keep procurement costs within acceptable limits.

In a national context, there is thus a conflict between the needs of competition, which requires more rather than fewer firms, and the need to achieve maximum scale economies. Other nations face a similar problem and this has encouraged the view that the solution to the competition and scale economies dilemma calls for a European solution. It is, therefore, the intention to open the European defence market to competition. At the same time, the completion by the end of 1992 of the European internal market for civil production will inevitably have a major impact on defence equipment producers because the majority also operate in the non-military sphere. Major restructuring of Western Europe's defence industries is thus in prospect as manufacturers strive to forge transnational links, so as to place themselves in an advantageous position to meet the challenges of a more competitive market place. The successful bid by GEC of the UK and Siemens of West Germany for the electronics firm Plessey, in 1989, is a prime example of major equipment producers adopting a pan-European strategy.

It appears inevitable that radical change of this kind will generate numerous problems for Britain's defence producers who, directly and indirectly, provide employment for some 400 000 people and generate exports of approximately £1bn a year.[6]

ALTERNATIVE INTERPRETATIONS

The political events in Central and Eastern Europe in the closing months of the 1980s may generate a significant reformulation of defence objectives. But before these changes there was considerable debate as to whether or not Britain's ambitious defence programme could be reconciled with the existing funding provision for defence very largely on the basis of more efficient resource use. Broadly, it is possible to discern two contrasting schools of thought on this question: these can be termed the 'official approach' and the 'funding gap' thesis.

The official approach to the funding position is optimistic. Outwardly at least the Government has consistently displayed a quiet confidence that an equilibrium between commitments and resources can be maintained without a major defence review. Each successive year of real rises between 1979–80 and 1985–6 provided the MoD with an expanding resource base and though there has been some slippage recently, defence provision remains considerably above that which was inherited. Furthermore, according to the plans laid down in November 1988,[7] some of the lost funding will be restored in the early nineties.

The alternative 'funding gap' approach argues that the annual amounts allocated for Britain's defence effort since the early 1980s have been inadequate to fully finance the existing programme. Two reasons are presented for this state of affairs. First, official predictions of defence inflation tend to be unrealistic. Second, the MoD's commitments were framed in the expectation of 3 per cent growth for some years, followed by continuing, if slower, growth in the final years of the 1980s. The view that the UK faces a funding gap is propounded by Mr David Greenwood, Director of the Centre for Defence Studies at the University of Aberdeen.[8] He contends that while in any one financial year a cash shortfall is not very significant, the gap between actual funding and required funding becomes considerable over a period of time. A gap of such magnitude cannot be bridged solely by more efficient resource utilization. In the short term, various devices – including delayed ordering of equipment and savings on operations outlays – can be deployed to contain the problem. Ultimately, however, the scale of the 'volume squeeze' implies that the problem must be solved, rather than merely accommodated. At that point, if adequate additional funds are not forthcoming, priorities need to be redefined.

Which view constitutes the more accurate interpretation of trends in the eighties? It is difficult to provide an unqualified answer to this question. On the one hand, there is evidence to suggest plenty of opportunity for increased efficiency in defence procurement. The MoD is making strenuous efforts to tap this potential and hopes, over a five-year period, to make savings equivalent to 10 per cent of the procurement budget through better costing, collaborative development of weapons and the like. Regrettably, however, there are numerous political and economic problems in the way of buying at minimum price, including the desire to keep certain producers in existence. Projects also encounter costly difficulties, as the Nimrod early-warning aircraft project illustrates.[9] Furthermore, the factor by which the cost of a new generation of defence equipment exceeds its predecessor in real terms shows little sign of declining; indeed, in the case of the most sophisticated products it appears to be increasing substantially. Eventually, the restructuring of the European arms industry should help to ease procurement cost pressures, but the timing and magnitude of the relief is, as yet, far from clear. Arguably therefore, while greater efficiency in the use of resources has as always, a useful role to play in easing resource constraints, it can only constitute a partial solution.

Unfortunately, the debate concerning the adequacy of defence resources tends to be clouded by difficulties in accurately quantifying 'full funding'. To begin with, it is unlikely that defence planners ever feel that they have sufficient resources to meet all obligations absolutely adequately. Second, UK commitments are defined in a manner which allows considerable latitude in the way they are performed; hence, inadequacies can often be glossed over.

These points notwithstanding, the existence of major resource problems during the past few years is highlighted by two developments. First, cancelled or delayed equipment purchases include tanks for the army, new vessels for the surface fleet and the upgrading of the UK's air defences. A second indicator of tight resource constraints is provided by the fall in the proportion of the defence budget spent on equipment from a peak of 45.7 per cent in 1985–86 to 40.9 per cent in 1989–90 – little higher than in 1979–80. In the past, the MoD has tended to regard a rise in the equipment share as leading to an improvement in the effectiveness of the Armed Forces. The extent of the slippage during a period of declining service manpower is therefore, disturbing.

Until the 1988 Autumn Statement indicated that military spending would rise in real terms during the early 1990s, there was a widespread feeling that the defence forces were in danger of losing credibility with both friends and foes. Arguably, therefore, the decision to increase funding in the early years of the nineties, rather than introduce broadly level provision as originally expected, constituted a recognition of how serious the resource problem had become. However, even if the planned rises in defence expenditure are not eroded by a general level of inflation in the economy above that forecast by the Treasury, real spending in 1991–92 (at 1987–88 prices) will amount to only £18.2bn, compared with £19.5bn in the last year of the UK's '3 per cent commitment'.[10] At the end of the eighties, financial pressures seemed to have eased slightly, but, as on previous occasions in recent decades, scarce defence resources are being overstretched by too many commitments. Improved efficiency, small injections of additional funds, delayed ordering of equipment and some reductions in manpower will permit the MoD to get by in the short term, but all is not well in terms of the balance between commitments and resources.

OPTIONS FOR THE 1990s

The strategically important political changes in Central and Eastern Europe in late 1989, however, may put a different complexion on the debate. The Soviet threat to Western Europe, the main concern of military planners since the mid 1940s, has been reduced by recent events. If the threat continues to decline, the UK may be able to reduce its defence commitments, by abandoning certain tasks and performing a number of other tasks less intensively. This would involve another major defence review, the outcome of which will depend upon consultations with NATO allies and observation of the continuing developments in the Warsaw Pact countries. The arms reduction talks between NATO and the Soviet Union would also be an important consideration.

Table 7.1 indicates the potential scope for retrenchment if the size and scope of Britain's military might were to be looked at afresh. The Trident programme is now too advanced to yield huge savings on its estimated £9.1bn cost, even if the Government were willing to consider the abandonment of an independent strategic nuclear force. Economies would therefore have to be fashioned from Britain's conventional capabilities. In practice, the choice would probably be the same as that which faced the Government at the time of the 1981 Defence Review: either to reduce the size of the navy, or reduce Britain's capacity for military operations in Central Europe.

If the arms negotiations make swift progress, questions may soon have to be asked with respect to the size and shape of the Armed Services. In the not-too-distant future Britain may thus be presented with a unique opportunity to recast the defence programme in such a way as to ensure that it is adequately funded. More specifically, the easing of tension in Europe could make it feasible to prune the manpower and equipment allocated to the defence of the Central Front.[11] Such action would alleviate the financial and demographic problems facing the MoD, whilst permitting greater emphasis to be placed on the defence of the home base and the protection of the Atlantic sea lanes. Ironically, the economic difficulties of the Soviet Union may thus be instrumental in resolving the long-term problem of matching Britain's security requirements with budgetary austerity.

The alternative policy strategies for the 1990s would be either full funding, or steering some middle course between that and defence cuts. The sums required to increase resources by an amount necessary to provide full funding of the existing defence programme are open to debate. However a significantly larger military budget in the recent past would, for example, have permitted earlier replacement of the army's Chieftain tanks, the ordering of more new naval vessels and better helicopter provision. In terms of the future, a substantial rise in defence appropriations would permit much more rapid replacement of existing equipment.[12] It would also enable the MoD to budget for some improvement in service pay and conditions relative to those in the civilian sector, as part of a strategy to maintain recruitment in the face of adverse demographic trends.[13] A substantial rise in military expenditure would be unlikely to receive public support at a time of greatly improved relations with the Soviet Union. Indeed, there will, understandably, be pressure for cuts in defence outlays if the threat from the Warsaw Pact continues to diminish. Furthermore, most other public expenditure programmes, including health, education and transport remain hungry for funds even while the Conservatives struggle to reduce the proportion of GDP accounted for by the state.[14] Consequently, greatly increased spending on defence is extremely unlikely in present circumstances.

The defence plans formulated at the end of the 1980s represent a middle course of action. This may be appropriate, pending the consolidation of events in Eastern Europe, and the outcome of arms reduction negotiations. In the meantime, the Government may be unwilling to base defence provision largely on Soviet good intentions. It can therefore pursue the remaining option of keeping resources and commitments broadly steady. This middle course has economic, political and military advantages. To begin with, tight constraints on defence spending ensure that the search for greater efficiency is pursued with vigour. At the same time, the rapid growth of the British economy during the past few years has provided somewhat greater flexibility in state finances than might have been anticipated. This has permitted the MoD to extract marginally better funding from the Treasury, thereby postponing the day when harsh decisions have to be taken. Militarily, the provision of a level of funding just sufficient to maintain all existing capabilities has the attraction of leaving all options open.

CONCLUSION

Little purpose is served by attempting to predict the exact outcome of any review of existing military arrangements. Indeed this nicely illustrates the uncertain conditions under which many decisions have to be taken. However, the transformation of East–West relations present Britain with an opportunity to establish a sustainable equilibrium between military commitments and resources, without compromising national security. This chapter provides the economic background for what promises to be a reassessment of both the scale and distribution of UK defence spending.

NOTES

1. See, for example, J. Le Grand (1982), *The Strategy of Equality*, George Allen & Unwin, and the biannual study by Central Statistical Office, 'The Effects of Taxes and Benefits on Household Income', published in *Economic Trends*.
2. For an overview of external defence commitments, with special reference to economic constraints in the period since the Second World War, see M. Asteris (1987), 'British Overseas Military Expenditure and the Balance of Payments' in M. Bateman and R. Riley (eds), *The Geography of Defence*, London: Croom Helm, pp 194–214.
3. The experience of the period 1975–78, when premature voluntary retirement from the armed services was at a disturbing level because of dissatisfaction with pay and conditions, provides ample evidence of this fact.

4. For a discussion of the economic performance of the industries from which defence equipment is purchased, see M.S. Levitt (1985), *The Economics of Defence Spending*, National Institute of Economic and Social Research, Discussion Paper No 92. There is also considerable relevant material in M.S. Levitt and M.A. Joyce (1987), *The Growth and Efficiency of Public Spending*, London: National Institute of Economic and Social Research, Chapter 8.

5. *Statement on the Defence Estimates 1988*, Cm 344-1, London: HMSO, p. 37.

6. A detailed examination of the problems and prospects of that part of British industry which provides military equipment is to be found in T. Taylor and K. Howard (1989), *The UK Defence Industrial Base*, London: Royal United Services Institute/Brassey's.

7. *The Autumn Statement 1988*, HCP 695, London: HMSO.

8. Mr Greenwood has presented his views on defence funding in numerous publications. See, for example, his Memorandum in the Third Report from the Defence Committee, *Defence Commitments and Resources and the Defence estimates 1985/6*, HC-37-11, London: HMSO. pp. 288–98.

9. This was cancelled in December 1986 after encountering major technical and cost problems. Consequently, a considerable sum is having to be spent on the purchase of seven Boeing E–3A aircraft from the United States.

10. These figures include expenditure relating to the Falkland Islands. See HC 383, Fourth Report from the Defence Committee, *Statement on the Defence Estimates 1989*, London: HMSO, p. viii.

11. There is already a strong economic case for reducing Britain's military presence on the Continent: see M. Asteris, (1987) *British Forces Germany: Size Versus Presence*, London: Royal United Services Institute for Defence Studies.

12. This, in turn, would help to ease manpower problems because new equipment is often considerably less labour intensive than that which it replaces. For example, Leander class frigates have a complement of around 250; the Type 23s require only about 150.

13. Between April 1988 and March 1989 the total strength of the Armed Forces declined by 5295: approximately 70 per cent of this reduction was unplanned. See HC 383, Fourth Report from the Defence Committee, *Statement on the Defence Estimates 1989*, London: HMSO, p. xxi.

14. Defence represents a pure public good, and so it differs from these three services in the sense that private funding is not an option for individuals.

FURTHER READING

Kennedy, G. (1983), *Defence Economies* London: Duckworth.

Kennedy, G. (1986), 'Managing the Defence Budget', *Royal Bank of Scotland Review* (ISO), June.

Smith, R. (1989) The Economics of Defence. *Economic Review*, January.

QUESTIONS FOR DISCUSSION

1. To what extent can economic principles assist in deciding the level and distribution of public expenditure?

2. Discuss the distributional implications of defence expenditures financed out of general taxation.

3. What factors would you consider when undertaking a cost–benefit analysis on a new piece of defence equipment? What problems would such an exercise encounter and how might they be overcome?

4. Explain the economic pressures on the UK defence budget. What

measures are the Government taking to alleviate these pressures? Are they proving successful?

5. Consider the case for and against the UK buying a far greater percentage of its defence equipment requirements from overseas.

6. Assuming agreement is reached to reduce greatly the armed forces of the East and West, which areas of the UK defence programme do you consider should be prime candidates for adjustment on economic grounds?

8. Pollution, Environment and Sustainable Development

Peter Pearson

INTRODUCTION: THE GROWTH OF CONCERN ABOUT POLLUTION

Pollution is now perceived as a major environmental, economic and political problem. It has become a 'green' issue that is securely on the political agenda, as voting patterns and opinion polls have demonstrated. Major areas of concern include acid rain, damage to the ozone layer, the greenhouse effect, oil spills (such as the Exxon Valdez incident in Alaska), and toxic waste dumping, as well as a variety of other forms of air, land and water pollution. Why might pollution problems and/or people's concern about them be expected to have increased over time? Of the many reasons here are four to consider:

1. As economic growth has occurred, more has been taken out of the natural environment as inputs to production and consumption, and more has gone back to the environment in the form of 'residuals' from production and consumption processes. This is not a new phenomenon but one that has been growing geometrically as both population and economic activity have expanded. It has posed an increasing challenge to the environment, since pollution occurs when waste residuals exceed the assimilative capacity of the environment in a given time-period, either because of their amount or their form. In some cases – for example, the 'greenhouse gases' – it can take decades or even centuries for pollution damage to occur and become evident.
2. The development and increasing use of some types of new and/or 'exotic' materials – for example, leaded petrol, some plastics and pesticides, other chemicals such as chlorofluorocarbons (CFCs), and radioactive materials – means that the environment and some of its inhabitants may have difficulty in adapting to and assimilating these

new irritants. Moreover, there are rising possibilities of irreversible changes occurring, such as the extinction of animal or plant species.

3. Increasing concern has also arisen out of recent developments in scientific and medical knowledge. There is now a fuller understanding of the impacts of certain pollutants – for example, the likely climatic effects of the greenhouse gases, the 'holes' in the ozone layer resulting from CFCs, the consequences of acid rain, and the carginogenic and mutagenic effects of exposure to radiation.

4. As per capita real incomes rise in some countries, especially the industrialized countries, there tends to be a growing demand for environmental quality. Demand increases rapidly for those types of environmental service that are luxuries and so exhibit high positive income elasticities. Hence as incomes rise we would expect increasing concern over the effects of some types of environmental pollution, especially those that are related to rising levels of consumption.

However, this is not to imply that all forms of environmental quality are always and everywhere a luxury. In the Third World, for example, many of the poorest people's ability to work, feed and clothe themselves depends on the quantity and quality of the services yielded by their natural environments and resources. For such people, the environmental quality of their land, their soil or their water is not a luxury consumer good but a necessary producer good. In many parts of the Third World, there has been increasing evidence and understanding of the damaging impacts of pollution and natural resource degradation.

As well as concern about the present impacts of pollution, there is also a growing awareness of the likely nature and scale of its future impacts. Influential recent work on the sustainability of development (for example, Pearce *et al.*, 1989) has emphasized how present choices about pollution can have major impacts on the stock of wealth, including environmental assets, that will be available to future generations. Such impacts constrain the choices open to future generations about how to meet their needs.

It is one thing to identify reasons for the increasing severity or urgency of pollution problems. It is quite another to devise appropriate and effective environmental policy strategies in response. This chapter first considers some of the difficulties of environmental policy-making. Then economy–environment interactions are discussed and three key pollution problems are outlined – the greenhouse effect, damage to the ozone layer, and acid rain. This provides a basis for the following discussion of the ways in which economic analysis can contribute to understanding why pollution problems arise and how they may be addressed. The final section focuses on pollution problems and the Third World. It discusses the problems and prospects of achieving workable international agreements to deal with global problems like the greenhouse effect and damage to the ozone layer.

DIFFICULTIES OF POLICY-MAKING

Despite advances in scientific understanding, in some areas there is still much uncertainty and controversy about the nature and extent of the relationships between, on the one hand, emissions of pollutants and changes in environmental quality and, on the other hand, between changes in environmental quality and damage to people, animals, vegetation and buildings. This is one of the main reasons why the formulation of pollution control strategies and policies is often both difficult and contentious.

The debate about appropriate policy strategies – and about the balance between the costs of preventing and controlling pollution and the costs of experiencing it – is complicated by the fact that pollution damage has three important aspects. It is spatial, temporal and sometimes irreversible:

1. The spatial aspect means that damage is often caused at a great distance from the point of emission. Thus effects can be local (noise pollution), transnational (acid rain in Europe, soil erosion in the Himalayas), or global (the greenhouse effect). On the one hand, this means that local or national policy-makers should not ignore impacts beyond their boundaries, while on the other it can also mean that local or national policies may be ineffectual unless accompanied by other national or international policy actions.

2. The temporal aspect means that damage often occurs many years after the original emissions. This is because the effects are long-lived (for example, some radioactive materials have 'half-lives' of more than a century) and sometimes because it takes a long time before the stock of the pollutant significantly exceeds the assimilative capacity of the environment (for example, the accumulation of greenhouse gases since the nineteenth century). Thus we have to deal today with polluting decisions taken many years ago; and, as has been suggested, we have also to be aware that our polluting decisions may have delayed and/or long-lived impacts far into the future.

3. The irreversibility aspect means that some forms of pollution damage either cannot be rectified, in the sense that the status quo can never be restored (an extinct species, for example), or could only be restored at an infinitely high cost. One implication of this relates to the interge-

nerational issue – it may not be impossible for future generations to benefit from some features of the natural environment because they[1] will not exist.

At an international conference held in the mid-1980s by the Organization for Economic Cooperation and Development (OECD), it was claimed that OECD countries were at a watershed in the evolution of their environmental policies. Among the new directions for policy that were identified, was the need to develop *proactive* or 'anticipate and prevent' strategies in addition to the *reactive* or 'react and cure' strategies which remain necessary to deal with already-identified environmental problems. As one of the conference participants emphasized:

> The advanced industrial societies must start to do what they have all too often failed to do in the past; that is to anticipate the environmental consequences of their economic activities and to take measures to prevent them, not only within their own boundaries but also with regard to their neighbours and with regard to the global commons. (OECD, 1985, p 23)

Moreover, it was argued that there is a danger of a vicious circle, whereby the resources available for proactive policies become limited because they have to be devoted to current environmental problems which themselves have been exacerbated by the absence of earlier proactive policies. Thus one of the key policy issues is how far governments should try either to take proactive action now in the face of scientific uncertainty and risk over-reacting, thus paying 'too much' now (in terms of the social opportunity costs of controlling pollution); or to postpone action and risk greater (and possibly irreversible) damage as a result, thus paying 'too much' in the future (in terms of the social costs of experiencing and reacting to pollution damage).

There has been considerable debate as to which is the more appropriate approach, both in general and for particular pollutants. Much of the debate has been about the balance between the costs of controlling pollution now and the costs of experiencing and controlling it in the future, with estimates of future costs being much the more uncertain. The balance of the debate has been influenced recently by the weight given to the interests of future generations in the concept of sustainable development. Thus Pearce *et al.* (1989) argued that policy should be directed towards ensuring sustainable development, where development implies achieving a set of desirable goals for society:

> Sustainable development involves devising a social and economic

system which ensures that these goals are sustained, i.e. that real incomes rise, that educational standards increase, that the health of the nation improves, that the general quality of life is enhanced. (Pearce *et al.*, 1989, pp 1–2)

And they describe the principle underlying sustainable development to be that '... future generations should be compensated for reductions in the endowments of resources brought about by the actions of present generations' (ibid, p. 3)

In the very recent past many governments have been moving slowly and often somewhat reluctantly from a largely reactive to a more proactive stance. In the case of the UK, as Pearce (1989) has noted, the practice of environmental regulation in this area was for a long time based on what is termed 'reactive bureaucratic accommodation'. It was reactive rather than anticipatory, and did not seek to develop clearly-articulated policies for the future. It tended also to operate through bargained 'accommodations' between regulators and regulated, rather than through the imposition of inflexible regulations. This resulted in an incremental approach which responded to problems as they were perceived to occur. Pearce suggested that while there can be considerable merit in the flexibility of this kind of approach, particularly in the face of uncertainty about scientific knowledge, there were serious doubts as to whether the reactive mode (although not necessarily the accommodatory approach to policy implementation) was appropriate to the new era of environmental concern. He recommended a more proactive stance.

Writing on energy and environmental policy in 1988, Pearce suggested that there was some evidence that in 1986 a limited 'green shift' towards the proactive mode had begun to occur in the UK, itself partly an accommodation to the increasing national and international pressures for policy change. But in his view, at that time:

If the green shift is to be successful – that is, if we are to accommodate anticipatory policy – there will be a major need to re-evaluate energy policy. For it will mean that we shall need to find mechanisms for internalising future uncertain damage costs into current decisions. It is neither clear that this message has been taken on board in the United Kingdom, nor is it obvious that we know how to go about this new challenge. (Pearce, 1989, p. 100)

In 1989, however, major green shifts in the UK's policy stance were signalled, both by the Prime Minister, Margaret Thatcher, and by Christopher Patten, the successor to Nicholas Ridley at the Department of the

Environment. Considerable improvements in a wide range of environmental protection measures were promised. At the time of writing, however, it is too early to be able to assess the extent to which the political rhetoric will be translated into significant impacts on policy, policy implementation and hence the control of pollution.

It is evident that proactive policy-making is neither simple nor uncontroversial, either to formulate or to implement. It requires consistency between environmental policies and related policies, including energy policy, and can require action ahead of established environmental damage and of scientific consensus about the relationships involved. It requires careful monitoring of current economy–environment relationships and of future physical and socio-economic impacts, as well as evaluation of the costs and benefits of alternative policies. All this places heavy demands on data and knowledge and is costly to implement. Reactive policy strategies, on the other hand, of their nature tend not to emphasize the forward-looking aspects nor to encourage such active and costly investigation, speculation and data-gathering. Thus in the UK, with its past lack of proactive policy-making, it is perhaps not surprising that the environmental database has been limited, much of it has not been open to public scrutiny, and relatively little economic modelling of pollution has been done (for example, few attempts have been made to measure the monetary value of environmental damage from pollution). There are some signs that this has begun to change and action has begun on all of these fronts.

INTERACTIONS BETWEEN THE ENVIRONMENT AND THE ECONOMY

It used to be customary to represent the economic system simply in terms of production processes using scarce inputs of capital, labour and material resources and transforming them into outputs of goods and services for consumption, the final act which the system existed to serve. However, environmental economics and the pursuit of sustainable development imply that this is a dangerously narrow view. Some of the key relationships involved in the broader view of economy–environment interactions can be represented in a simplified flowchart (see Figure 8.1). This indicates that there are, in particular, three aspects of the interaction with the environment that require attention from economists. They are that the environment is first, the source of natural resources; second the source of natural goods and amenities; and third, the assimilator of waste products. Let us consider briefly each aspect and the important economic questions that it raises:

1. *The source of natural resources.* The raw materials, such as iron ore, coal and oil, that are used in production processes, are taken out of the natural environment and used as inputs into production. Some of these resources also go directly to consumption, as with domestic fuels like coal, but most go to production as intermediate inputs. Economic growth tends to lead to a rapid rise in the demand for natural resources – consider energy consumption, for example. In the past this has led to concern about the implications of having an increasing flow of demands placed on a limited stock of resources, especially in cases where the economic system has been thought not to be giving the right signals about the scarcity and value of these resources.

    Thus a key economic question about natural resources is: at what rate should we use each resource and how does the present rate compare with this? For example, how fast should the UK deplete its stock of petroleum in the North Sea?[2]

2. *The source of natural goods.* The natural environment provides us with life-enhancing services, such as those of scenic views, species of wildlife, and so on. The stock of such resources is limited. Using them for one purpose may preclude using them for any other (for example, you cannot use a field simultaneously as a spoil tip and a beauty spot), sometimes irreversibly. Thus there is an opportunity cost associated with using natural goods.

    A question economists address is: which of several competing uses for natural goods makes the most contribution to society's economic welfare, in terms of broadly-defined benefits to society net of costs? Thus in the case of potential damage to natural goods caused by pollutants, it is often appropriate to carry out a cost–benefit analysis of the benefits of pollution control.[3]

3. *The environment as a waste assimilator.* We tend to use the environment as though it were a kind of sink for the waste products from our activities. Thus we make use of the atmosphere, land and water as repositories of waste from production and consumption processes. The 'materials balance principle' reminds us, however, that the residuals from material goods do not disappear into a bottomless pit but are returned to the natural environment. Physically, apart from recycling and storage in the form of capital goods, whatever is removed from the environment in the form of physical resources must eventually reappear in equal weight as waste. Thus whatever is consumed eventually reappears as waste residuals disposed of in the environment. And, as we have seen, pollution occurs when waste residuals exceed the assimilative capacity of the environment, either because of their amount or because of their form.

Figure 8.1   Economy–environment interactions

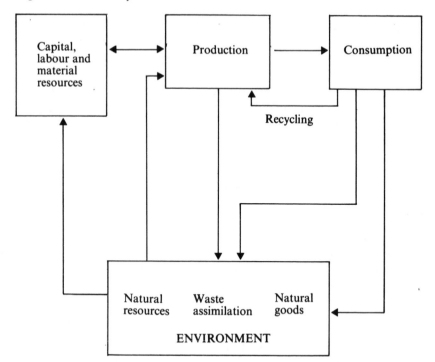

Important economic questions here include: (i) since the assimilative capacity of the environment is limited, how should we use this scarce resource? (ii) what are the consequences for both present and future generations of exceeding the assimilative capacity? and (iii) if the impacts are reversible, what is the cost of reversing them? These questions are central to the pursuit of sustainable development.

Pollution abatement is expensive and so we would not expect a society to choose to have zero pollution – even if this were possible – because the social benefits of having zero pollution could well be outweighed by the social costs of obtaining it. Zero pollution would imply that production and consumption activities (and indeed pollution abatement activities, which also have residuals) would have to be conducted at levels such that their residuals never exceeded, even temporarily, the assimilative capacity of any part of the environment. An important question, therefore, is whether for many populations this might imply exceedingly low, possibly infeasibly low, levels of consumption. For social efficiency, of course, marginal analysis suggests that pollution abatement should proceed until the point where the marginal social benefits (MSB) of abatement are equal to the marginal social costs (MSC) of abatement (see below for the derivation of the rule that for social efficiency MSB = MSC). Thus what we have to choose between is not a pollution-free versus a polluted environment but rather which pattern of pollution seems likely to contribute most to (or detract least from) economic welfare now and in the future.

POLLUTION PROBLEMS

Before moving on to consider in more detail the ways in which economics can help to analyse pollution problems and formulate control policies, it may be helpful to have a brief description of three current pollution problems: the greenhouse effect, damage to the ozone layer, and acid rain. Unfortunately it is not possible in limited space to give adequate explanations, even if there were a clear scientific consensus about the nature of these three problems.[4] It must be stressed that there is still much uncertainty and controversy surrounding the science of the greenhouse effect in particular, although it also extends to a number of aspects of the other two problems.

The Greenhouse Effect

This refers to the physical effects of the accumulation of increased concentrations of 'greenhouse gases' in the atmosphere. The greenhouse gases warm the atmosphere by trapping the heat radiated back into the atmosphere by the earth's surface. The greenhouse gases have been dominated by carbon dioxide (CO_2), with a contribution of around 50 per cent, but they also include chlorofluorocarbons (CFCs), methane (CH_4) and nitrous oxide (N_2O). Carbon dioxide is particularly associated with the combustion of fossil fuels (particularly coal, but also to a lesser extent oil and then gas), while emissions of methane and nitrous oxide are linked to the growth of human populations and agricultural development. CFCs are discussed below, in relation to the ozone layer.

The greenhouse effect is projected to lead over the coming decades to increased global temperatures, with associated climatic changes, such as altered rainfall patterns and eventually significant increases in the global mean sea level. The major consequences of global warming include impacts on natural vegetation, including forests and grassland, and agricultural production (which is very sensitive to climatic change). They also include the possibility of severe problems for low-lying, island and coastal nations; indeed it has been suggested that almost every country with significant regions near sea level may be eventually affected. Because of the potentially enormous scale of the costs of either controlling the rate of global warming (for example, cutting down the use of fossil fuels, with all that that might entail) or trying to adjust to the impacts of global warming (for example, population migrations, constructing coastal defences), the greenhouse effect raises the issue of proactive and reactive policy strategies in a major way.

Damage to the Ozone Layer

The ozone layer (located in the stratosphere, 20–25 km above the surface of the earth) filters incoming ultraviolet (UV) radiation, including harmful UV–B radiation. Exposure to UV–B is believed to increase the incidence of skin cancers and cataracts. The main cause of ozone depletion has come from CFCs – which have been widely used as aerosol propellants, as refrigerants, in insulation materials and as industrial solvents. CFCs act by releasing chlorine which destroys the ozone molecules. Nitrous oxide and methane, industrial and agricultural by-products, also damage the ozone layer. Action has begun to control CFCs and ultimately it is hoped to phase them out altogether. However, it is worth noting that ozone-friendly substitutes for CFCs are not necessarily also greenhouse-friendly; this demonstrates the complexity of atmospheric pollution problems.

Acid Rain

Sulphur dioxide, chiefly from fossil-fuel combustion such as coal-fired electricity generation, and nitrogen oxides, especially from vehicle exhausts, are emitted into the atmosphere. Complex transformation processes then precede the fallout of acidic pollutants, in the form of both wet deposition (hence 'acid rain') and dry deposition. Subsequent processes can lead to damage to vegetation, animal and human health, physical structures, such as buildings, and more generally to the beauty of the natural environment. As fossil fuel consumption increases, the extent of the acid rain problem tends to expand, although control measures (for example, flue-gas desulphurization in coal-burning power stations) now exist. In recent years transnational deposits (for example, across Europe) have been exacerbated by the widespread use of very tall chimney stacks. Slow but increasing progress has been made recently in negotiating and implementing international agreements to control sulphur and nitrogen oxide emissions.

MARKET FAILURE, ENVIRONMENTAL RESOURCES AND POLLUTION

A major issue in pollution policy is the extent to which the market can be expected or relied upon to allocate environmental resources efficiently and appropriately. Some economists claim that there are scarce environmental resources that markets tend not to allocate effectively – and that these include the atmosphere, the oceans and sometimes forests. They argue that the services of the environment tend to be underpriced, so people overuse, indeed, abuse them. The key feature of the market as a decentralized resource allocator is that prices convey signals about the relative scarcity and value of resources. If the right kind of market operates then its prices will reflect the social opportunity costs and benefits of resource use. So when people use a resource they bear and hence are aware of the social costs of doing so and adjust their behaviour accordingly. But, as A.C. Pigou pointed out decades ago, where there are differences between the private and the social costs of resource use – where the price that individuals or groups have to pay to use a resource is less than what it costs society – where, to use the jargon, there are harmful 'externalities', then from society's point of view, too much of the resource will be used (Cornes & Sandler, 1986). The market has failed to convey appropriate price signals – and where environmental services are underpriced, people, firms and governments will tend to overuse them. This, of course, is what lies behind the 'polluter pays principle' (the PPP) – the idea that the polluter should be made to pay the external costs, the difference between private and social costs, and so will adjust his or her behaviour accordingly.[5]

It may be helpful at this point to review the condition for a Pareto-efficient resource allocation and to consider externalities within this framework. We begin with the 'product-mix' or 'top-level' condition. For two goods, x and y, we want: MRS = MRT, that is the marginal rate of substitution, the rate at which consumers are *willing* to substitute between x and y, equals the marginal rate of transformation, the rate at which they *can* be transformed into each other in production. This condition can be expressed for only one good x in the following way. We want to maximize net social benefit NSB, that is, to maximize the difference between total social benefit TSB and total social cost TSC. The necessary condition for this is that marginal *net* social benefit MNSB, that is, marginal social benefit MSB minus marginal social cost MSC, equals zero: this, of course, implies that MSB = MSC. This result can be derived a little more formally, with the aid of simple calculus:

We want to maximize $NSB(x) = TSB(x) - TSC(x)$
The first-order condition for a maximum is:

$$dNSB/dx = dTSB/dx - dTSC/dx = 0$$

or $\quad MNSB = MSB - MSC = 0$

So $\quad MSB = MSC$

is necessary for efficiency.

Externalities (also known as 'spillovers') can be defined in the following way:

> Externalities arise where the activities of one agent affect the profit or utility functions of others in ways not fully reflected in market transactions or prices, that is in ways not involving legally recognized and enforceable rights of compensation.

Thus externalities are sources of social gain or loss that do not get translated into the market signals that constitute the 'invisible hand'.

Another way of looking at externalities, as we have seen, is to say that they reflect divergences between private and social costs, such that in the absence of intervention, activities with harmful externalities may be expanded above the socially efficient level where MSB = MSC. For example, if there are marginal external costs MEC, then a market agent's private profit-maximizing decision to set price equal to marginal cost, $P = MC$, ensures only that marginal social benefits equal marginal private costs MPC, and thus that MSB < MSC and price is too low and the output of the polluting activity too high.

Since $MSC = MPC + MEC$, the social efficiency condition can be written more fully as $MSB = MPC + MEC$. The PPP requires that the market prices should be corrected by making the polluter pay the MEC as well as the MPC, so we want $P = MPC + MEC = MSC$, and the polluter would pay a charge equal to MEC at the socially efficient level of the externality. Alternatively, the PPP might be implemented by operating on the output rather than the price. The authorities could sell emissions permits allowing pollution emissions only up to the socially efficient level, and the agent could buy them. Again, the authorities might choose to regulate the polluter directly by prohibiting emissions above the socially efficient level.

In what circumstances do such polluting externalities occur? One of them is where people have uncontrolled access to a resource – what are often called 'open-access' or 'common-pool' resources. People tend to overuse such resources because access is not rationed and they do not have to pay the full social costs involved (for example, the few extra drivers whose arrival on the M25 motorway slows the entire traffic stream to a crawl, or the emitters of greenhouse gases and toxic waste who use the atmosphere, land and oceans as a free waste sink). The problems tend to result because of the difficulties of limiting access – in some cases, such as the atmosphere, it is hard to assign and enforce legal property rights of ownership and control – or they arise because of a lack of awareness of the need to limit access, because the nature of the environmental damage is not perceived. In these circumstances the market 'fails' to allocate resources appropriately, and it does so in two ways. First, there is an incentive to overuse; and second, there are no means of generating the revenues that may be necessary for environmental maintenance to prevent the depreciation of the stock of environmental capital – and this may threaten sustainability.

The next stage in the argument of course is to suggest that where there is market failure in the allocation of environmental resources, some form of action on the part of society may be desirable in order to improve welfare. As we have seen, the regulatory activity can be some method of implementing the polluter pays principle directly, either through using 'economic instruments', such as pollution charges/taxes or marketable pollution permits, or regulations limiting discharges of pollutants. It might also involve assignments of property rights allowing people either the right to be free of pollution, or to pollute. However, this method faces difficulties in dealing with the sort of multiple source/multiple recipient situations common to most air and water pollutants; this is because the 'transaction costs' of information, negotiation and enforcement tend to be prohibitively high.

I want to return to regulation later. At this point it is important to be clear about what we can take from the theory here: while in principle we might identify an efficient resource allocation – one where no opportunities to make people better off are unnecessarily wasted and MSB = MSC – in practice we do not have the information to do this (Baumol & Oates, 1988), because scientific knowledge is incomplete and/or the costs of obtaining complete information are excessive. What we settle for in the practice of policy-making are decisions where a change is thought to be an improvement on the status quo for society. In other words, governments select 'acceptable' or 'satisficing' rather than optimal, socially efficient standards of environmental quality. Economic analysis is then used to help devise ways of achieving these standards effectively, for example by minimizing unnecessary abatement costs. And here is an added complexity, mentioned earlier. When we talk of social costs, which society do we mean? And how external are external costs? The original formulators of the theory tended to use examples like a farmer's crops being set alight by the sparks from a passing train. But when we talk of acid rain or fallout from Chernobyl, the externalities are transnational, while for greenhouse gases they are global. So we have to define what we mean by 'society' in order to delineate social costs – and it is clear that we can no longer formulate our environmental policies on the basis of damage caused only within territorial boundaries. This adds great difficulty to the task of devising, implementing and monitoring environmental control strategies – it implies the need for international agreements and monitoring. It also makes it very difficult to estimate social costs if we wish to adjust prices.

Just to add an extra spanner to a works already festooned with them, there is the temporal as well as the spatial dimension to defining social costs. This used to be cited as no more than the sort of theoretical nicety that economists like to play with. However, as we have seen, it is now recognized as a fundamental issue (Spash and D'Arge, 1989). If our decision-making time horizon is limited to our own lifetime, we are likely to take very different decisions from those we might take if we considered the welfare of future generations. This time dimension not only influences policy choices but also brings problems in particular to the application of cost–benefit analysis.[6]

COUNTER ARGUMENTS

Not everybody would agree that we need to regulate because the market misallocates some environmental resources. Let us look at the counter-argument that says that even if the market signals are not appropriate now, they will be in the future – that is when the problems of environmental degradation are serious enough, successful adaptation will occur. At that time, it is argued, prices will signal appropriate reallocations of resources, including technological innovation, and political processes will also ensure the taking of necessary steps, so we do not need to worry now.

The problem with this argument is that by that time there may be significant irreversible damage – and even though there may also have been (conventionally recorded) economic growth,[7] we will not necessarily be able to undo the damage. The adaptations are not guaranteed to maintain and improve on our existing standard of living – for example, new technology might find a way round climate change but it might not be comfortable – how would you like to live indoors all the time, munching only on new-style forest-friendly eco-burgers? A further point is that even if the price signals are promoting adaptation in the right direction, they may not be able to ensure that it is at the right speed or that different types of adaptation will interact benignly. For example, the physical processes of adaptation may not be able to respond quickly enough – how rapidly can agriculture adapt to rapid climate change and species adapt to changed habitats? Moreover, this approach is essentially reactive rather than proactive, so that although there is adaptation to new environmental situations (climate change, sea level rise, for example) this might not mean that action would be taken to slow the continued accumulation of greenhouse gases. We would be continually trying to adapt *ex post* to a dynamically worsening situation.

This is about choices, in the sense that if what we do now causes irreversible changes on a significant scale, then we are restricting the set of opportunities open in the future, no matter how ingenious we are. We have to decide how likely and how important we think these options are. As an example, global warming could alter the whole framework within which we operate – and although it is conceivable that for some people it will alter it for the better, the prognostications are that it may alter it for the worse – for example, one of the latest scenarios from one of the American Global Climate Models suggests that regions that do not suffer from increased droughts seem likely to suffer from too much rain, frequently in the form of devastating storms and floods.

Now I am not arguing that the end of the world is nigh – nor am I naive enough to think that government intervention is a panacea; it could conceivably make things much worse.[8] But there is in my view no guarantee that the market will find satisfactory solutions to all of the major energy-related environmental problems, especially if it seems not to be giving the right signals to slow down the causes of the problems. If we want an example of technology unfolding in response to market incentives then we have only to think of Thomas Midgley, the inventor of leaded petrol, who also conceived the use of CFCs in refrigerators. He would – quite reasonably – have viewed himself as responding creatively to the market signals of his day.

POLICY OPTIONS

Suppose you accept that the market unaided gives inappropriate or badly-timed signals, then what can be done? Clearly, there is a range of possible policy responses to pollution problems, none of them costless to implement. Here is a very brief list of some of the most widely canvassed policy responses:

1. Adaptation, for example in the case of the greenhouse effect, population migrations, coastal defences, modified farming, and so on.

Figure 8.2   Environmental policy instruments and applications

Instrument	Examples of applications
Economic Instruments	
Taxes (polluter pays principle)/ Marketable pollution permits	Greenhouse gases Acid deposition (acid rain)
Subsidy/tax relief	Energy conserving investments Research (private) Unleaded fuels; catalytic converters
Direct public investment	Afforestation programmes Research (private)
Grant aid	Third World afforestation; soil conservation; agrarian reform & land settlement programmes Regional programmes in industrial countries
The Law	
Public regulation; law; legal liability	CFCs Toxic wastes Community property rights Unleaded fuels; catalytic converters
Zoning	Location of polluting activities
Negotiation	Localized issues; emissions; wastes; compliance with local land use and building codes
Values	
Self-regulation	Green consumers and producers
Education/Propaganda	Consumers and producers

Source: Adapted from Anderson (1989, p. 3)

2. Reduction of pollutant emissions either by direct abatement at the source (for example flue-gas desulphurization in the case of coal-fired electricity generation) or by indirect abatement, for example by reducing the levels of polluting consumption or production activities (this can be done either by reducing the demand for the activities or by using alternative materials).

3. For transnational and global pollution problems, the formation of international groups to examine evidence, consider policy responses and develop agreements.

Figure 8.2 illustrates some of the policy instruments that can be used in order to achieve policy objectives, together with some of the applications for which they can be used. When we consider policy instruments, it is here that economists have been saying for years, 'use the market to "internalise" the externalities'. In other words, implement the polluter pays principle by using market-based instruments like charges or tradable pollution permits – set appropriate prices/quantities which allow for social costs. The market may not set the right prices of its own accord, but you can use the market to encourage people to make their own adaptive choices at the prices/quantities you set. In this way they may have more choice than if you regulate their emissions by law, and the costs of abating pollution emissions may in many circumstances be minimized. Moreover, charging systems raise finance which may be essential for environmental maintenance.

It is in the area of greenhouse gases, particularly carbon dioxide, that proposals for charges – the 'carbon tax' – are currently being considered much more seriously. The level of the tax would vary according to the carbon content of fuels, so that coal would be more highly taxed than oil, and oil would be more highly taxed than natural gas. The tax would be borne partly by producers and partly by consumers, depending on the price elasticities of demand and supply. As an example, electricity generators, soon to be privately-owned in the UK, might pay the tax on carbon-based fuels. The tax would be expected to stimulate substitution away from the taxed fuels by both producers (including electricity producers) and domestic consumers. It would also encourage energy efficiency in all fuel-using sectors. In the case of the carbon tax system, it is of course exceedingly difficult to estimate how much the externality premium should be, although some iterative experimentation might permit the market's responsiveness to be gauged.[9]

However, it must be said that pricing is neither the only nor necessarily the best way of dealing with all forms of pollution in all circumstances. It can have major drawbacks. For example, pollution taxes raise revenues which could be but often may not be used to remedy environmental damage. And, as we shall see below, it is not clear that such taxes could effectively be implemented in all countries. Moreover, the fact is that government have in practice shown much reluctance to use pollution charges to achieve environmental quality targets, preferring regulations, zoning and often subsidies (which do not give polluters the incentive to seek more effective ways of abating pollution). It is, however, beginning to look as though the challenges posed by current pollution problems – and the need for revenue to finance responses to them – is giving governments an incentive to look more seriously at the use of market-based policy instruments.

Although there are obvious reasons why polluters would prefer not to face a regime of taxes, there are other reasons why governments tend not to implement them. One of these is the issue of equity or fairness – a reluctance to subject certain groups to the explicit, visible impact of taxes in the pursuit of efficiency. And on the international scene the issue of equity is of major significance.

POLLUTION, THE THIRD WORLD AND INTERNATIONAL CO-OPERATION

Growing economic activity in the Third World both threatens and is threatened by pollution damage, especially energy-related environmental damage. Sustainable development in the Third World is fundamental to the well-being of the majority of the world's population. Furthermore, projected Third World economic growth patterns have also been widely touted as key determinants of future global levels of greenhouse gases, both through increased fossil fuel combustion and the destruction of tropical forests. In addition, the loss of tropical forests threatens a serious diminution of biodiversity through the extinction of animal and plant species (Wilson, 1988).

Thus it can be argued that the pollution problems of the Third World matter for at least three reasons:

1. Their populations are so poor, so numerous and so rapidly expanding – consequently the sustainability of their development is crucial.
2. Although their per capita energy use is very low, their aggregate economic growth rates tend to be higher than those of industrialized countries – hence it is likely that this is where relatively fast increases in energy use and other polluting activities will come from.
3. Their populations are highly vulnerable – both to the disruption of food supplies through climatic change, and to the flooding of low-lying land areas in which many people live – the Nile Delta, Bangladesh, the Maldives, for example.

International discussion and negotiation over CFCs and other greenhouse gases have already begun. Why might we think that some of the major difficulties over reaching and implementing agreements are likely to arise between the Third World and the other country groupings? Anderson (1989) suggests that there are two important reasons:

1. Within the Third World the effective institutional arrangements for

environmental maintenance and pollution control are often not in place: '... the weaknesses of institutions, laws and administration in many LDCs are bound to impede the implementation of environmental policy, whether the issue is local or global. The fate of the rainforests illustrates the dilemma perfectly' (Anderson, 1989, p. 7).

2. Because of the relatively low levels of per capita income and energy consumption in the LDCs, the issue of equity in international environmental policy-making cannot be sidestepped, as the Third World delegates to conferences on the ozone layer and the greenhouse effect have themselves pointed out.

Thus the Third World is likely to co-operate with the industrialized world only at a price – if the countries are, in various ways, compensated for this. As Anderson notes, the fact that subsidies to agriculture in Europe, Japan and the US cost these countries $75 billion per year, more than twice the level of official development assistance, has not been lost in the discussions.

International agreements are, therefore, likely to be dependent on major financial (and probably technological) transfers from the industrialized countries to the Third World through aid programmes or other means. If through aid programmes, it has been pointed out that current programmes are based on principles of project-based capital finance, whereas what will be needed is a system of international public finance to implement and monitor arrangements for regulating the global commons. A number of alternative schemes have already been mooted but it is clear that developing appropriate, workable institutions will be far from easy.

What about using the market and the prospects for carbon taxation here? Third World countries understandably ask why in equity they should pay high prices for their current use of the atmosphere, when there is a problem now because in the past the industrialized countries added so rapidly to the stock of pollutants, free of charge, while their own economies were maturing. In principle, however, it would still make sense to apply the carbon tax while also finding ways of compensating Third World countries on the grounds of equity. Whether in practice a carbon tax would be implemented is another matter – the wide variations in the passing on of changes in oil prices since 1973–74 in the Third World suggest that implementation might be very patchy, quite apart from any administrative problems. One recent suggestion has been to have leasable, marketable carbon emission permits initially allocated on an adult per capita basis (Grubb, 1989). The allocation rule attempts to address one aspect of the equity issue, since it is derived from the idea that every human being has an equal right to use the atmospheric resource.

It is noticeable that in some of their more recent public pronounce-ments, commentators for the industrialized countries have begun to stress the need for population control in the Third World, presumably partly because this might be one way of limiting the growth of energy demand. However, not only are Third World countries unlikely to welcome outside admonitions to limit their populations, they may also be unable to do so in the absence of that most effective of birth control devices, the rapidly rising income level.

CONCLUSION

I conclude with a passage from an article written by the late Professor Alan Coddington in 1972, entitled – with intended irony – 'The Cheer-mongers – or How to Stop Worrying and Love Economic Growth':

> Samuel Butler hit on a great insight when he wrote: 'All progress is based upon a universal innate desire on the part of every organism to live beyond its income.' Since the industrial revolution industrialised societies have been able to fulfil this desire by consuming their natural wealth at unprecedented rates. Is this cause for celebration or disquiet?

In my view it is cause for both celebration and disquiet.

NOTES

1. The ambiguity in this use of 'they' is not unintentional, since the consequences of pollution may mean that the membership of future generations will be different than it might have been.
2. Some natural resources, such as timber and fish stocks are renewable (although in practice they are also sometimes extinguishable). Others, such as fossil fuels, are non-renewable or exhaustible. None the less, the question about the rate at which to deplete them is important in both cases.
3. For more discussion of cost–benefit analysis applied to environmental issues, see Common (1988), Mishan (1988) and Pearce *et al.* (1989).
4. And even if I could claim to have studied and understood all the science myself, which I cannot.
5. For more discussion of the PPP, see Pearce *et al.* (1989, pp 156–61).
6. See Pearce *et al.* (1989, pp 132–52) for a helpful discussion of the problems involved in using discounting procedures in cost–benefit analyses of environmental issues.
7. See Pearce *et al.* (1989, chap. 4) for a discussion of environmental accounting and ways of modifying the system of national accounts to allow for: (*a*) measures of welfare loss due to environmental pollution; and (*b*) measures of depreciation in the environmental resource base.
8. The work of Niskanen, Peacock and others (Buchanan *et al.* (1978)) reminds us that politicians and bureaucrats are not necessarily either altruistic or efficient. Moreover,

government regulatory activity is expensive, both to implement and to monitor. The question of the extent to which markets or governments will 'fail' to allocate environmental resources appropriately cannot be answered by theoretical reasoning alone. It also requires empirical analysis.

9. Space does not allow further discussion of the carbon tax. However, see Pearce *et al.* (1989, pp. 162–66) for more analysis. See also Grubb (1989) on marketable emission permits.

REFERENCES

Anderson, D. (1989), 'Environmental Maintenance and Investment', in Pearson, P. (ed.) *Energy and the Environment in the Third World*, Surrey Energy Economics Centre Discussion Paper No. 46, Guildford: University of Surrey.

Baumol, W. J. and Oates, W. E. (1988), *The Theory of Environmental Policy* (2nd edn), Cambridge: Cambridge University Press.

Buchanan, J. M. *et al.* (1978), *The Economics of Politics*, London: Institute of Economic Affairs.

Coddington, A. (1972), 'The Cheermongers or How to Stop Worrying and Love Economic Growth', *Your Environment*, Autumn.

Cornes, R. and Sandler, T. (1986), *The Theory of Externalities, Public Goods, and Club Goods*, Cambridge: Cambridge University Press.

Grubb, M. (1989), *The Greenhouse Effect: Negotiating Targets*, London: Royal Institute of International Affairs.

Mishan, E. J. (1988), *Cost-Benefit Analysis*, 4th edn, London: George Allen and Unwin.

OECD (1985), *Economy and Environment*, Paris: Organization for Economic Cooperation and Development.

Pearce, D. (1989), 'Energy and Environmental Policy in the UK', in Pearson, P.J.G. (ed.), *Energy Policies in an Uncertain World*, London: Macmillan.

Pearce, D., Markandya, A and Barbier, E. B. (1989), *Blueprint for a Green Economy*, London: Earthscan.

Spash, C. L. and D'Arge, R. C. (1989), 'The Greenhouse Effect and Intergenerational Transfers', *Energy Policy*, 17(2), pp. 88–96.

Wilson, E. O. (ed.) (1988), *Biodiversity*, Washington, DC: National Academy Press.

FURTHER READING

Baumol, W. J. and Blinder, A. S, (1988), *Economics* (4th edn), San Diego: Harcourt, Brace, Jovanovich, Ch. 34.

Common, M. S. (1988), *Resource and Environmental Economics: an Introduction*, London: Longman, especially Chs. 5 and 8.

Downing, P. B. (1984), *Environmental Economics and Policy*, Boston: Little, Brown.

Energy Policy, Butterworths. Recent issues contain a number of relevant articles, including: Everest, D.A. (1989), 'The Greenhouse Effect: Issues for Policymakers', **17**, pp. 177–81; Skea, J. (1988), 'UK Policy on Acid Rain', **16**, (3), pp. 252–69.

Goldsmith, E. and Hildyard, N. (eds) (1990), *The Earth Report II*, London: Mitchell, Beazley.

Hartwick, J. M. and Olewiler, N. D. (1986), *The Economics of Natural Resource Use*, New York: Harper & Row, chs. 12 and 13.

Park, C. C. (ed.) (1986), *Environmental Policies: An International Review*, London: Croom Helm.

Pearce, D., Markandya, A. and Barbier, E.B. (1989), *Blueprint for a Green Economy*, London: Earthscan. Useful and inexpensive.

QUESTIONS FOR DISCUSSION

1. Collect, graph and interpret data on economic activity (for example, GDP, sectoral output), energy use and pollution for at least a decade.
2. What criteria might you use to evaluate: (*a*) an environmental policy strategy; (*b*) an environmental policy instrument?
3. For what reasons might governments and others prefer to use regulations rather than pollution charges or emissions permits to control pollution?
4. Why do economists so often recommend the use of market-based policy instruments like pollution charges or permits?
5. What are the differences between private property, common property and open-access resources, and why are these relevant to pollution control?
6. If you were trying to decide between proactive and reactive environmental policy approaches to deal with one pollution problem, what criteria would you adopt and what information might you need?

9.   Wage Bargaining in the 1980s

Peter Ingram

The purpose of this chapter is to investigate the process by which the size of periodic increases in pay received by separate groups of employees was determined in the British economy during the 1980s. Strictly speaking the terms 'pay negotiations' or 'collective pay bargaining' need to be qualified because they imply the presence of a trade union in the process. While this is the case in the majority of instances,[1] regular wage reviews are also present in non-union environments. Where unions are recognized by management, wage settlements are normally negotiated through collective bargaining. However, in circumstances where no union is present, wage rises are typically determined by management award. It is important to stress that wage reviews take place in both union and non-union sectors and that the influences on these reviews is essentially similar.[2] As a result, in this chapter the two sectors of the economy are largely treated together. Where distinctions are drawn between the experience of union and non-union groups this is made apparent in the text. Otherwise for both sectors of the economy the terms collective bargaining, pay negotiations and wage reviews are interchanged for the purpose of variation.

Wage bargaining and its tendency to give rise to inflationary increases in money wages has represented an enduring problem for the British economy during the post-war period. The rationale behind the imposition of incomes policy is to attempt to contain the rate of growth of earnings in the economy to a defined upper limit. In 1979 the election of a Conservative Government with a commitment to free-markets heralded the end of the most recent period of statutory wage restraint – the Social Contract – and a return to free collective bargaining. The period from 1979 to date represents the longest consecutive period of free collective bargaining since the Second World War. In this chapter we focus on the outcome of the process of collective bargaining during the 1980s and the factors that have influenced these outcomes. In the final section the impact of wage growth on the macroeconomy is addressed.

119

PERIODIC WAGE REVIEWS

The rate of growth of money wages is largely determined by the size of pay increase awarded in periodic wage negotiations between employers and employees, frequently referred to as wage settlements. There are many dimensions to wage settlements: the duration of wage settlements, that is the period between each periodic review; the settlement calendar, that is the date which the parties undertake a review of wages; the level and distribution of the increase in wages across workplaces as a consequence of the wage settlement; the influences contributing to upward and downward pressures on the size of the settlement and finally the extent to which the influences reflect movements in the macroeconomy.

Although the process of wage review is present throughout the economy we focus attention in this chapter on the manufacturing sector, first, because manufacturing represents the largest relatively homogeneous sector of the economy and second, because the pattern and influences on pay determination are most complex here. Other sectors of the economy, particularly the non-traded public sector and the private services sector display many characteristics that are present in manufacturing, although typically the range of influences on wage demands are not so diverse.

In order to address these issues we shall use data from a survey of wage settlements in private manufacturing industry conducted by the Confederation of British Industry (CBI). This data set provides a continuous series of details on wage settlements since it was established in 1979. The questionnaire survey is completed by a member of the management negotiating team who has had direct involvement in the settlement process. In addition to determining the rate of increase in wages as a result of the settlement, the survey asks its respondents further questions covering the implementation date and expected duration of the settlement; the level of wage claim, if any; an evaluation of an extensive set of factors potentially influencing the settlement; and information relating to any industrial action taken in support of the claim.[3]

SETTLEMENT DURATIONS AND CALENDAR

The vast majority of collective agreements have a 'contract' duration of twelve months. In 1989 fewer than 10 per cent of agreements were 'longer-term' in the sense of lasting for more than a year. In effect therefore most employees receive a wage review annually. The increase in pay as a result of these reviews is usually expressed as a percentage increase in the level of earnings negotiated at the start of the previous contract, in other words, as

Table 9.1   The settlement calendar 1988/89

	Wage settlements (%)
August	2
September	3
October	6
November	6
December	4
January	23
February	4
March	5
April	21
May	7
June	8
July	11
TOTAL	100

an annual percentage increase. Moreover individual companies' wage settlements are located at different 'anniversary' dates throughout the year (see Table 9.1), and as a result the pattern of pay bargaining throughout the economy is a continuous process. The twelve-month duration of a wage settlement and the notion of an annual settlement 'year' starting in August each year became an established feature of wage bargaining following the implementation date for the £6 pay limit incomes policy on 1 August 1975. This and subsequent stages of the Social Contract prohibited the introduction of more than one pay settlement within any given twelve-month period. The convention of a twelve-month pay review with a settlement year running from the 1 August to 31 July the following year endured through the 1980s despite the return to free collective bargaining in 1979.

Following this convention, Table 9.2 examines the process of wage bargaining over ten complete 'pay years'. It is important to stress the point, implicit in the notion of a 'settlement calendar' that the process which gives rise to the demand for higher wages in the UK is both institutional and regular.

FACTORS AFFECTING THE PAY INCREASE

Much of the literature on wage determination in economics is directed towards explaining differences in wage levels between individuals and occupations.[4] Wage equations typically explain observed differences in

Table 9.2   Average settlement and properties of the distribution (annually 1979/80–1988/89)

Year	Mean	Mode	(percentage at mode)	Zero settlements	RPI
1977/78*	10.0	10.0	(85.0)	–	11.1
1979/80	16.3	15.0	(16.8)	0.9	18.6
1980/81	9.0	8.0	(14.1)	1.3	13.5
1981/82	7.0	5.0	(12.9)	3.1	10.7
1982/83	5.7	5.0	(18.5)	5.1	5.3
1983/84	6.0	5.0	(18.3)	1.6	5.0
1984/85	6.4	6.0	(16.8)	1.1	5.7
1985/86	6.1	6.0	(18.7)	1.6	4.5
1986/87	5.2	5.0	(20.0)	3.4	3.6
1987/88	6.0	5.0	(18.3)	0.9	4.0
1988/89	7.4	7.0	(14.2)	–	7.3

Source: CBI Pay Databank, RPI Department of Employment

Note: *Preliminary data from pilot survey

wage rates in terms of human capital and the nature of employment. The observed differences in wages are therefore dependent on education, age, experience and other factors embodying the heterogeneity of labour and the type of job in which the individual or occupational group are employed including the size of the company, the concentration ratio of the industry and capital intensity. While such wage equations can account for the observed differences in wage levels between individuals, occupations, or industries, in practice the process of wage bargaining is about negotiations over rates of change in money wages. We have already shown that in more than 90 per cent of firms in any given year, wages are the subject of annual negotiations over the extent of the percentage increase in pay. A wage function, at the individual company level, therefore needs to be developed to explain the rate of change in the wage rate.

The variables defined in the equation explaining wage differentials are not ideally suited to explaining the process of wage growth. The rate of change needs to be defined in terms of more volatile, company specific variables. The main explanatory variables in such an equation, in no particular order of importance are changes in company profits; changes in productivity; the company's demand for labour; comparisons with other groups of employees; changes in the cost of living and the size of wage increase in the previous period. Each of these variables can affect the pressure for the demand for higher wages by employees and influence the employer's capacity to award a given increase.

Profits

The level of company profits and particularly changes in the level of profits play an influential role in determining the size of a wage increase. Improving company profitability, reflecting improvement in the company's fortunes is likely to fuel employee expectations for a higher wage increase. Correspondingly the firm's ability to award an increase in wages is strengthened. Conversely at times of reduced or falling profitability employee expectations are dampened and the firm's ability to award increases in wages is diminished.

Productivity

Changes in output per person employed operate in the wage equation in the same way as profitability. Clearly an increase in output per person gives rise to claims or expectations from employees for wage increases that reflect this improved performance. Improving output per head is also likely to enhance the employer's ability to concede a higher wage increase. Likewise falling productivity reduces the demand for higher wages and diminishes the employer's capacity to award increased wages.

In certain circumstances the process of wage negotiation may be explicitly broadened to include productivity enhancing changes in working arrangements, whereby an element of the pay offer is made contingent on employees accepting changes in working practices. In effect this process represents a *de facto* process of productivity bargaining where pay is used to secure change to improve workplace efficiency.[5]

Cost Competition

Th extent of competition in the product market for a company's goods and services will have a significant impact on its ability to award a given pay increase. Research into variations in the size of the trade union wage differential has argued that the size of the union wage differential is likely to be larger, the greater the firm's monopoly power in the market for its output. During the 1980s, with the increased presence of competitive forces as a commercial constraint, price competition in the marketplace has greatly restricted companies' ability to award sizeable pay increases. In manufacturing, labour costs represent on average about 70 per cent of value added (Williams, Williams and Haslam, 1989), so an increase in a firm's wage bill can be significant. Other substantial cost components, particularly raw materials and fuel, are usually purchased at prevailing world commodity prices and their price is beyond the control of the individual enterprise. The control of increases in labour costs is however, located within the firm. Clearly, while external as well as internal forces influence the demand for a wage increase, an individual firm's ability to meet a wage demand will be restricted by its capacity to absorb the increased costs it generates, without passing them on in the form of increased product market prices. This pressure will be particularly acute in the traded sector where the demand for the company's product is extremely price sensitive. Thus the ability to raise prices will greatly affect a company's ability to fund a pay demand.

Buoyancy of the Labour Market

Movements in the state of the labour market represent a crucial variable in the wage change equation. In effect, this is the demand for labour relative to its available supply. The interaction between these two forces at any given time is crucial in determining the balance of power in collective bargaining. If employers are shedding labour through redundancy, employees will perceive their position or job security to be weakened, and this effectively shifts the balance of power towards the employer. If however the company is seeking to recruit new labour in order to expand or make good the attrition of employees retiring or leaving the company, existing workers will perceive their position to be relatively secure and the balance of power in collective bargaining will shift towards the employees. Moreover, in a situation where there is a scarcity of potential recruits, those individuals in demand will be able to choose between competing employers as to which job they take. Thus in a time of labour shortage a company will have to offer a competitive wage increase to attract the labour it requires. Such a wage increase will serve the dual purpose of retaining its existing employees as well as attracting new recruits. In this respect awarding a competitive wage increase will reduce the likelihood of another employer poaching a company's existing employees. The task of retaining employees and preventing poaching can represent a major pressure on management wage offers within local labour markets where movement of workers between firms can be widespread.

In addition to recruitment and retention pressures from the labour market, management also has to ensure that its workers are motivated to perform the task they are employed to do effectively. Eliciting the required performance and commitment to a job requires that employees are properly motivated. This is analogous to the efficiency wage theory of wage determination. Efficiency wage theory, rather than treating labour as a factor of production that can be purchased in varying quantities, argues that improved reward gives rise to improved effort and efficiency of employees. In order to feel motivated or committed employees must perceive the rate of increase in wages they are awarded to be right or consistent with their notions of what represents a fair pay increase. Failure to achieve this by violating employees' perceptions of what is right may reduce their performance or may result in increased absenteeism and costly labour turnover. Motivation can therefore often depend on how employees compare themselves with other workers or movements in the price level.

The problem of recruiting, retaining and motivating employees represents a complex balance of forces acting on the wage negotiation process. It is clear that employers have to be mindful of other companies' wage decisions for fear of becoming uncompetitive in terms of recruitment of employees, or risking retention problems, or giving rise to a perception that the wage rise is a low one and thus demotivating employees. This pressure emphasizes the intense interdependence between companies recruiting from the same labour market.

Comparability

This interdependence is manifested in the interrelated notion of comparability in British wage determination, that is comparisons with other groups of employees. The maintenance of customary differentials or relativities between different groups of workers through comparability effectively maintains the structure of earnings levels throughout the economy and ensures that the rate of growth in earnings in the economy over time is not widely divergent. The influence of comparability therefore involves an employee demand that they receive an increase in pay on a parity with other groups of workers. This pressure can exert itself over a number of years. The rate of change in wages is a dynamic, usually annual process. As a result, the size of the wage increase in previous years can exert an influence on the level of pay settlement in any given period. An individual wage settlement may diverge from the mean due to particular company circumstances in any given year; however over time the forces of comparison tend to exert themselves. As a result, over a series of years pay relativities demonstrate greater stability, through a process known as regression towards the mean.

Prices and Inflation

In addition to comparisons with other groups of employees are the comparisons made with movements in retail prices, or the retail price index (RPI). Changes in the cost of living act as a major source in fuelling wage

Figure 9.1   Manufacturing wage settlements 1979–89

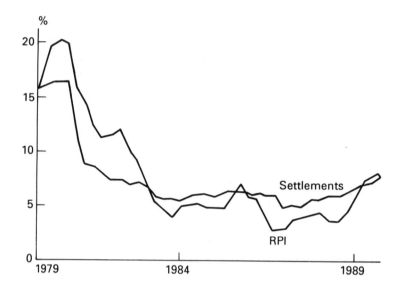

expectations. Employees expect this wage increase at least to make good the erosion in the real value of their living standards through the effects of inflation. The fact that inflation is usually expressed as an annual figure probably represents the greatest institutional force for having annual wage reviews.

OUTCOMES OF WAGE NEGOTIATIONS

Having outlined the important variables that will determine the extent of pressure for a change in money wages it is worth stressing that the impact of these influences will vary over time and exert differing forces according to first, the state of the individual workplace (that is, the prosperity of the company) and second, the state of the economy.

The annual average outcomes of wage negotiations from 1979/80 to 1988/89 are shown in Table 9.2. Figure 9.1 shows the average level of wage settlements plotted quarterly during the 1980s contrasted with movements in the RPI. From an initial level of 16.3 per cent in 1979, settlements fell steeply from the summer of 1980 through midwinter 1980/81, during which time the rate of increase reduced by over a half. Since 1982, settlement averages have displayed considerable stability moving within a narrow range reaching a high of 6.5 per cent in mid 1985 and a low of 4.8 per cent in late 1986. During this period settlements appear to have varied with some sluggishness, with movements in the RPI. After decreasing appreciably in the first two years of the 1980s, the RPI reached a peak of over 7 per cent in mid 1985, coinciding with the peak in wage settlements of 6.5 per cent. The price index then fell to its lowest level of twenty years to 2.4 per cent in the autumn of 1986, at which time average settlements fell to their lowest level since monitoring began. Towards the end of the decade settlements edged up beyond this plateau to reach 7.5 per cent by 1989 when significantly, inflation was at its highest level since 1982.

In addition to the average settlement level, Table 9.2 also shows the modal wage increase in each year and the percentage of wage awards settling at that rate of increase. Of particular interest in this respect is the inclusion of data from the year 1977/78, during a time in which an incomes policy allowing a 10 per cent maximum wage settlement was in force. During that year preliminary research for the CBI survey identified some 85 per cent of all negotiations at precisely 10 per cent. Effectively the statutory limit of 10 per cent had become both a 'ceiling' and a 'floor' for negotiators, giving rise to a strongly unimodal distribution of outcomes. Since then, with the ending of statutory wage restraint the percentage of groups settling at the mode has never been above 20 per cent, generating a widespread though still unimodal distribution of outcomes as shown in Figure 9.2. The existence of a distribution of outcomes reflects the differential impact between individual companies and workplaces of their ability to pay or particular pay pressures they face. What is demonstrated by this distribution is that the notion of a 'going rate' – a prevailing percentage increase representing a target for employee wage demands, has been replaced by a greater diversity of outcomes reflecting flexibility in company wage decisions. A notably important feature of the wage bargaining process in Britain evident both in Table 9.2 and in Figure 9.2 is that throughout the 1980s, including the economic recession of 1981–82, wage settlements were seldom negative.

The most extreme outcome is represented by a zero settlement. The fourth column in Table 9.2 gives the percentage of zero settlements – in effect no change in money wages in each year. The proportion of zero settlements reached a peak in 1982/83 at just 5.1 per cent of all groups. By 1988/89, none were recorded. This suggests that even in very adverse economic conditions, pay increases were still negotiated or awarded in 95 per cent of companies and that at worst a company would award a 'zero increase'. In effect therefore, throughout the economic recession money wage cuts were rarely negotiated or implemented. This evidence also

Figure 9.2   Distribution of manufacturing wage settlements 1988/89

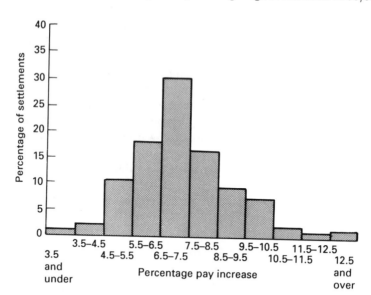

emphasizes the developed institutional basis to wage bargaining over pay increases in so far that the pattern or calendar of bargaining was adhered to even in circumstances where the firm was unable to award any increase at all.

NEGOTIATING PRESSURES

We focused above on the main variables that might explain the outcomes and range of outcomes of wage settlements in any given year. We now turn to the impact that these variables exerted on wage determination during the 1980s.

The question of the influence of negotiating pressures on wage increases was approached by Millward and Stevens (1986) pp. 245–9. Here however we use similar data from the CBI's Pay Databank survey which provides a continuous series on the influence of an extensive list of negotiating pressure throughout the 1980s and categorizes the pressures into upward or downward influences on the wage settlement process. The Databank survey asks a member of the company's management team closely involved in the pay review process, 'What were the main factors which you think influenced the level of your settlement?' Table 9.3 lists the responses to the most significant pressures during the 1980s. The figures in the table represent the percentage of companies in each year indicating whether each factor was a very important upward or downward influence on the consequent wage settlement. For example, if we take the variable 'profitability', this can exert either an upward or a downward influence on a company's wage negotiations. The influence of profits as an upward pressure on wages, shown in Table 9.3, reached a low point of just 10 per cent of companies in 1980/81 and progressively increased through the decade to 23 per cent of companies by 1987/88. Conversely, in the opposite direction, the downward influence of falling or low profits reached a peak in 1981/82 at 63 per cent of firms, and has since reduced in impact to 19 per cent of firms by 1988/89. Expressing the impact of profits as both an upward or downward pressure on wage negotiations enables a net balance to be derived of the overall effect of profits on wage demands. Taking the year 1980/81, the trough of the recession, the net impact of the profits variable exerted a downward influence in 49 per cent of cases. Since 1980/81 however, the aggregate impact of company profitability emerged from being negative in 1987/88, to exerting a net positive impact on wage demands. This intensification of the pressure on wage bargaining from profits reflects the increase in the rate of return on capital employed in the industrial and commercial sector from just 3 per cent in 1981 to 12 per cent by 1989.

The second pressure in Table 9.3 addresses the impact of the labour market on wage negotiations. Here the upward pressure of the need to recruit, retain and motivate employees is offset by the risk of redundancy. The upward pressure from the need to recruit and retain employees again increased consistently from 1981/82 to nearly a third of all companies by the late 1980s. Conversely the downward pressure from the risk of job losses was at its peak in 1980/81 and reduced to just 10 per cent by the end of the decade. As a result, the net balance of pressure from the labour market exerted its greatest downward impact in 1980/81 (35 per cent of companies) coinciding with a peak in the national rate of redundancy, and has since exerted progressively less of a downward impact on wage growth, moving into positive balance in 1986/87. This corresponds with the pronounced reduction in the rate of redundancy in the economy and latterly the fall in unemployment in the late 1980s.

The movements in the balance of the impact of profitability and labour market factors during the 1980s invite comparisons with movements in macro variables in the economy (see Figures 9.3 and 9.4). Figure 9.3 tracks movements in the net balance of companies, citing profits as a very important upward or downward pressure with movements in the rate of return on capital employed in industrial and commercial companies.

Table 9.3 Trends in company pressures on wage settlements 1979/80–1988/89 (percentage of respondents indicating very important upward/downward pressure)

	1979/80 %	80/81 %	81/82 %	82/83 %	83/84 %	84/85 %	85/86 %	86/87 %	87/88 %	88/89 %
Profitability										
Higher profits (u)	12	10	15	19	20	23	19	20	23	20
Lower profits (d)	45	59	63	54	48	40	32	26	20	19
(Balance +/−)	−33	−49	−48	−35	−28	−17	−13	−6	+3	+2
Labour Market										
Need to recruit (u) & retain	24	7	6	6	8	12	11	12	21	31
Risk of redundancy (d)	18	42	38	29	23	17	16	14	11	10
(Balance +/−)	+6	−35	−32	−23	−15	−5	−5	+2	+10	+21
Inability to raise prices (d)	37	55	54	53	52	44	41	43	37	38
Cost of Living (u)	60	47	45	36	40	45	31	23	23	60
Industrial Action (u)	3	1	1	1	2	2	1	1	2	1
Comparability	63	50	49	48	51	53	51	48	51	57

Source: CBI Pay Databank

Notes: (u) = upward pressure
(d) = downward pressure
Respondents are private manufacturing companies.

Figure 9.3 Profitability 1979–89

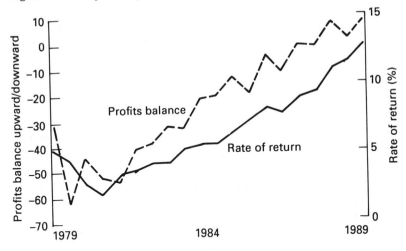

Figure 9.4 tracks the net balance of the influence of labour market factors on wage demands against the rate of redundancy and the level of unemployment. What emerges from both of these Figures is the degree of correspondence between macro economic variables and the pressure cited by companies as influencing contemporaneous wage negotiations.

Figure 9.4 The labour market 1979–89

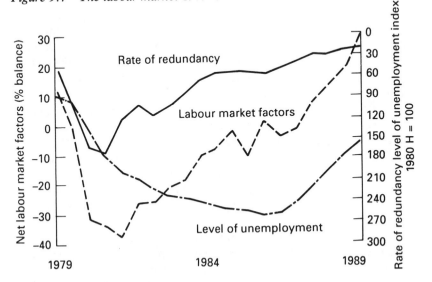

Returning to the data in Table 9.3, the greatest downward pressure on company wage settlements throughout the 1980s was the inability of firms to pass on wage increases into price increases – the inability to raise prices. This is a measure of the extent of cost/price competition companies face in their product markets. The intensification of international competition in the traded sector, both in export markets and with overseas imports in domestic markets represented one of the greatest influences on workplace industrial relations of the 1980s (Brown 1985).

The increased presence of cost competition exerted a considerable impact in terms of limiting the ability of companies to respond to wage demands. The downward pressure from the 'inability to raise prices' was at its peak in 1980/81 at the height of the recession, affecting over half of all firms. While the intensity of this pressure ameliorated towards the end of the 1980s, it remained a very important downward pressure in 38 per cent of instances by 1988/89.

The role of the cost of living as a factor in the formulation of wage demands, as would be expected, closely reflects movements in the RPI. However the number of companies where the cost of living is invoked as a very important upward pressure over time, appears to be particularly sensitive to upward movements in the rate of price inflation. Thus towards the end of the 1980s, as inflationary expectations had been progressively reduced, the sharp increase in price inflation from an average of 4 per cent in 1987/88 to 7.5 per cent in 1988/89 was accompanied by a jump from the joint lowest figure of 23 per cent of companies citing the cost of living as an upward pressure, to the joint highest figure of 60 per cent (since 1979/80 when inflation averaged 18 per cent). Finally, despite the pronounced increase in the dispersion of outcomes of individual company wage settlements, the influence of some form of comparability remained throughout the 1980s a very important influence on wage settlements in around half of all instances in any given year.

The data in Table 9.3 present an interesting perspective on the aggregate influences on wage bargaining throughout the 1980s. By the end of the decade the extent of upward pressure on pay from profits, the labour market, the cost of living and comparability had intensified, and this was reflected by an increase in the average percentage pay settlement from 6.0 per cent in 1987/88 to 7.4 per cent in 1988/89. While these results are drawn from the private traded sector they are broadly representative of the economy as a whole.

Millward and Stevens (1986 pp. 246–7) show little difference in the influence on pay settlements between those employees covered by collective bargaining and those affected by managerial award, or between manual and non-manual employees. This is largely due to the pervasive nature of the

Table 9.4 *Annual percentage changes in pay, productivity, unit labour costs and prices in manufacturing industry*

	Settlements	Earnings	Productivity	Unit Labour Costs UK	Unit Labour Costs Competitors
1979	15.9	15.6	0.6	15.2	5.2
1980	15.3	17.8	−3.8	22.3	8.5
1981	8.2	13.2	3.5	9.3	7.0
1982	7.0	11.2	6.6	4.2	4.8
1983	5.7	9.0	8.6	0.5	0.5
1984	6.1	8.6	5.5	2.8	0.3
1985	6.4	9.0	3.4	6.0	1.4
1986	5.7	7.7	3.2	4.5	1.9
1987	5.4	8.0	7.0	1.5	−0.3
1988	6.0	8.5	5.4	2.8	−1.8

Source: CBI Pay Databank, Department of Employment and OECD

factors that give rise to a demand for an increase in wages. All employers and employees are faced with the same circumstances prevailing in the economy as a whole. In the public services sector the pressures on pay demands are similar. Public sector employers face the same labour market and thus a similar necessity to retain and motivate their employees. The inability to pay, rather than being determined by the product market, is determined by cash limits on expenditure imposed by Government. Moreover, comparisons with other groups of employees and the price index form a major feature of collective bargaining in the non-traded public sector.

THE IMPACT OF WAGE GROWTH ON THE ECONOMY

The overall rate of growth in wages or earnings is of considerable importance to the state of the macroeconomy. Throughout the post-war period, nominal wage growth in Britain has tended to increase in excess of productivity growth. This has given rise to inflationary pressure, thus reducing the competitiveness of British firms and severely limiting the scope for manoeuvre in other areas of economic policy. In the past, Governments have introduced periods of incomes policy to attempt to contain the rate of wage growth in the economy. The effect of this has often resulted in pay determination becoming a political issue. How does the experience of free collective bargaining in the 1980s compare with the record of the past?

Table 9.4 shows the annual percentage changes in settlements, earnings, productivity and unit labour costs in manufacturing during the 1980s.

Employees' earnings include overtime premia and performance payments above the rate of increase in pay rates negotiated in wage settlement. Despite favourable performance during the 1980s, productivity, the annual rate of growth of output per person, consistently lagged behind earnings in each year of the decade. As a result, unit labour costs, which express the cost of labour per unit of output – essentially wage growth adjusted for productivity growth – increased in each of the last ten years. This means that the nominal cost of the labour input in production increased in each year. Moreover if we compare domestic movements in unit labour costs with an average of our main trading partners, our unit labour costs have increased relative to those of our competitors. There are two adverse consequences of this. First, deteriorating relative unit labour costs imply a loss of international cost competitiveness, necessitating either a devaluation of sterling to maintain the price competitiveness of domestic production or risking loss of market share. Second, increases in the cost of labour in relation to its productivity increase the price of a unit of production, therefore giving rise to domestically generated inflation. This is fuelled by the inflationary effects of devaluation, which in turn further erodes the value of the currency and puts further upward pressure on wage demands.

The experience of the 1980s has been less adverse than earlier decades when high wage and price inflation, low productivity growth and a depreciating currency gave rise to serious constraints on the economic management of the country. However, the increased flexibility in labour markets of the 1980s has not manifested itself sufficiently to ensure that wage growth is more closely reflective of productivity growth. As a result, UK unit labour costs increased faster than those witnessed among other G7 nations over the period.

The most recent figures in the series of indicators in Table 9.4 highlight the extent of the problem of pay bargaining and wage growth as a contemporary economic issue. Wage settlements and earnings are, at the time of writing, increasingly reflecting the intensification of pressures on wage demands. At the same time, the domestic rate of productivity growth has fallen sharply. The result of this has been an increase in the rate of deterioration in UK unit labour cost performance. The issue of wage growth in the British economy, as we enter the 1990s with the country now in the ERM, clearly represents an issue of considerable importance.

So what factors prevent a slowdown in the rate of growth of pay, or an amelioration in pressures for higher wages? What is the mechanism explaining why wage growth is increasing as it is and why the annual rate of wage inflation never dropped below 7.5 per cent during the 1980s, despite high unemployment and increased labour flexibility? Company labour market strategies may provide the best answer. As this chapter has argued, the need to recruit, retain and motivate employees represent a major influence on pay. Firms need to ensure that their employees are motivated and committed to corporate goals to achieve success. Pay is central to this motivational process; if employees' rewards do not match their notion of what is 'right', eliciting the requisite level of commitment and motivation becomes more difficult. The factors that determine employees' notions of what is 'fair' or 'right' therefore have to be assessed carefully.

Table 9.3 shows that the importance of comparability has changed little over the period since 1979. For many firms the use of comparisons is tied up with labour market positioning, with firms placing themselves relative to each other in order to ensure they remain able to recruit, retain and motivate the employees they require. Firms are understandably concerned to maintain competitive rates of pay in order to minimize recruitment and, crucially, retention difficulties. Added to this, in circumstances of increasingly increased fragmentation of decision-making about pay, individual firms are having to anticipate, in circumstances of imperfect information, other firms' decisions on pay. In this situation, pay increases set by the best performing companies can put pressure on pay awards in other firms who have not performed as well. What is clear however from the results in Table 9.3 is that trade union wage pressure does not appear to be a feature of the current upward pressure on pay. Only 1 per cent of wage settlements in 1988/89 cited industrial action as a negotiating pressure.

NOTES

1. Millward and Stevens (1986), Table 3.1 p. 51 and Table 9.1 p. 226.
2. See for example, Millward and Stevens (1986), p. 246.
3. For a full description of the data set see Gregory, Lobban and Thomson (1985).
4. See for example, King (1980), pp. 234–304 and Marsden (1983).
5. For analysis of this process in the first half of the 1980s see Cahill and Ingram (1987).
6. For an explanation see for example, Hamermesh and Rees (1988).
7. For an econometric assessment of the impact of separate wage pressures on the level of pay settlements see Gregory, Lobban and Thomson (1987).

REFERENCES AND FURTHER READING

Blanchflower, D. G. and Oswald, A. J. (1988), 'Internal and External Influences Upon Pay Settlements', *British Journal of Industrial Relations* **26** pp. 363–70.

Brown, W. (1985), 'The Effect of Recent Changes in the World Economy on British Industrial Relations', in H. A. Juris, M. Thompson, and W Daniels (eds) *Industrial Relations in a Climate of Change*, IRRA.

Cahill, J. P. and Ingram, P. N. (1987), 'Changes in Working Practices in British Manufacturing Industry in the 1980s: a study of employee concessions made during wage negotiations', mimeo, CBI.

Daniel, W. (1976), *Wage Determination in Industry* London: PEP.

Gregory, M., Lobban, P. and Thomson, A. (1985), 'Wage Settlements in Manufacturing 1979–1984: Evidence from the CBI Pay Databank', *British Journal of Industrial Relations* **23** pp. 339–57.

Gregory, M., Lobban, P. and Thomson, A. (1986), 'Bargaining Structure, Pay Settlements and Perceived Pressures in Manufacturing 1979–1984: Further Analysis from the CBI Databank', *British Journal of Industrial Relations* **24** pp. 215–32.

Gregory, M., Lobban, P. and Thomson, A. (1987), 'Pay Settlements in Manufacturing Industry 1979–84: A Micro-Data Study of the Impact of Product and Labour Market Pressures', *Oxford Bulletin of Economics and Statistics* **49** pp. 129–50.

Hamermesh, D. S. and Rees, A. (1988), *The Economics and Work and Pay*, 4th edn, New York: Harper and Row.

King, J. E. (ed.) (1980), *Readings in Labour Economics*, Oxford: OUP.

Marsden, D. W. (1983), 'Wage Structure' in G. S. Bain (ed) *Industrial Relations in Britain*, Oxford: Basil Blackwell.

Millward, N. and Stevens, M. (1986), *British Workplace Industrial Relations 1980–1984* Aldershot: Gower.

Williams, K., Williams, J., and Haslam, C. (1989), 'Do Labour Costs Really Matter?', *Work, Employment and Society,* **3** pp. 281–305.

QUESTIONS FOR DISCUSSION

1. What are the major economic principles illustrated in the process of wage determination?

2. Why might wages continue to rise even though unemployment is very high?

3. In what ways are the variables defined in the equation explaining wage differentials not ideally suited to explaining the process of wage growth?

4. Explain the relationship between improving productivity and wages.

5. Discuss the role of trade unions in wage determination both in theory and practice.

6. Examine the statement that 'the problem of recruiting, retaining and motivating employees represents a complex balance of forces acting on the wage negotiation process'.

10.   Britain's Economic Recovery

Geoffrey Maynard[1]

Mrs. Thatcher's Conservative government which came into power in 1979 was determined to make a complete break with the past in the management of the British economy.

The new strategy effectively abandoned Keynesian short run demand management aimed at full or high employment. Instead, emphasis was placed on improving the long run supply side performance of the economy. Deregulation, the abandonment of controls over prices, incomes and capital movements, the return of state-owned industries to private ownership and management, and, as urgent as anything, reduction in the power of trade unions and reform of labour laws, were all seen to be necessary. An urgent priority was to reduce inflation and to establish an environment of price stability, since without this the supply side performance of the economy could not be improved. The proposed method of doing this was by monetary control, incomes policy being rejected partly on grounds of its demonstrable ineffectiveness and partly because control over incomes was incompatible with improved supply side performance. With the abandonment of short run demand management, fiscal policy became a matter of reducing both government expenditure and taxation relatively to GDP, as a means of increasing incentives and resources for the private sector. Although it was clearly unrealistic to think of balancing the fiscal budget in any quick period of time, this seemed to constitute a long-term aim.

At the centre of macroeconomic policy lay a Medium Term Financial Strategy (MTFS) which incorporated declining targets for monetary growth and budgetary deficits over an initial four-year-period. With modifications made in the light of out-turn and experience, the MTFS was then extended throughout the life of the government, although by 1987 targets relating to broad money supply had been virtually abandoned.

Initially, with the abandonment of short-term demand management, the government had no explicit policy for employment. The government subscribed to the view that a weakening, through legislation, of the monopoly power of the trade unions would produce a more competitive labour market, and consequently the greater flexibility of money and real wages that was necessary if full employment was to be restored and maintained. However, the failure of the labour market to behave in the expected way forced the government to undertake a series of micro-measures to alleviate the unemployment problem.

The government was also committed to raising work and saving incentives through structural reform of the tax system and cuts in the burden of tax, but the scale at which changes were introduced in its first budget surprised many of its own supporters, let alone opponents, and it had macro effects that were probably not fully expected.

In brief, the policies aimed at by Mrs. Thatcher's first administration represented a substantial change from those pursued in the post-war period. The new approach seemed to represent a return to classical macroeconomics prior to Keynes: ideas of balanced budgets, of the quantity theory of money, of equilibrating labour markets, of supply determining demand rather than demand determining supply, returned to the centre of the stage. Naturally it didn't work out quite like this, but none the less there was a significant change of philosophy which might be summarized as the substitution of an attitude of 'non-accommodation' of wage and other price-raising pressures for an attitude of 'accommodation' to them. Critics of the change in attitude saw it of course as the replacement of 'conciliation' with 'confrontation'. Few can deny however that the change has had a significant impact on the performance of the British economy.[2]

Early results appeared to be catastrophic. By 1981, the country's gross national product had fallen by 4 per cent, industrial production by even more, with manufacturing production being particularly affected; and unemployment had more than doubled. Only policy with respect to inflation appeared to be a success. Such was the scale of the apparent catastrophe that, in an unprecedented (for economists!) show of agreement, 364 of the country's economists, including many of the most distinguished and influential, put their signatures to a letter to The Times (31 March 1981) deploring the policy being pursued and predicting dire consequences if it were continued. Somewhat ironically, although the government remained unimpressed and broadly continued with its policy, the publication of this letter coincided with the low point of the downturn in output. Although employment continued to fall and unemployment to rise for the next year or two, output began to rise strongly; and this was broadly sustained over the next seven years, accelerating in pace the longer the recovery continued. By 1987 even unemployment had begun to fall.

The impressive performance of the economy since 1981 is summarized in Table 10.1. GDP growth averaged over 3 per cent per annum including

Table 10.1 UK macroeconomic performance 1979–88

	1979–88	1979–81	1981–88	1979–88 (% p.a.)	1981–88 (% p.a.)	1979	1981	1988
	% change over period							
GDP incl. oil	+20.0	−3.6	+24.5	2.0	3.2			
excl. oil	+25.2	−2.0	+27.6	2.5	3.5			
Manufacturing output	+9.9	−14.2	+28.0	1.0	3.6			
Employment								
total	−4.5	−5.5	+1.0					
manufacturing	−30.0	−13.3	−18.3					
Productivity								
whole economy	+21.7	−0.1	+22.2	2.2	2.9			
manufacturing	+51.0	−0.5	+52.0	4.2	6.0			
Unemployment (% labour force)						4.7	9.4	8.2
Inflation (%)						13.5	12.0	4.5
Companies' real rate of return (%)						5.0	3.0	11.0
Share of world trade in manufactures (%)						8.5	7.0	6.6

139

oil, and 3.5 per cent per annum, excluding it (compared with barely 2 per cent in the previous decade). Manufacturing output, having been pulled down sharply in 1979–81, rose by 28 per cent, at an annual average rate of 3.6 per cent. In the last two years alone, it rose by almost 13 per cent. Unemployment has fallen from the peak level of 1986 and the inflation rate was cut by about two-thirds, although for reasons referred to later, it started rising again towards the end of 1988.

The most significant feature recorded by Table 10.1 is the substantial increase in labour productivity that has taken place in manufacturing industry. This has risen by over 4.5 per cent per annum since 1979 and by 6 per cent per annum since 1981. This performance is superior to that experienced in the 1950s and 1960s and, of course, far better than in the 1970s. Despite the relative improvement since 1980, labour productivity in the UK still lags well behind that in its major competitor countries, showing that much remains to be achieved. The so-called Thatcher productivity miracle is the subject of Chapter 11.

THE CONTRIBUTION OF MACROECONOMIC POLICY

Can the undoubted absolute and relative improvement in Britain's productivity performance, which has taken place be ascribed in any specific way to the economic policy pursued by the Thatcher government? There would probably be general agreement that the government's legislative attack on trade union power and privilege and its willingness to stand up against crucial strikes (such as that of the miners in 1984), or to provide explicit or implicit support for others who have done so (for example, during the printers' strike of 1986–7), have played a significant role in reducing trade union opposition to the introduction of new technology and to changes in working practices.

But there is perhaps less agreement on the precise part played by macroeconomic policy *per se*, except perhaps that the government's willingness to accept or (as some would say) deliberately create massive unemployment through its fiscal and monetary policies may be given credit for weakening the power of labour and strengthening the power of management.

On the surface, a macroeconomic policy which (at least until recently) appears to have constrained aggregate demand for both goods and labour excessively, which has produced high nominal and real interest rates and (so it is argued) an overvalued exchange rate, and which by the abolition of exchange control has diverted British saving and North Sea oil revenue away from investment in the UK to investment overseas, would seem to have been designed to weaken manufacturing industry and the British economy generally rather than strengthen it. This has certainly been the view of the government's critics.

There is no doubt that policy pursued by the Thatcher administration since 1979 has run greatly counter to that advocated by many influential economists (for example, Lord Kaldor) in the 1960s and 1970s. This held that the way out for the British economy was export-led growth based on an undervalued exchange rate and perhaps subsidized labour costs, emulating, so it was thought, the example of other highly successful countries such as West Germany and Japan.

Of course the parallel drawn with Germany and Japan (by the proponents of export-led growth) was always highly misleading: it failed to note that although Germany's and Japan's export success was related to depreciation of the *real* exchange rates, their *nominal* exchange rates remained strong throughout. The bases of success in fact lay in these countries' superior productivity performance, which enabled competitiveness to be combined with a strong nominal exchange rate, low inflation and rising real wages, rather than the reverse. Advocates of the undervalued exchange rate approach often seem to overlook that they are in effect advocating a low real wage strategy that would keep the UK competing in low value-added product areas in which competition from Third World countries is already acute and likely to become more so. In fact, UK export performance has been poorest in those high technology and high quality product areas where price competition is less important than nonprice competitiveness, and where world demand has been increasing fastest. A policy of exchange rate depreciation to maintain price competitiveness discourages, rather than encourages, British industry from changing its pattern of output in a direction that is necessary if Britain is to join the high productivity, high real wage league.

It is in this context, namely, the central role of the exchange rate, that macro-policy under the Thatcher administration must be judged. Admittedly, partly because of the coming on stream of North Sea oil which coincided with a rise in world oil price, and partly because of unintended tightness of monetary policy, the real exchange rate initially appreciated too severely. Also, in the early stages of its strategy, the government undoubtedly saw the key role of a strong exchange rate as the major instrument for pulling inflation down rather than as a key element in long-term industrial strategy, and it was happy to see the exchange rate fall from the excessively high level of 1979–80.

Even so, it rightly stood up to pressure from political opponents, academics and industrialists to embark on a policy of exchange rate depreciation to increase short run competitiveness. By refusing to 'accommodate' rising costs and poor productivity with exchange rate depreciation, macro-policy imposed pressure on industry to raise productivity, lower costs and generally up-market its products. It is significant that many firms whose management were often vociferous in their criticism of government policy with respect to the exchange rate in the early years of the strategy, subsequently achieved productivity improvement and product upgrading to a degree that was almost revolutionary.

NORTH SEA OIL

Of course it is obvious that a policy of maintaining a strong ('overvalued') exchange rate in the interest of encouraging a change in industrial structure and a rise in labour and capital productivity – which is necessary if international competitiveness is to be combined with high real wages – would be difficult if not impossible without some short run support to the balance of payments. Fortunately for the Thatcher government and the country, the balance of payments had that support in the shape of North Sea Oil.

The government has been attacked for wasting North Sea Oil in a consumption splurge. In fact by the end of 1986, between a third and a half of the economic rent from the North Sea had been invested in overseas assets, yielding a substantial return in the form of dividends and interest to the British economy. Perhaps more important than this, North Sea Oil revenue enabled the country's real income to be maintained at a reasonably high level whilst necessary structural changes in the economy were taking place. As a result of this income support, the willingness to accept change was probably greater than would otherwise have been the case.[3]

The years 1979–81 are generally viewed as a disaster for British manufacturing, but future historians may well judge them less as a period that pulled the Conservative government's record down than as one in which the essential basis for sustained long run improvement in economic performance was laid down. It is hard to overstate the significance of the economic shock of 1979–81, whether one takes the view that in these years UK manufacturing industry was virtually destroyed or on the contrary, forced to accept changes in its management and work practices which now give it a serious chance to survive. Indeed, although it seems unlikely that the government did in fact favour 'shock' treatment as against 'gradualism' when it first came into office in 1979, it can well be argued that the intractable nature of the UK's problems at the end of the 1970s necessitated shock treatment if the country was to escape from them. Given this view, the government's apparent overdoing of monetary restriction in 1979–81 may have been a blessing in disguise, despite its high cost in terms of unemployment, and the steep fall in UK manufacturing output (16 per cent) which occurred in those years, is, on a long-term view, irrelevant. The real test of policy is perhaps still to come, in the performance of British industry as North Sea oil runs out.

While the evidence of the years since 1981 suggests that UK manufacturing does have a future, one better than could conceivably have been expected in the traumas of the 1970s, doubts as to the substainability of the improved economic trends in the British economy can certainly not be dismissed. One such doubt arises from the low level of capital formation in UK industry in the 1980s; and indeed the government is accused of pursuing monetary and exchange rates policies that have discouraged investment. Also it might well be asked today: if the underlying supply side performance of the UK economy has improved so markedly, why has the overseas trade balance deteriorated so badly in the course of 1987/8? Why does the UK seem to be facing a balance of payments crisis once again?

As to the first point, it is certainly the case that capital formation in British industry was at a low level in the 1980s. The fixed investment – GDP ratio averaged around 19 per cent in the years 1980–7, and only about 38 per cent of this took place in industry. However, as recorded earlier, capital productivity and the rate of profit on capital were at abysmally low levels in 1979, making further investment unattractive. It can be said that the prior need in the early 1980s was to raise the productivity of the existing capital stock rather than to increase its size. Against a background of declining trade union power and more effective shop floor management, this was largely achieved by the mid 1980s and the rate of profit on capital employed in manufacturing industry has returned closer to the levels of the 1960s. It is not surprising therefore that Britain is now enjoying a substantial investment boom which is certainly necessary if economic recovery is to continue. Indeed the present investment boom has contributed significantly to the recent deterioration in the UK's balance of payments.

A BALANCE OF PAYMENTS PROBLEM ONCE AGAIN?

That there has been such a deterioration is shown in Table 10.2. In the period 1979–85, current account surpluses averaged almost £3 billion a

Table 10.2   UK balance of payments

	Non-oil balance	Oil balance	Goods and services balance	IPD balance	Current balance
1985	−4.5	8.1	3.6	−0.3	3.3
1986	−7.2	4.1	−3.1	2.9	−0.2
1987	−8.7	4.2	−4.5	2.2	−2.5
1988(e)	−18.7	2.5	−16.2	2.0	−14.2

year. 1986 saw rough balance and 1987 a deficit of £2.5 billion. In 1988 however the deficit seems likely to approach £15 billion (almost 4 per cent of GDP) and not much, if any less in 1989. While these deficits do not represent a crisis situation for the UK, since the country has sizeable overseas asset and foreign exchange reserves, it is evident that deficits of this size cannot continue without eventually creating serious problems for the UK.

A deficit in the current account of the balance of payments indicates that a country is attempting to consume more than it is producing; and a deterioration in the balance would indicate that aggregate demand has risen relative to aggregate supply, or that supply has fallen relative to demand. Even when a country is not running a trade deficit, supply side deficiencies can still exist if aggregate demand and employment have to be restrained by policy measures in order to keep overseas payments and receipts in balance.

The worsening trade situation does not seem to have been connected with a worsening in Britain's supply side performance at least in a short run: on the contrary, GDP rose by more than 4 per cent per annum in the course of 1987/8, a significantly faster rate than in the preceding five years, and employment rose quite strongly. The output of manufacturing industry, which is the source of the greater part of UK tradeables, that is, exports and import substitutes, also rose at an exceptionally rapid rate – by more than 6 per cent per annum in the two years. Thus a failure of the supply side of the economy in 1987/8 does not in itself provide the answer, and we must look to demand.

Table 10.3 summarizes the behaviour of domestic demand and its major components in recent years, as well as that of GDP and exports and imports. The acceleration of domestic demand, particularly in 1988, stands out, as do the rapid rise in imports in 1987 and 1988, and the sharp fall in export growth in 1988. Evidently imports have been sucked in by the strength of demand in the economy, and exports have also been sidetracked from meeting foreign demand to satisfying home consumers.

Table 10.3 Domestic demand and GDP (1985–88) (1985 prices)

	Domestic demand	Consumers' expenditure	Fixed investment	Government consumption	Exports	Imports	GDP average measure
1985	300.7	215.3	60.3	74.0	102.8	99.2	304.7
1986	311.8	226.8	60.8	75.4	106.6	105.6	314.0
1987	324.8	238.5	64.2	76.0	112.5	113.3	327.1
1988 (prov)	345.0	251.4	72.9	76.3	114.4	126.6	345.1
Annual percentage change							
1985	2.9	3.5	3.8	0.0	5.9	2.6	3.8
1986	3.7	5.4	0.9	1.9	3.8	6.5	3.1
1987	4.2	5.1	5.5	0.9	5.5	7.3	4.2
1988	6.2	5.4	13.6	0.4	1.7	11.7	4.4

Source: Shearson Lehman Hutton (UK Economics): UK Macroeconomic Forecast, 15 November 1988.

Note: Stock building and factor cost adjustment are omitted from this table.

The alternative view that the problem lies in a loss of competitiveness of UK tradeable goods and services – although supported by the IMF index of normalized unit labour costs which indicates a loss of competitiveness by some 20 per cent since the fourth quarter of 1986 – is not borne out by other, perhaps more telling, developments.

First, despite high earnings growth of 9 per cent per annum, unit labour costs in manufacturing have been virtually flat through 1987/8 when the trade balance worsened so markedly; second, the profitability of UK exports relative to home production, which has increased significantly since 1981, shows no deterioration in 1987/8; and third, the UK share of world manufactured exports which has steadily fallen for over 100 years, stabilized in the 1980s, and indeed may actually have risen in 1987/8.

It is significant that 40 per cent of the increase in domestic demand in 1988 represented fixed investment, a large part of which took place in industry (gross capital formation rose from 19.5 per cent of GDP in 1987 to 21.5 per cent in 1988): indeed, the increase in fixed investment between 1987 and 1988 may have approached almost two-thirds of the increase of net imports of goods and services between those two years. Thus there is reason for believing that Britain's recovery has not yet run out of steam.

RECOVERY AT RISK

Even so, although Britain's foreign trade problem in 1988 does not bear witness to the failure of the government's supply side strategy, the government cannot be exculpated from allowing domestic demand to increase too fast in 1988. The failure of policy lay mainly in the explosion of credit and money (M3) of the last two years which fuelled a substantial boom in house prices and, through an associated withdrawal of equity from house ownership, led to a boom in consumer spending. The substantial cut in taxes in the 1988 budget also contributed.

Unfortunately the government's failure to adhere to its own monetary policies and targets (its own Medium Term Financial Strategy) may put at risk some of the gains of its long-term strategy. Although labour cost inflation was restrained through 1988 by exceptionally rapid productivity growth, any slowing down of the economy in 1989/90 – which may be enforced by the threat of inflation – could cut productivity growth, so that unless money wage increases are correspondingly slowed down, labour cost inflation could accelerate markedly. A longish period of relatively slow growth and even rising unemployment might then become necessary to pull inflation back to a more acceptable level. Worse still, the present investment boom might then not be sustainable. The government's record would then look much less good.

Moreover, although the recent deterioration in the UK's balance of payments with the rest of the world does not prove that the government's supply side policies have failed, it is too soon to claim overwhelming success for them. While the government can claim that the stance of macroeconomic policy – that is, the abandonment of short run demand management and a determination not to accommodate price and cost raising pressures by deliberate exchange rate depreciation – has been consistent with the need to bring about urgently needed changes in the structure and efficiency of Britain's industry, it can hardly claim that its actions so far have been sufficient to bring about long-term industrial rejuvenation. Much remains to be done, particularly in the area of education and training. Indeed the government is much more vulnerable to an attack for things it did not do in its first two terms of office than for the things it did do. Thus convincing evidence of the success of the government's strategy is not likely to be seen before the end of its third term in office and, given the deep rooted nature of Britain's educational and training problems, perhaps not even then.

NOTES

1. This is an abridged version of a paper originally appearing in *Economics*, Autumn 1989.
2. For a more detailed account of the policies of Mrs Thatcher's government see Maynard, G., (1988), *The Economy under Mrs Thatcher*, Oxford: Basil Blackwell.
3. For an amplification of the opportunity and problems presented by North Sea Oil, see Maynard, op cit, Chapters 2 and 7.

QUESTIONS FOR DISCUSSION

1. How did the strategy of the Thatcher government in the 1980s differ from that pursued by other governments in the earlier post-war period?
2. How can the performance of the macroeconomy be assessed? How well did the UK economy perform in the 1980s compared with earlier post-war periods?
3. Evaluate the view that 'the way out for the British economy was export-led growth based on an undervalued exchange rate'.
4. Discuss the contribution of North Sea oil to the British economy. How might this contribution alter over time?
5. Account for recent UK Balance of Payments problems. How might they be alleviated?
6. Assess the longer-term prospects for the UK economy.

11. Reflections on the so-called 'Thatcher Productivity Miracle'

Lester Hunt[1]

INTRODUCTION

After more than ten years of Mrs Thatcher's Conservative government there has been much written analysing the performance of the UK economy over this period (see, for example, Godley, 1989; Layard and Nickell, 1989 and 1990; Matthews, 1989; Matthews and Stoney, 1990; Maynard, 1989; and Wells, 1989). These tend to discuss a wide range of issues, such as unemployment, inflation, trade performance, income distribution and productivity. This chapter, however, focuses on one where the government has claimed particular success, namely, productivity.

Growth in productivity is a major contributor to a nation's prosperity. Higher living standards can normally only be obtained through higher productivity, which, in turn, is an important determinant of international competitiveness. A country's competitive position in international markets improves when its productivity increases faster than that of its international competitors, unless there are offsetting adjustments in exchange rates or real labour costs. Given the importance of productivity, it is not surprising that it attracts much political and media attention. Nigel Lawson, the former Chancellor of the Exchequer, (among others), often claimed a productivity 'miracle' for the Thatcher era:

> The plain fact is that the British economy has been transformed. Prudent financial policies have given business and industry the confidence to expand, while supply-side reforms have progressively removed the barriers to enterprise.
>
> Nowhere has this transformation been more marked than in manufacturing where output rose by 5½%. This outstanding performance was founded on a further big improvement in productivity. In the 1980s, output per head in manufacturing has gone up faster in Britain than in any other major industrial country, and we led the way once again last year. This is in stark contrast to the 1960s and the 1970s, when in the growth of manufacturing productivity, as in

148

so much else, we were at the bottom of the league. (Budget Speech, March 1988)

The 'miracle' hypothesis has been questioned however. With manufacturing output and investment only recently returning to 1979 levels and manufacturing employment still lower than 1979, some argue that the long-standing problems of UK industry have yet to be tackled. This chapter attempts to answer the following two questions:

1. Has there been a productivity 'miracle', (or at least a significant breakthrough)?
2. If the answer to (1) is yes (with or without qualifications) is the recent productivity performance sustainable?

THE FACTS ABOUT THE UK'S PRODUCTIVITY PERFORMANCE

Before looking at the evidence it is necessary to clarify exactly what is meant by 'productivity'. The debate has largely centred around 'labour productivity', and in particular 'output per person employed'. This is by no means the only measure of labour productivity. It may also be measured by 'output per person hour' by adjusting for changes in the utilization of labour over time (due to changes in the length of the working day, week or year). Another useful measure is the more comprehensive 'total factor productivity', which is output per unit of average input, where average input is a weighted average of the factors of production. Here attention is focused on the measure that has been at the centre of the debate in the 1980s, namely, 'output per person employed', hereafter referred to as just 'productivity'.

The growth in UK productivity for manufacturing and non-manufacturing sectors and for the whole economy are shown in Table 11.1.[2] Both broad sectors of the economy suffered a marked slowdown in productivity growth during the 1970s after the first OPEC oil crisis of 1973/4. Since 1979, however, there has been a considerable improvement, with manufacturing productivity rising much faster than during the 1973–79 period. Moreover, manufacturing productivity has grown faster in the 1980s than in the period before the first OPEC oil crisis leading the present Government to claim that:

Underlying growth in labour productivity in manufacturing now appears to be

Table 11.1   UK labour productivity (Average annual percentage changes)

	1964–73	1973–79	1979–88
Manufacturing	3.8	0.7	4.2
Non-manufacturing	3	½	1¾
Whole Economy	2.7	1.1	2.1

Source: Central Statistical Office (CSO) data bank at the University of Bath and *HM Treasury*, 1988(b).

Note: Manufacturing and whole economy figures calculated from the output per head index. Non-manufacturing are H.M. Treasury figures which exclude public services and North Sea oil and gas extraction (includes estimate for 1988).

higher than the rate experienced in the 1960s. (H.M. Treasury, *Autumn Statement*, 1988b, emphasis added)

Non-manufacturing and 'whole economy' productivity growth has also shown some improvement in the 1980s, but, unlike manufacturing, growth is still less than during the 1964–73 period.

Most analyses of productivity concentrate on the manufacturing sector, justified on the grounds that it is the key to the growth and transformation of the whole economy. The idea is that a country will not achieve strong output growth without strong manufacturing output growth which, in turn, is unlikely to occur without strong manufacturing productivity growth. It is of some interest, therefore, to look at the productivity growth of the sub-sectors of manufacturing given in Table 11.2. Most sub-sectors experienced an improvement in productivity growth in the period 1979–88 compared with 1973–79. These improvements, however, are by no means evenly distributed. Productivity growth in the Clothing, Footwear and Leather sector was actually less in the 1979–88 than the 1973–79 period (when it had well above average growth), while Food, Drink and Tobacco and All Other Manufacturing improved by less than 2 per cent per year on average. Motor Vehicles and Parts and Other Transport Equipment, on the other hand, showed improvements of over 6 per cent per year on average.

It is the UK's position *vis-à-vis* its international competitors, however, that is of major importance. Table 11.3 shows the UK's productivity growth in manufacturing and in the whole economy along with those of the other six major industrialized countries.[3] The UK's recent growth performance in productivity has out-performed that of the other countries cited. During the 1960s, when many countries experienced strong productivity growth, the UK lagged well behind. During the 1970s all countries

Table 11.2 UK manufacturing labour productivity (Average annual percentage changes)

1980 SIC	Sector name	1973–79	1979–88
21–24	Metals, Other Minerals and Mineral Products	−0.2	7.9
25–26	Chemicals and Man-Made Fibres	1.6	5.7
31	Metal Goods n.e.s.	−0.9	3.6
32	Mechanical Engineering	−0.8	2.3
33–34, 37	Office Machinery, Electrical Engineering and Instruments	2.0	7.6
35	Motor Vehicles and Parts	−1.3	5.1
36	Other Transport Equipment	−0.6	5.9
41–42	Food, Drink and Tobacco	1.8	3.6
43	Textiles	0.8	3.3
44–45	Clothing, Footwear and Leather	3.2	2.6
47	Paper, Printing and Publishing	0.1	3.0
46, 48–49	All Other Manufacturing (including Timber, Furniture, Rubber and Plastics)	0.9	2.7
2–4	TOTAL MANUFACTURING	0.6	4.6

Source: CSO data bank at the University of Bath and the Department of Employment.

Note: Calculated from the index of output for each year and employees in employment as of June of each year. The CSO does produce an output per head index for these sub-sectors which includes self-employment in the denominator. However the revised index only goes back to 1978 and the actual self-employment data are not published at a disaggregated level. Thus the average annual growth for total manufacturing differs slightly from that in Table 11.1. (Although self-employment has grown significantly in the 1980s it is still a small proportion of total manufacturing employment, about 4 per cent in 1986.)

experienced a slowdown in productivity growth, but the UK was again near the bottom of the international league table. In the 1980s, however, manufacturing productivity growth in the UK outstripped that of all major OECD countries, with productivity growth in the economy as a whole second only to Japan. This is what has led many commentators to talk of the British or Thatcher productivity 'miracle'.

It would appear from the data, therefore, that there has been some kind of productivity growth breakthrough in the 1980s. But this is only one half of the story. As well as the *growth* in productivity, the UK's relative position in terms of the *level* of productivity is also important. Unfortunately the productivity *gap* in relation to competitor countries is still considerable. After many decades of slow productivity growth, the UK's

Table 11.3 *International comparison of labour productivity (Average annual percentage changes)*

	1960–70	*1970–80*	*1980–88*
Whole economy			
UK	2.4	1.3	2.5
US	2.0	0.4	1.2
Japan	8.9	3.8	2.9
Germany	4.4	2.8	1.8
France	4.6	2.8	2.0
Italy	6.3	2.6	2.0
Canada	2.4	1.5	1.4
G7 average	3.5	1.7	1.8
Manufacturing industry			
UK	3.0	1.6	5.2
US	3.5	3.0	4.0
Japan	8.8	5.3	3.1
Germany	4.1	2.9	2.2
France	5.4	3.2	3.1
Italy	5.4	3.0	3.5
Canada	3.4	3.0	3.6
G7 average	4.5	3.3	3.6

Source: HM Treasury (1988a)

Notes: 1. Whole economy: UK data from CSO. Other countries' data from OECD except 1988 which are calculated from national GNP or GDP figures and OECD employment estimates.
2. Manufacturing industry: UK data from CSO. Other countries' data from OECD, except France and Italy which use IMF employment data. 1988 data for France and Italy cover first three quarters only.

relative level of productivity lagged well behind many other industrialized countries at the beginning of the 1980s. Thus, although the UK's productivity has grown faster than most of these other countries since 1980, this has only been making up for lost ground in terms of productivity levels and the UK still remains far behind its major competitors. The CBI estimates that labour productivity in West Germany is 22 per cent higher than the UK, 27 per cent higher in France, 16 per cent in Japan and over 30 per cent in the USA. Moreover, if the UK and its chief competitors continue with the productivity growth rates achieved in the mid 1980s it should be another seven or eight years before the UK catches up with West Germany and France, some 20 years to match Japan and longer, if at all, before the UK matches the USA (see PA/CBI, 1988 and Williams, 1988).

POSSIBLE REASONS FOR IMPROVEMENTS IN THE 1980s

A number of attempts have been made to analyse the reasons for the Thatcher productivity 'miracle' in UK manufacturing. Probably the most influential has been the work by Muellbauer (see Mendis and Muellbauer, 1984, Muellbauer, 1984, and Muellbauer, 1986). He has put forward five main hypotheses to explain these productivity gains in the 1980s: 'micro-chip', 'capital scrapping and utilization', 'shedding of the below-average', 'labour utilization' and 'industrial relations'.[4]

The 'Microchip' Hypothesis

The surge of innovation and growth of new technology in the 1980s through the spread of computer controlled machines and computer-aided design gives rise to the 'micro-chip' hypothesis. This new technology, however, is generally available to other industrialized countries. Thus this may not necessarily explain the relative improvement in the UK's position, unless the UK has been able to incorporate these advances faster than other countries and make better use of the new technology (assisted, perhaps, by the industrial relations changes mentioned below).

This hypothesis depends heavily on the assumption that adequate new investment embodying the latest technology has taken place since the recession of the early Thatcher years. But, as Nolan (1989) points out, this may not be the case. Manufacturing investment more or less collapsed during the first half of the 1980s, and although it has recovered somewhat, it is only now returning to the levels attained in 1979. This is further highlighted by the historically high levels of capital utilization recorded in the 1980s.

The 'Capital Scrapping and Utilization' Hypothesis

This hypothesis rests first, on the above-average capital scrapping and below-average capital utilization which occurred over the 1973–80 period following the large rise in energy prices and second, on the fall in capital scrapping and improved utilization that occurred after 1981, thus assisting productivity growth to return to something like its pre-OPEC rate.

The 'Shedding of the Below-average' Hypothesis

This hypothesis, also commonly called the 'batting-average' hypothesis, suggests that the improvement in the average quality of workers, management and plant, from the shedding of less productive resources (or, as Matthews, 1988, puts it 'the elimination of tail-enders') is responsible for a once-and-for-all improvement in productivity growth. However, some doubt has been expressed as to whether this has been of any practical importance. Oulton (1987) noted that it was the largest plants which were closed in the 1980–81 recession, with employment shifting away from the size of plant which had the highest level of productivity in 1979 and the highest growth in subsequent years. Blackaby and Hunt (1989) find that the increase in total manufacturing productivity growth of the 1980s is attributable to the productivity growth of the individual sub-sectors of manufacturing and not from a reallocation of resources from low-productivity to high-productivity sectors.

The 'Labour Utilization' Hypothesis

This rests on the idea that employers 'hoard' labour as output changes in order to cut hiring and firing costs. In other words, labour is treated as a quasi-fixed factor of production so that firms facing large changes in output would face large adjustment costs if they responded by hiring or firing workers. Instead, firms have responded by changing the rate at which the employed workers are utilized as demand for the product changes. Thus, if output falls labour utilization falls, but not the size of the workforce, resulting in a fall in measured output per person employed. This, according to Muellbauer, is what happened in the early Thatcher years. Output collapsed during the 1979–80 period. The shedding of labour lagged behind, but eventually caught up as output stabilized at a lower level. Thus, after the initial fall in measured manufacturing productivity, adjustment did take place with rapidly declining employment and reasonably stable output, resulting in a short-term increase in manufacturing labour productivity.

Nolan (1989) casts some doubt on this hypothesis. Since 1986 manufacturing output has grown very fast. The 'labour utilization' hypothesis would predict, therefore, that after the adjustment period has passed, there would be a corresponding rise in employment. But this has not happened; although the decline in manufacturing employment slowed and reversed slightly in 1988, the downward trend has continued, with utilization rates increasing as firms attempt to increase output without additional hiring and firing costs. This could, however, reflect a change in the attitude and expectations of managers about the government's ability or will to avoid future recession following the events of the late 1970s and early 1980s.

The 'Industrial Relations' Hypothesis

This hypothesis has attracted the most attention. It refers to the reduced strength of trade unions caused by the rise in unemployment and by government legislation, a development which enabled 'managers to manage' and to introduce new technology and flexible working practices. This, Muellbauer claims, would be consistent with a permanently higher rate of productivity growth. His view is supported by Boakes (1988), who claims that the most striking labour market development in the 1980s has been the change in balance of power in industrial relations. Managers have won back considerable control and have successfully introduced widespread changes in work practices, leading to the general adoption of a more flexible working pattern in a large number of UK companies. All of this has combined to increase productivity growth. Freeman and Medoff (1984) accept that the restrictive practices of unions could lead to lower productivity, but argue that two other channels exist whereby they could actually do the opposite. First, firms could respond to strong unions that push up the cost of labour by substituting capital and/or better quality workers for the existing labour. If the amount of capital per worker increases, labour productivity could increase. Second, by reducing turnover, the unions might raise productivity by lowering training and recruitment costs. In addition, the managers' response to unions may take the form of more rational personnel policies and more careful monitoring of work. All of this could help raise productivity by reducing organizational slack. Empirical evidence for the UK is mixed. Metcalf (1988) has suggested that unions tend to be associated with low productivity in the UK economy; thus the diminishing influence of the unions in the 1980s has contributed to the improvements in productivity growth rates, particularly in manufacturing. This result is disputed by Wadhwani (1989), however, who finds that unionized firms actually experienced faster productivity growth than non-unionized firms over the period 1980–84, whilst there was no difference in productivity between the two sectors during 1975–79 and 1985–86.[5]

ASSESSMENT AND A LOOK TO THE FUTURE

In returning to the first of the two questions posed at the end of the introduction, ('Has there been a productivity miracle?'), it is clear from the previous section that there is no unequivocal answer. Total manufacturing output has only recently returned to its 1979 level and employment is still some two million below its 1979 level. Although this leads to an increase in

Table 11.4   UK manufacturing output and employment (Average annual percentage changes)

1980 SIC	Sector name	Output 1973–79	Output 1979–88	Employees in employment 1973–79	Employees in employment 1979–88
21–24	Metals, Other Minerals and Mineral Products	−2.3	0.3	−2.1	−7.0
25–26	Chemicals and Man-Made Fibres	1.8	2.1	0.2	−3.5
31	Metal Goods n.e.s.	−2.5	−1.0	−1.6	−4.5
32	Mechanical Engineering	−1.0	−1.1	−0.3	−3.4
33–34, 37	Office Machinery, Electrical Engineering and Instruments	1.0	4.6	−1.0	−2.8
35	Motor Vehicles and Parts	−2.9	−1.1	−1.6	−5.9
36	Other Transport Equipment	−1.5	0.6	−1.0	−5.1
41–42	Food, Drink and Tobacco	0.8	0.6	−1.0	−2.8
43	Textiles	−3.4	−2.1	−4.1	−5.2
44–45	Clothing, Footwear and Leather	0.6	−0.7	−2.5	−3.2
47	Paper, Printing and Publishing	−0.3	1.5	−0.4	−1.4
46, 48–49	All Other Manufacturing (including Timber, Furniture, Rubber and Plastics)	−0.6	1.3	−1.5	−1.3
2–4	TOTAL	−0.7	0.8	−1.3	−3.6

Source: CSO data bank at the University of Bath and the Department of Employment.

Note: Calculated from the index of output for each year and employees in employment as of June of each year. The CSO does produce an output per head index for these sub-sectors which includes self-employment in the denominator. However the revised index only goes back to 1978 and the actual self-employment data are not published at a disaggregated level. Thus the average annual growth for total manufacturing differs slightly from that in Table 11.1. (Although self-employment has grown significantly in the 1980s it is still a small proportion of total manufacturing employment, about 4 per cent in 1986.)

measured manufacturing productivity,[6] it is not obvious that this constitutes a 'miracle'. This is also true of the sub-sectors of manufacturing highlighted in Table 11.4. Seven sectors, during the period 1979–88, experienced positive average annual growth, which is only a slight improvement over the earlier period. The figures for employment are more dramatic, with Chemicals and Man-Made Fibres the only sector experiencing employment growth in the first period. No sectors at all experienced this in the latter. Most sub-sectors experienced a bigger decline in employment over the period 1979–88 compared with 1973–79 (the All Other Manufacturing sector being the exception). As a result, the low productivity growth in the first period was associated with a small decline in output and a slightly larger decline in employment while in the latter period the so-called productivity 'miracle' is associated with negligible growth in output and rapidly declining employment. Thus, while the growth in total manufacturing productivity in the 1980s is a distinct improvement on the 1970s, this productivity 'miracle' is not evenly distributed across manufacturing and does not seem to have been accompanied by a supply-side output 'miracle'.

Consequently, it would seem difficult to describe the recent UK productivity performance as a 'miracle'. At best it appears that some structural changes took place in the deep recession of 1979–81, which have lead to increased productivity growth over the Thatcher era. The real test of the 'miracle' hypothesis, therefore, lies in the second of the questions posed at the end of the introduction, namely, whether or not the recent gains are sustainable across the whole of manufacturing (with productivity continuing to rise faster than its competitors, accompanied by a continued growth in output and, possibly, stabilized employment). The likelihood of this happening, however, depends upon a number of factors.

It is possible that the factors mentioned by Muellbauer may continue to help improve productivity in the years to come. In particular, the momentum of change, in terms of 'flexible working practices' and the managers' 'right to manage', that has built up during the 1980s, is unlikely to diminish immediately. But this, in isolation, is unlikely to be enough for sustainable productivity improvements. For one thing the economic climate of the late 1980s and early 1990s is very different to that of the early 1980s. No longer is unemployment high and rising and so weakening the position of unions and giving the upper hand to managers. Instead unemployment is lower and falling,[7] allowing unions to renew their strength and improve their bargaining position. Already commentators have spoken about the 1989 'summer of discontent', as industrial problems hit the headlines again, with 2.4 million days lost through strikes in July 1989 (the highest since November 1984, the year of the miners strike).

In addition, there are a number of other factors that suggest that such optimism may be short-lived and that future productivity growth may be less impressive in years to come. It has been shown that the productivity 'miracle' does not seem to have been accompanied by an output 'miracle'. Rather, the recent strong growth of demand has not just been translated into rising domestic production, but also rising prices and a widening trade deficit, as the economy tended to overheat. These developments are reflected in the quarterly CBI Industrial Trends Survey of Manufacturing

Firms, which show that the number of respondents working below capacity fell from 50 per cent in January 1987 to 31 per cent in January 1989, compared to 84 per cent in October 1980. These trends partly reflect the relatively low levels of investment undertaken by firms in the 1980s; although the UK may be at the top of the international league table for productivity growth it remains at the bottom of the league for investment.

This situation is unlikely to be eased in the immediate future, given the interest rate policy used by the present Government in order to take the heat out of the economy. This policy is particularly damaging to manufacturing industry. High interest rates both directly and indirectly (via their effect on the exchange rate) are likely to squeeze manufacturing, and so lead to adverse affects on investment as managers delay new investment or possibly cancel it altogether.[8] An economy already short on capacity can well do without this. Manufacturing, as a result, is doubly hit by the Government's present policy of using interest rates as its main anti-inflationary instrument and could well hinder future productivity growth.

Furthermore, the UK is not only poor in terms of physical investment, but also in terms of investment in training and in research and development (R&D). The January 1989 CBI survey reports that 25 per cent of respondents felt that shortage of skilled labour would be an important factor limiting future output, a similar percentage to 1978. This skills problem is further highlighted by the work of Davies and Caves (1987). They suggest that an important factor limiting growth of the UK economy (and leading to a reduction in the quality of output compared to its competitors), is underinvestment in human capital, in everything from simple technical skills to business administration. This, in conjunction with the UK's deteriorating position in the field of R&D, will possibly constrain future productivity growth. R&D employment fell by 5 per cent between 1981 and 1983 and by 16 per cent between 1983 and 1985, although the decline in supporting staff was greater than that for scientists and engineers (*British Business*, 1987). In 1967 the UK was second in terms of the proportion of GDP spent on R&D, but by 1983 it was sixth, with the lowest rate of the ten major OECD countries between 1967 and 1983 (Patel and Pavitt, 1987).

SUMMARY

In summary it would appear that the UK's productivity growth in the 1980s represents an advancement on the previous decade with notable improvements *vis-à-vis* other countries. Whether this constitutes a 'miracle' or not is less clear. For anything like a 'miracle' to emerge, these improvements must endure for some time to come with a continued rise in manufacturing output and at least some distinct slowing up in the decline in manufacturing employment. It is possible, however, that this may not be the case. With strike frequency increasing, skill shortages developing and relatively low investment, the prospects for continued productivity growth may not be that great, especially as the economy seems to be slowing down in response to the Government's high interest rate policy. A repeat of the high interest rate and exchange rate policies adopted in 1979–80 would have disastrous consequences, since labour hoarding is less of a problem today. Hence the possibility of high productivity growth accompanying falling investment is less likely in the future.

NOTES

1. This is a shortened version of a joint paper with David Blackaby published in *Economics* (Blackaby and Hunt, 1990) and the ideas here are very much his as mine. I am, of course, extremely grateful to David and also to Rosalind Levačič, the Economics Editor of *Economics*, for comments on earlier versions of the paper.
2. When comparing long-term trends in productivity, the peaks of the business cycle are usually taken for the starting and end years in order to abstract, as far as possible, from cyclical influences and thus give an estimate of the *underlying* growth in productivity. Thus 1964, 1973 and 1979 represent these peaks, as identified by the CSO's Coincident Index (see *Economic Trends*, January 1990, pp. 71–4). This index does suggest peaks in 1984 and 1988. But the cyclical movements are significantly smaller than those in the 1970s and somewhat smaller than those seen in the 1960s, (see *Economic Trends*, p. 71). 1988 has thus been used as the end year since it is the latest data point.
3. Ideally the cyclical peaks should be used (see Note 1), but the results are not radically altered by the use of decades. In addition, other countries may not necessarily have the same cyclical peaks as the UK.
4. Muellbauer also mentions the 'sub-contracting' hypothesis. As manufacturing firms hived off parts of their activities (such as cleaning) to sub-contractors in the service sector, measured output stayed the same and measured employment fell, resulting in an increase in measured manufacturing productivity.
5. Freeman and Medoff (1984) conclude that for the USA, productivity is generally higher in unionized establishments than in similar non-unionized establishments, but that the relationship is far from stable and has notable exceptions.
6. Given that labour productivity growth is approximately the difference between the growth in output and the growth in employment.
7. Since the time of writing, however, the seasonally adjusted unemployment figures have increased for the first time since 1986.
8. The October 1989 CBI Industry Trends Survey showed a decline in investment intentions compared with April 1988, with 19 per cent specifying the cost of finance as a factor limiting investment programmes, compared with only 5 per cent in April 1988.

REFERENCES

Blackaby, D. H. and Hunt, L. C. (1989), 'The Manufacturing Productivity "Miracle": A Sectoral Analysis', Ch. 6 in F. Green, (ed.), *The Restructuring of the UK Economy*, Hemel Hempstead: Harvester Wheatsheaf.

Blackaby, D. H. and Hunt, L. C. (1990), 'An Assessment of the UK's Productivity Record in the 1980s: Has there been a "miracle"?', *Economics*, **26**, Autumn, pp. 111–19.

Boakes, K. (1988), *Britain's Productivity Miracle – More to Come*, Greenwell Montague Gilt-Edged, Economic Research Paper, May.

British Business (1987), 'Business Trends: Industrial R&D', HMSO, 27 February, pp. 24–5.

Davies, S. and Caves, R. E. (1987), *Britain's Productivity Gap*, Cambridge: Cambridge University Press.

Economic Trends (1990), HMSO, No. 435, January.

Freeman, R. B. and Medoff, J. L. (1984), *What Do Unions Do?*, New York: Basic Books.

Godley, W. (1989), 'The British Economy During the Thatcher Era', *Economics*, **25**, Winter, pp. 158–62.

HM Treasury (1988a), 'Productivity in the 1980s', *Economic Progress Report*, HMSO, No. 201, April, pp. 1–4.

HM Treasury (1988b), *Autumn Statement*, HMSO, November.

Layard, R. and Nickell, S. (1989), 'The Thatcher Miracle?' *American Economic Association Papers and Proceedings*, **79**, (2), pp. 215–9.

Layard, R. and Nickell, S. (1990), 'Mrs Thatcher's Miracle?' *Economic Affairs*, **10**, (2), December/January, pp. 6–9.

Matthews, K. and Stoney, P. (1990), 'Explaining Mrs Thatcher's Success', *Economic Affairs*, **10**, (2), December/January, pp. 10–16.

Matthews, K. G. P. (1989), 'The UK Economic Renaissance', *Economics*, **25**, Autumn, pp. 103–10.

Matthews, R. C. O. (1988), 'Research on Productivity and the Productivity Gap', *National Institute Economic Review*, (124), May, pp. 66–72.

Maynard, G. (1989), 'Britain's Economic Recovery', *Economics*, **25**, Autumn, pp. 96–101.

Mendis, L. and Muellbauer, J. (1984), *British Manufacturing Productivity 1955–1983: Measurement Problems, Oil Shocks and Thatcher Effects*, Centre for Economic Policy Research, Discussion Paper No. 32.

Metcalf, D. (1988), *Trade Unions and Economic Performance: The British Evidence*, London School of Economics, Centre for Labour Economics, Discussion Paper No. 320.

Muellbauer, J. (1984), *Aggregate Production Functions and Productivity Measurement: A New Look*, Centre for Economic Policy Research, Discussion Paper No. 34.

Muellbauer, J. (1986), 'Productivity and Competitiveness in British Manufacturing', *Oxford Review of Economic Policy*, **2**, (3), pp. I–XXV.

Nolan, P. (1989), 'The Productivity "Miracle"?', Ch. 5 in F. Green (ed.), *The Restructuring of the UK Economy*, Hemel Hempstead: Harvester Wheatsheaf.

Oulton, N. (1987), 'Plant Closures and the Productivity "Miracle" in Manufacturing', *National Institute Economic Review*, (121), August, pp. 53–9.

PA/CBI (1988), *UK Productivity: Closing the Gap*.

Patel, P. and Pavitt, K. (1987), 'The Elements of British Technological Competitiveness' *National Institute Economic Review*, No. 122, November, pp. 72–83.

Wadhwani, S. (1989), *The Effect of Unions on Productivity Growth, Investment and Employment: A Report on Some Recent Work*, London School of Economics Discussion Paper, No. 356.

Wells, J. (1989), 'The Economy After Ten Years: Stronger or Weaker?', *Economics*, **25**, Winter, pp. 151–7.

Williams, N. (1988), 'Productivity: Will the UK Close the Gap?', *CBI Economic Situation Report*, October, pp. 26–31.

QUESTIONS FOR DISCUSSION

1. What is meant by productivity? Discuss the problems associated with measuring productivity and productivity growth.
2. To what extent do you think that the relatively fast rate of productivity growth in the UK in the 1980s was due to:
   (a) the UK 'catching up' with other countries which had experienced stronger productivity growth than the UK during the 1960s, and
   (b) the policies of the Thatcher Government?
3. Discuss the ways in which labour market conditions might influence productivity changes.
4. Attempt to explain why 'the so-called productivity "miracle" is associated with negligible growth in output and rapidly declining employment'.
5. What conditions are required to ensure continued productivity increases in the UK economy in the future?
6. How do productivity increases contribute to economic growth?

12. Unemployment: Facts and Theories

John Treble[1]

Unemployment is at the centre of the current economic debate. On the one hand there is the practical debate concerning the method of counting the unemployed; whilst on the other hand there is the more theoretical debate concerning the working of the labour market and, in particular, the relationship between unemployment and wages. This chapter looks at both aspects of the debate on unemployment.

There are always two debates going on about unemployment. One is the much publicized and often acrimonious discussion of how unemployed workers are counted. The other is a less well publicized and, to some, arid argument about why unemployment exists.

Strangely, there is little debate about the definition of unemployment. It is counting the unemployed that causes all the problems. The definition involves two concepts: the labour force and those in work. The labour force comprises those people in work together with those actively seeking work. The unemployed are then those members of the labour force who are not in work. The problem with this definition is that when it actually comes to counting the numbers, it is not easy to decide who is in work, or who is in the labour force. The government itself is in two minds about this, and it collects two separate sets of unemployment statistics, one of which (the 'claimant count') is published monthly and is the cause of much of the acrimony referred to above. The other set of statistics is called the Labour Force Survey (LFS), which is administered annually. The LFS attracts little media attention, perhaps because it usually does not appear until about 11 months after the end of the year to which it refers.

In the first part of this chapter I want to explain how these two sets of statistics are constructed and how they can be compared. I will then move on to some recent theoretical ideas about unemployment, which have been the subject of much of the recent discussion among economists. These theories focus on wage-stickiness and address the question of why wage rates may not fall in the presence of widespread unemployment. They also

162

Figure 12.1 *Reconciling the unemployment statistics: not all claimants are unemployed and not all unemployed are claimants*

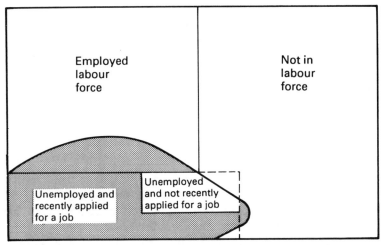

Notes:

░░ Benefit claimants

—--Disputed frontier. According to the Labour Force Survey, those who are not in work, and who have not recently applied for a job are not in the labour force. However, they can claim benefits and can be included in the official claimant count

challenge our preconceptions of what a properly functioning labour market should do.

MEASURING UNEMPLOYMENT

First, how are unemployment statistics calculated? The 'claimant count' figures are derived from the returns of the Unemployment Benefit Offices, and are simply a count of people claiming unemployment benefit, supplementary benefits or national insurance credits on a particular day each month. (Students claiming during the university vacation are excluded.) The debate about the meaning of these figures has arisen because the unemployed are not necessarily the same as claimants, and because there is confusion about who is unemployed and who is not in the labour force. The Venn diagram in Figure 12.1 may help you to sort out how the various categories of people relate to one another. Some unemployed people may not claim benefit, while some claimants may not be unem-

Table 12.1   Reconciliation of LFS and official unemployment counts, Great Britain, Spring 1988, (millions)

	All	Male	Female
LFS unemployment	2.37	1.40	0.98
of which non-claimants	0.75	0.24	0.52
claimants	1.62	1.16	0.46
Claimants not unemployed	0.79	0.52	0.28
of which inactive	0.63	0.41	0.22
employed	0.16	0.10	0.06

Source: Employment Gazette, August 1989

ployed. To add further complexity, the rules as to who may claim benefits are often changed, leading to charges that the Government is fiddling the figures. The latest change of this sort, introduced in October 1988, has arisen because of the provision of a new, comprehensive training scheme. Since everyone under 18 will either be in full-time education, have a job, or can be on a training scheme if they want, the government argues that anyone who is not doing one of these things is not in the labour force, and therefore cannot be unemployed. The change is expected to remove about 100 000 from the claimant count.

The Labour Force Survey (LFS) conforms to a set of guidelines that were set up by the International Labour Organization to encourage comparability in unemployment statistics both over time and between countries. They are calculated from a survey of 60 000 adults in Great Britain. The survey asks people if they have a job and, if they do not, whether they have applied for one in the previous week or previous four weeks. The LFS thus gives two estimates of the unemployment level, because the phrase 'actively seeking work', which determines whether or not an individual who is not in work is in the labour force, is given two different meanings. It might mean 'applied for a job in the last week' or it might mean 'applied for a job in the previous four weeks'. Furthermore, because it is based on a sample of the population, the LFS measure is subject to measurement error.

How do the claimant counts and LFS measures compare? It is possible to do a complete reconciliation of the numbers yielded by the two methods. This is an instructive exercise because it makes clear how the two methods of calculation differ, and also gives an idea of how important the claimant/unemployed distinction is. Table 12.1 shows the reconciliation for Spring 1988. In Spring 1988, the official claimant count was 2.41 million unemployed, while the LFS estimate was only 2.37 million. Thus the official unemployment count was 1.69 per cent above the LFS estimate. (The discrepancy is usually larger than this). The reconciliation is shown in the Table which contains figures from the LFS. According to Table 12.1, 1.62 million of the 2.37 million unemployed were claimants. These were included in the claimant count together with 0.79 million who claimed but were not unemployed by the LFS definition. Thus the 2.41 million who were officially unemployed, consisted of 1.62 million claimants who were unemployed by the LFS definition, plus 0.79 million who were not unemployed by the LFS definition. The LFS total of 2.37 million is made up of the 1.62 million unemployed claimants, plus 0.75 million unemployed non-claimants. There are two ways in which a claimant can be not unemployed by the LFS definition. He or she can be employed and claiming benefit, or be claiming benefit and unemployed by the benefit rules, but not have sought work in the last four weeks. The important point to note is that the definition of unemployed accounts for 630 000 of the 790 000 difference between LFS claimants and official claimants. These people are unemployed according to the official definition but they are not in the labour force according to the LFS.

EQUILIBRIUM OR DISEQUILIBRIUM

With such a large degree of controversy in the measurement of unemployment, it is no surprise to find a wide variety of theoretical views about why the figures turn out the way they do, and what, if anything, should be done about unemployment. Economists think of the labour market in much the same way as they think of the market for any other commodity. We think of a supply of labour, determined by the decisions of households and trade unions; and a demand for labour, determined by the activity of firms in the private sector and of public sector employers. The market can be summarized in the usual way, by drawing a supply curve and a demand curve (see Figures 12.2 and 12.3). The supply curve (L_s) shows the relationship between the real wage rate (w/p) and the quantity of labour that households would be prepared to supply at that wage rate. The demand curve (L_D) shows the relationship between the real wage rate and the quantity of labour that firms would be prepared to use at that wage rate.

Now there are some economists who argue that the labour market works well and that the observed level of unemployment is consistent with equilibrium in the labour market. To make this argument stick, one needs to be able to show that all workers who are not in work are also not in the labour force – that is, that it is possible for anyone who searches diligently enough to obtain a job at the market wage rate. If someone demands more

Figure 12.2 Unemployment as an equilibrium

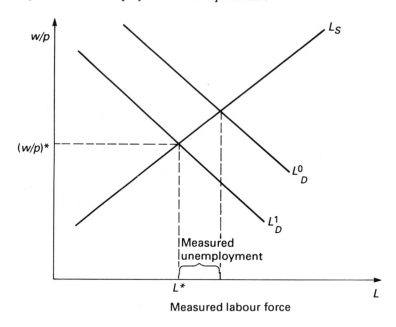

Figure 12.3 Unemployment as a disequilibrium

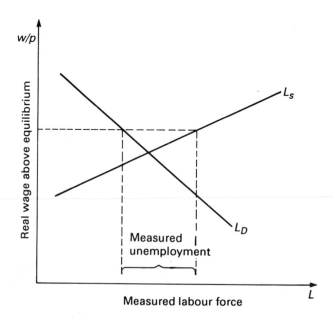

than the market wage rate they cannot properly be described as being in the labour market. According to this view the measured unemployment rate does not measure unemployment at all; it is simply a count of claimants, or of people who say that they would take a job if the market wage rate were higher than it actually is (see Figure 12.2). This viewpoint is sometimes expressed by saying that all unemployment is voluntary.

Perhaps the leading academic exponent of this view in Britain is Patrick Minford. In Professor Minford's work, voluntary unemployment is made possible by the operation of the benefit system and the black economy. His major policy prescription is thus the reform of the benefit system.

Equilibrium models of this sort can be contrasted with models in which unemployment is treated as a disequilibrium phenomenon (see Figure 12.3). For such models to be credible there needs to be some mechanism at work that prevents the real wage rate adjusting to shifts in the supply and demand curves. This is commonly referred to as the idea that wages are 'sticky', even though widespread unemployment may exist. The most common explanation that students of economics meet is that *unions* play a crucial role in creating wage stickiness. Thus unionized industries have been predicted to experience greater unemployment fluctuations than non-unionized ones, and economies that are heavily unionized are expected to experience greater fluctuations than those that have only a small fraction of unionized workers. This old idea has received a new twist with '*insider–outsider*' models, which have proposed that, even in the absence of formally established unions, currently employed workers (insiders) may be in a powerful position *vis-à-vis* the employer and be able to resist wage cuts. This enables the 'insiders' to resist the recruitment of 'outsiders'. How is this possible in non-union settings? The firm in each period must choose a wage and employment level. To lay off all its employees and replace them would be expensive, given their skills and local knowledge. In this situation employees will be able to bargain informally for some of the benefits of the continuing relationship with the firm and earn a wage above that which clears the labour market. In this way insiders may for a very long period frustrate the ability of wages to fall even in the face of mass unemployment.

The remainder of this chapter discusses some recent economic ideas about why wage rates might be sticky. These ideas are important and interesting not only because they have implications for unemployment policy but also because they attempt to incorporate institutional structure into economic theory. Nothing new about that, you may say, but the novelty of these theories is that the institutional set-up itself is seen as a consequence of the operation of the market, and not simply as a framework within which the market operates.

A THEORY OF WAGE STICKINESS

When a worker is paid to do a job, a problem of supervision is instantly created. To take an example, suppose you were employed to sell magazine subscriptions by telephone. If you were paid by the hour, you would not have much incentive to make your phone calls quickly or effectively. At some cost in time and effort your employer could check the log of your telephone to make sure that you had made the necessary calls, but without actually standing over you all the time, he could not make sure that you were really using effective selling methods. The same would apply if you were being paid by the call. In this particular case there is a fairly simple solution to the supervision problem, which is one often adopted in sales jobs. All or part of the pay is related to success in making sales. Notice, however, that this solution depends crucially on the employer being able to identify sales with the person who makes them.

If you were employed as one of four quality control inspectors in a chocolate factory, and you occasionally decided that gazing at coffee creams and picking out the misshapes was a less than ideal way of spending time, you could probably get away with letting your concentration lapse a little. You could get away with it because there is no way, short of direct supervision by another person, in which the lapse could be attributed to you rather than to one of your co-workers. Working situations in which output cannot be attributed to a specific worker are of course quite common in modern industry, and so we can take it that the problem of shirking in the fashion described above is a genuine problem. Note also that direct supervision of each worker would be a very expensive method of controlling shirking. Furthermore, it is doubtful if it would be effective since there is no reason to suppose that supervisors would work diligently either!

There is, however, a deeper problem here. Suppose that you had a method by which you could tell which workers were shirking and which were not. What penalty could you impose on shirkers? One possibility (there are others) might be to threaten shirkers with dismissal, but this is an effective threat only if dismissal imposes some sort of cost on workers. If they are made unemployed and the labour market is in the kind of equilibrium illustrated in Figure 12.2, then they will either be able to get another job at the going wage, or would prefer not to work. If, on the other hand, the labour market has an excess supply of labour at the current wage as in Figure 12.3, dismissal will impose a real cost on the shirking worker, since he may be unable to get another job.

These ideas suggest that it might be fruitful to think of unemployment as a method of discouraging shirking by workers. The way the story might run is this: suppose a firm has imperfect monitoring of its workers and there is full employment. Then there will be no cost to workers in any particular firm if they are caught shirking unless the firm they are working for pays a higher wage than that of other firms, so that each firm will think it worthwhile to raise its wage. Since all firms raise their wages, the demand for labour will fall and unemployment will result.

There are several interesting features of this story: the first is that the firms achieve their goal of discouraging shirking, but not by the means with which they set out to do this. They say 'We must pay high wages to discourage shirking' (or reduce turnover), but since all firms will find it worthwhile to pay high wages, there is no wage incentive to discourage shirking. However, at these higher wages there is an excess of labour supply over labour demand – that is, some unemployment. The threat of unemployment is costly to the worker because he or she would rather be employed in the high-wage job. Thus employment serves as the workers' discipline device.

Second, it is worthwhile comparing this story with the standard model of labour demand as derived from the demand in the output market. According to that theory, there exists a labour demand curve with diminishing marginal product as workers are added. The firm will find it worthwhile to continue adding workers to its workforce until such time as the value of the marginal product is exactly equal to the money wage. This is because if it were to add a further worker, the value of the extra output produced by that worker would be less than the wage, and the firm's profit would therefore fall. If, on the other hand, it were to reduce its labour force, the saving in the wage bill would be less than the value of the lost output. What happens in the shirking model is that output is directly increased if the wage increases, because the level of shirking is reduced, and the simple standard model no longer applies. Because the firm must allow for the fact that output is influenced when the wage changes, the models we have been discussing here are called *efficiency wage* models of unemployment.

The third point to make about the efficiency wage models is that they have some rather unfamiliar policy implications. If unemployment is really caused by the kind of mechanism described above, then it is clearly an institution that has its positive side as well as the negative ones that are usually emphasized. If the model is right, then reductions in unemployment will have the unwanted side effect of reducing industrial efficiency.

Finally, note that the basic problem in the shirking model is that the worker knows better than the employer what his or her own productivity is. Workers can take advantage of this by not revealing their true productivity. Shirking workers would not tell an employer that they were not producing as much as they could.

The central proposition of these efficiency wage ideas is that potential employees queue for higher-wage jobs. Several of the economists who have studied this argument further have argued that the evidence that workers do this is stronger for manual workers than it is for white-collar workers. In the case of white-collar jobs there exist a variety of sophisticated effort-creating mechanisms, such as wages that rise over the length of time that an individual works for a firm, that are cheaper for the firm than paying wages higher than required by the market. A second criticism of this approach to wage rigidity is that it provides a good explanation of the presence of 'involuntary' unemployment in an unchanging labour market, but a poor explanation of why unemployment might fluctuate quite sharply over time. Thus some consider it doubtful that the increase in unemployment since 1979 can be usefully explained by this model. At the same time it is also unclear why the pattern of unemployment – with more unemployment amongst the young and the old – has changed over the past decade in a way which this idea based on job monitoring and 'efficiency wages' helps us understand.

It will be clear from these criticisms that exactly why wages are not flexible in the face of fluctuations in the demand for labour remains controversial and unsettled. We have simply depicted one argument that has attracted economists in the past few years.

CONCLUSION

While the debate concerning the measurement of unemployment rages on, observers have frequently noted that the official count has been repeatedly adjusted to eliminate various categories of workers, many of whom are not actively searching and would be excluded from many economists' definition of the 'labour force'. However, at the same time there are a large number of searching workers who are not eligible for benefit and most economists would also hope that the official statistic will eventually include these workers.

To help understand unemployment, both 'insider–outsider' and 'efficiency wage' models have been widely used by economists to explain why wages have not fallen in the face of unemployment, but there is as yet no widespread consensus as to the best way of explaining the coincidence of rising real wages and mass unemployment.

NOTES

1. An earlier version of this Chapter was first published in *The Economic Review*, November 1988.

FURTHER READING

The quantity of literature on unemployment is, of course, vast. Two major academic figures who are prominent in the debate are Richard Layard of the London School of Economics and Patrick Minford of Liverpool University. Their respective views have recently been explained in:

Layard, R, (1986), *How to Beat Unemployment*, Oxford: Oxford University Press.
Minford, P, (1985), *Unemployment: Cause and Cure*, Oxford: Basil Blackwell.

QUESTIONS FOR DISCUSSION

1. What are the principal costs of unemployment?
2. What is the natural rate of unemployment and why might it change through time?
3. Why does the rate of unemployment differ between countries? Why did unemployment rise rapidly in the United Kingdom during the first half of the 1980s?
4. What is the concept of the efficiency wage? Why did wages in the UK rise rapidly during the 1980s even though the level of unemployment was high?
5. What supply-side measures might be adopted in an attempt to reduce the level of unemployment?
6. What is Keynesian unemployment? How would you seek to reduce this type of unemployment and what changes might be associated with such a policy?

13. How Important is it to Defeat Inflation?

Roger Bootle[1]

INTRODUCTION

The fundamental aim of Mrs Thatcher's Government was to defeat inflation and as far as we can tell this remains Mr. Major's top priority. The importance of this aim has been reiterated time and again by Government spokesmen, and it is clear that the pursuit of this end subordinates all others, including not only the traditional policy objective of 'full' employment, but also the particularly Conservative objective of reducing taxation. The overwhelming importance accredited to this aim derives from the belief that persistent inflation has lain at the root of Britain's economic *malaise*, and that its defeat is a prerequisite for the achievement and maintenance of higher rates of real economic growth. Yet although the debate has raged about how best to defeat inflation, the basic premise has gone largely unchallenged. Why should the defeat of inflation be so important? What is wrong with inflation anyway?

To ask this question is not to deny the costs which inflation can bring; although there have probably been occasions when inflation has brought net benefits by overcoming some blockage in the economic system, at the very least it is inefficient, and on occasions it has brought terrible injustice and even the virtual collapse of the economic and social system. Rather the purpose of asking this question is to establish perspective, for few Western governments either face the danger of hyper-inflation on the one hand, or can reasonably envisage achieving complete price stability on the other. Their choice is between having more or less inflation, within the range 0 – 30 per cent per annum, and by general consensus it is better to have less. But how much better?

This chapter examines the theoretical and empirical evidence on the costs of inflation. Its objective is not to provide a definitive measure of those costs; that would in any case be thwarted by the intangible nature of so many of the elements. Instead, its aim is, by analysing the nature of the costs involved, and such estimates of these costs as can be readily made, to assess how far the primacy of the anti-inflation objective is justified by the evidence.

The chapter begins by examining the costs of inflation in the macro sphere, and in particular the links between inflation and unemployment. It concludes that, contrary to common belief, generalized inflation does not necessarily cause macro problems, and that the source of any difficulties at this level arises from changes in relative values which cannot properly be ascribed to inflation as such. Turning to the micro level, it argues that although unanticipated inflation may cause countless distortions of far-reaching consequence, when it is anticipated the problems come down to only two. The evidence that inflation is more likely to be less well anticipated the higher it is, is discussed and found to be unsatisfactory, which throws the spotlight onto the two costs of anticipated inflation. The evidence on one of these – the cost of actually changing wages and prices – suggests that it is fairly small, and whilst some existing theoretical and empirical material on the other – the welfare losses from reduced money holdings – suggests that these are highly significant, this material is shown to be based on invalid assumptions. Finally, there are some concluding remarks on the implications for current UK economic policy.

INFLATION AND UNEMPLOYMENT

Such costs as inflation imposes reduce economic welfare below what it would otherwise have been, and in so far as the relevant welfare items enter into the national accounts, they will lower national product as well, and may directly affect the rate at which national product grows. Analysis of the effect of inflation on unemployment is a useful, though imperfect guide to this effect on national product. It is given great weight in the following discussion largely because it is an aspect most strongly emphasized by Government ministers. Nevertheless, it should be noted that the message of this analysis also applies to the national product more generally, and not simply to the employment of labour.

Until some years ago the policy maker's view of the connection between inflation and unemployment was dominated by the Phillips Curve – higher inflation was the cost (some would have said the cause) of lower unemployment. When it was realized that the combination in many Western countries of sharply increased levels of both unemployment and inflation required a reinterpretation, the Friedman–Phelps view that the Phillips relation rested on the assumption of money illusion, and that in the long run there was no relation between the two variables, was a popular choice. Many people, including Government ministers, however, have gone further and have seen the explanation of increased employment at the time of higher inflation, not as the result of slowly adjusting expectations, or changes in the natural rate of unemployment (as Friedman and the monetarists do), but as evidence of the harm done by inflation; in short, they have come to believe that inflation creates unemployment, and that reducing inflation would reduce unemployment.

It is difficult to know exactly what the Government has in mind when it says that inflation creates unemployment. Of course, in a trivial sense inflation 'creates' unemployment because the attempt to reduce it by deflation creates unemployment. This amounts to saying that something is bad because when you try to stop it bad things follow, which will hardly do. There are, however, a number of ways in which inflation may legitimately be said to create unemployment, once it is posited that the inflation is uneven, that is once it is assumed that the structure of relative values is changed adversely by inflation.

If inflation is greater in the UK, for instance, than it is abroad, and if the exchange rate does not adjust sufficiently to correct this imbalance, domestic producers will lose price competitiveness in markets both at home and abroad, thus tending to worsen the trade balance, impair profitability, and reduce levels of output and employment. But the exchange rate is crucial; if the rate adjusted to the excess of domestic inflation over inflation abroad (net of productivity changes) there would be no problem on the score of competitiveness.

An examination of the implications of inflation for competitiveness which does not take account of the exchange rate effects is rather like a production of Hamlet without the Prince of Denmark. It is by no means obvious that getting a lower rate of increase in domestic costs will succeed in improving competitiveness for, *ceteris paribus*, this will tend to increase the exchange rate. Indeed, even countries with very low rates of increase of domestic costs have experienced very large losses of competitiveness, solely as a result of exchange rate changes.

The question of exchange rate behaviour is especially interesting in the context of UK policy since the Government has openly looked to an appreciation of the exchange rate as one of the prime agents for lowering inflation. It is difficult for the same Government to cite loss of competitiveness as one of the evils which justify the primacy of the anti-inflation objective.

This difficulty is perhaps best illustrated in an international context. Nearly all governments now attach a very high degree of importance to defeating inflation, and attempt to reconcile this pursuit with the objective of promoting employment. But just as monetary policy cannot work as a cure for inflation for all countries by raising exchange rates, so inflation cannot cause unemployment for all countries through impairing competitiveness. Competitiveness is impaired only when one country's costs rise relative to costs elsewhere; it is clearly impossible for all countries' relative costs to increase.

Perhaps the most fundamental way in which inflation may be thought to create unemployment is through increasing real personal incomes at the expense of profits, and thereby shifting income from capital to labour. Such a shift would inhibit employment directly, but would also tend to have indirect effects through the discouragement of investment. For this transfer to occur during inflation, of course, wages must rise faster than prices, but if this does indeed occur, it is not enough to conclude that inflation has caused the change in relative values. Clearly, shifts in relative income shares may take place without inflation, or inflation may itself be the result of an attempt to increase labour incomes at the expense of profits.

Certainly there is no real evidence that pressure on profits in the UK has been caused by inflation as such (although clearly pay inflation has been a very significant contributor). Moreover, attempts to reduce inflation by deflation of demand has undoubtedly been largely responsible for sharp twists against profits.

Of course much of the Government's effort has been directed towards trying to reduce pay inflation, but short of an incomes policy, and apart from exhortation the Government can only hope to reduce pay inflation in the private sector by putting pressure on companies through high interest rates, low demand, and a high exchange rate – pressure which limits the rate at which companies can raise prices. The likely result of such pressure is that the rate of pay inflation will indeed fall, but not necessarily faster than price inflation. Once again, looking at the absolute rate of increase (of pay, in this case), is misleading; the key concept is a relative value which is not certain to move in the desired direction as pressure is exerted to lower the absolute rate of increase.

Increased uncertainty is another channel, however, through which inflation could reduce real incomes and employment. But again this problem is substantially one of relative values – does the high nominal interest rate at which investment funds can be borrowed accurately reflect the prospective increase in prices over the investment period? Will the rate of increase of product prices keep pace with the cost of raw materials and labour? Will the exchange rate depreciate to offset any excess of domestic inflation over inflation abroad? These are the key issues which will affect the investment decision, but it is not obvious that the uncertainty concerning the answers to these questions will increase as the inflation rate increases. Moreover, if the chief worry about inflation is its effects on investment, then the policy of combating it by deflation of demand again appears self-defeating, for both through its effects on profits, and by reducing pressure on productive capacity, deflation acts as a disincentive to investment.

A further sense in which inflation may be said to cause unemployment is by depressing consumption expenditures. Inflation erodes the real value of savings fixed in money terms, and since individuals like to maintain a fairly stable relationship between their incomes and their liquid assets, it may be argued, faster inflation causes individuals to reduce consumption in order to rebuild their real assets by further saving.

There seems no reason to object to this as a description of the way people may react to inflation, but even if it is accurate, it is perverse to argue from it that inflation creates unemployment, for all it accounts for is a deflation of demand through one channel which can easily be offset through another. There would be no reason for the Government to wait for inflation to fall to re-stimulate consumption expenditures when they would be stimulated (and with the same effect in extra-inflationary pressure) by tax cuts. Moreover, it would be ridiculous to try to justify support for a policy of deflating demand to reduce inflation, on the grounds that inflation causes unemployment by depressing consumption expenditures.

This analysis has identified three senses in which inflation could legitimately be said to cause unemployment – but all of them operate through changing a relative value, or by creating uncertainty about relative values. Yet there is no evidence that inflation must necessarily change relative values in the directions required by the explanation. So far, however, this discussion has dealt only with the macro aspects; inflation can also have profound implications on a micro level, most notably through its effects on the whole structure of relative prices and other values (including incomes). If these effects reduced efficiency, or reduced investment, by making economic activity less productive, they would in themselves tend to increase unemployment.

ANTICIPATED AND UNANTICIPATED INFLATION

Modern theory on the welfare costs of inflation has centred around the distinction between perfectly and imperfectly anticipated inflation. This does not imply that anyone thinks that perfectly anticipated inflation has ever occurred; indeed the conditions required for perfectly anticipated inflation are so stringent as to make this virtually impossible, since not only is it necessary that the actual inflation rate conforms to the 'expected' rate, but also that this expectation be held confidently by every member of society. Nevertheless, the analytical distinction between perfectly and imperfectly anticipated inflation is of key importance; its point is to distinguish between costs of inflation which can be expected to fall as the general level of inflation falls, and costs which can be expected to fall as the general level of inflation is better anticipated.

As long as inflation is not perfectly anticipated, it distorts the structure of relative prices and both income distribution and allocative signals are thereby disturbed in an essentially arbitary fashion. Except in particular instances where such disturbances redress a prior imbalance in the structure, they are bound to impair economic efficiency, and to create unfairness. Moreover, without full anticipation, economic agents will find it difficult to distinguish genuine relative price changes from inflationary price changes, and their consequent uncertainty about the relative price structure will both cause them to make wrong decisions, and to put extra resources into shopping around in order to avoid such mistakes.

The difference which would be made by the complete anticipation of inflation is profound. Prices, incomes, all sorts of money values and contracts in money, could be fixed with the rate of inflation firmly in view, so that the structure of relative values need not be disturbed. (Of course, in order to preserve the structure of relative values, at faster rates of inflation the frequency of price and other money value changes would have to be increased. Changing prices is an expensive business and the cost of doing this more frequently may be legitimately counted as one of the losses from even perfectly anticipated inflation.) Indeed nearly all the major problems associated with inflation disappear once it is assumed that the inflation is perfectly anticipated.

A good example of this is shown in the analysis developed by the late Arthur Okun (1975) in which he divided the economy into what he termed auction markets and customer markets. Auction (for example, commodities) markets are those in which the price responds flexibly to the pressure of supply and demand; in customer markets, (for example, in the service industries) by contrast, prices are administered with a view to maintaining a relationship between supplier and customer. Although prices in customer markets might seem in a pure sense to be inefficient, in fact the economy derives great benefits from this system of price determination since it economizes on shopping and information gathering, which are expensive.

What about the argument that in order to protect themselves against inflation, economic agents will hold a higher proportion of real assets in their portfolios, thereby incurring increased transaction costs of switching from financial to real assets, and wasting the resources tied up in the assets themselves? The attempt by individuals to protect themselves in this way, and therefore these associated costs, will increase not only with the dispersion of the distribution of anticipated possible inflation rates about their mean, but also with the mean itself. Thus, if higher rates of inflation lead to higher expectations of inflation, as seems reasonable, these costs will increase with the rate of inflation.

For the costs of holding financial assets to increase with the mean expected rate of inflation, however, it must be true that the nominal yield on financial assets does not rise to reflect these expectations. Yet there are strong theoretical reasons for supposing that the nominal yield does rise to reflect inflation. It has to be admitted, of course, that in the UK, on an *ex post* basis, fixed interest securities have failed to show a positive real rate of return for most of the post-war period. It is very doubtful, though, that this is because fund managers and others have been satisfied with a negative real return. More probably, this result is due to persistent underestimation of the prospective inflation rate.

Of course, increases in nominal yields on financial assets are of no assistance to the holders of existing fixed interest stock; they quite definitely lose, just as the holders of fixed interest liabilities gain. But what is relevant to the investment decision is the prospective return, and provided that the prospective nominal return adjusts to compensate for inflation, then the costs incurred by holding more real assets should remain invariant to its level.

Nevertheless, it must be admitted that even perfect anticipation of inflation would not be able to reduce the losses from inflation if economic agents were unable to fix and re-fix prices in accordance with anticipations. This will happen with contracts negotiated before inflation is anticipated, and when administrative arrangements preclude changes to keep up with inflation. There is no doubt that losses from this source can be substantial when an inflation begins, or when it changes pace, but beyond the immediate short run it need not present much of a problem. Contracts and administrative arrangements can be made with the prospective inflation rate firmly in view, or altered (via indexation) to keep pace with inflation. The fact that this sometimes is not done is often due, not so much to an inherent characteristic of inflation, but rather to the characteristics of the agents concerned. A frequently cited cost of inflation is, for instance, the diminution of the real value of fixed incomes such as old age pensions. Yet the solution to the problem of state pensions (and many others) is in the hands of the government, namely the automatic increase of such benefits in line with inflation.

As inflation is currently experienced in the UK, there can be no doubt that even though it is fairly well anticipated, substantial distortions arise from the varying degrees to which these anticipations are reflected in setting money values. Some money values (such as wages) are set with an eagle eye on past, current and prospective rates of inflation, whilst others (for example fines) are entrapped by a web of administrative procedure, and adjust only slowly. This discrepancy must cause losses compared to the position in which inflation is zero and is expected to be zero. It is not obvious, however, that starting from the position in which we find ourselves, a sharp reduction in inflation would bring net benefits on this score. For large parts of the economy are built on the assumption of continued inflation, and if there were a substantial reduction, considerable distortions would follow. A notable example of this is the housing market. The scale on which millions of people have taken on nominal liabilities (mortgages) to acquire real assets (houses) has been heavily influenced by the experience of the last generation. Such large nominal liabilities have tended to be rapidly eroded in real value by inflation.

The distinction between anticipated and unanticipated inflation holds clear policy implications. Provided that the costs of even perfectly anticipated inflation are not great, there is a good case for trying to cope with inflation by improving the degree to which inflation is anticipated, and ensuring that all parts of the economy are allowed to adjust to it. Anticipation would probably be more easily achieved if the inflation rate were stable, but there is a suggestion that higher inflation rates are associated with great variability of inflation. If this were true, it would follow that inflation would tend to be steadier, and hence better anticipated, the lower it was; the objective of perfectly anticipated inflation would then be coincident with the objective of no inflation.

THE RELATIONSHIP BETWEEN THE LEVEL AND VARIABILITY OF INFLATION

Assessing the ease with which an inflation rate may be anticipated is a tricky business. Depending on the circumstances of the time and the quality of information dissemination, a wide variety of inflation experience may be capable of ready anticipation. Nevertheless, the variability of inflation provides a starting point. If inflation is steady, we may be reasonably sure that it may be more readily anticipated than if it is variable.

At the outset, we should be clear that what matters is the absolute amount of variation in inflation. The variation between, say, 10 per cent and 12 per cent is comparable in its effects with the variation between, say, 1 per cent and 3 per cent, rather than between 1 per cent and 1.2 per cent. Even so, it is far from clear that higher rates of inflation are more variable than lower rates. Moreover, the attempts to provide a theoretical backing for this proposition look decidedly lame.

In so far as there is any association, it could well be due to the struggle between competing interest groups for income shares. The greater the intensity of this struggle, the greater may be the tendency to variability of inflation rates, due to the ebb and flow of periods of advancement, catching up, and acceptance, by the various groups. But inflation, at least in the first instance, presents an easy way of accommodating mutually incompatible income demands. It may, therefore, tend to be higher in societies where the struggle over income shares is most intense. If that were so, despite a statistical association between the level and variability of inflation, deflating demand in order to reduce the average rate of inflation might leave its variability unaffected.

A further difficulty concerns the use of statistical measures of variability as an index of uncertainty. This is particularly important with regard to Latin America, where the data are dominated by powerful inflationary and deflationary trends. These are bound to increase dispersion about the mean, and hence increase variability in a statistical sense, but variability such as this could easily be consistent with complete anticipation of inflation. It is surprise which is the problem, and surprise may occur when the inflation rate does not increase in line with trend.

Despite the theoretical and empirical problems surrounding the relationship between the level and the variability of inflation, Minford and Hilliard (1978) have made an estimate of the cost of inflation from greater uncertainty, assuming that the variability of inflation does increase with the level of inflation. The results are reproduced here in column three of Table 13.1. The size of these estimated losses is not insignificant, but the most noteworthy feature of the results is how little the losses increase as the rate of inflation increases. Indeed, the losses are little different at 30 per cent and 2 per cent.

THE COSTS OF CHANGING WAGES AND PRICES

However well an economy may be brought to anticipate inflation in its setting of all sorts of money values, inflation could still cause large losses, since even perfectly anticipated inflation has its costs. The first of these arises from the greater frequency of money value changes required in an inflationary system in order to keep the structure of relative values

Table 13.1   The non-monetary costs of inflation (per cent of GDP)[1]

Annual rate of inflation (%)	Costs of known inflation	Costs of uncertainty due to inflation
0	0.000	0.000
2	0.06	0.25
4	0.065	0.25
6	0.07	0.25
8	0.075	0.25
10	0.08	0.255
15	0.09	0.26
20	0.10	0.27
25	0.11	0.28
30	0.115	0.295

Source: Minford and Hilliard (1978)

Note: 1. Calculated on the basis of 1976 (Quarter 3) GDP figures (as per Minford and Hilliard)

unchanged through time. The business of changing these values is costly – making the decisions, changing the price tags, slot machines, wage arrangements, and disseminating the information, all take time, effort and money.

Any estimate of this factor is bound to be a shot in the dark, although it is more directly measurable than uncertainty. In their study, Minford and Hilliard took the number of days lost due to wage disputes in proportion to total days worked as an estimate of the costs of negotiations, and were able to use direct data from a firm in manufacturing industry to calculate the total salary bill of all staff working full-time on implementing price increases, and the costs of new price lists.

This procedure produced results which the authors felt were an underestimate. They are reproduced here in column two of Table 13.1. Once again these estimated losses, although not insignificant, are hardly substantial and again they increase much less than proportionately with the level of inflation.

THE COSTS OF PERFECTLY ANTICIPATED INFLATION – LOWER REAL MONEY HOLDINGS

The second (and apparently only other major) source of loss from perfectly anticipated inflation is its tendency to encourage people to reduce their holdings of money balances in real terms. This may seem obscure to the non-specialist but it is an aspect of inflation on which an

Figure 13.1   The losses from reduced holdings of money balances

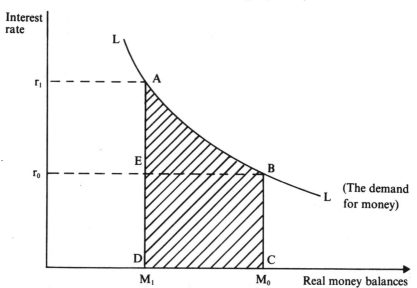

enormous research effort has been lavished. In many studies, losses from this source constitute a large proportion of the total losses from inflation.

An approach to this question which has generated much empirical research derives from an analysis developed by Bailey (1956). If inflation is perfectly anticipated, he argued, nominal rates of interest would rise but the rate of return on money would not. Yet the nominal return on other assets is the opportunity cost of holding money, and as (anticipated) inflation increases, therefore, this opportunity cost would increase, which would provide an incentive to economize on money holdings. As a result, although the nominal amount of money held would tend to rise with the price level, it would tend not to rise by quite as much, giving a fall in real money balances as inflation increased. The effects of this reduction in the holdings of a particular asset can be likened to the welfare loss induced by taxation; there is a loss of consumers' surplus on the reduced money holdings. Yet since money is virtually costless to produce, the total loss from this reduction comprises not only the consumers' surplus, but also the amount which would normally constitute the cost of production, in other words, the whole of the relevant area under the demand curve. In Figure 13.1 this is represented by the area ABCD, as opposed to the consumers' surplus ABE. So far, so good, but actually attributing meaning to this loss, and measuring its size is a different matter.

There is no doubt that, at very high rates of inflation, the losses connected with lower real money holdings can be enormous. In the limit, money is no longer acceptable in exchange for goods and services, and the established system of production and exchange breaks down. During the German hyperinflation of 1923, for instance, shops opened for only short periods so that shopkeepers could rush out to spend their receipts before they lost almost all value. It is noteworthy, however, just how much the inflation rate had to accelerate to reach this point. During the early part of even this most terrible of inflations, production in Germany was booming, and although it is possible to dispute how much of this effort was worthwhile, there is no doubt that the system of production and exchange worked. Moreover, many countries (for example, Brazil) have more recently managed to combine very high inflation rates with high real growth rates. In the majority of industrial countries which, like the UK, have experienced more moderate rates of growth of both real output and prices, it is difficult even to recognize the ways in which lower real money holdings have brought substantial losses of welfare.

Friedman (1969) has suggested that a reduction in real money holdings involves costs by necessitating more trips to the bank, but this can be no more than a starting point. Indeed Hicks has cast aspersions on the significance of this point when noting that 'there is just one sophisticated reason why (perfectly anticipated inflation) may be of some importance, a reason why has been brought to our attention by Milton Friedman and other American economists who (notoriously) live in their thinking in just such a world.' (Hicks, 1974, p. 77.)

Nevertheless, this has not inhibited economists from continuing to attach great importance to reduced money holdings. Laidler (1977) has tried to bolster the significance of the point by stressing that money is a social phenomenon; the result of my conducting fewer transactions with other people due to my lower money holdings is a loss for them also. Furthermore, he argues, money holdings derive partly from the need to conduct exchange on markets. Inflation will reduce money holdings, partly by encouraging production to be conducted on a command basis within organizations rather than on markets, which would be detrimental to economic efficiency.

Feldstein (1979) has argued that many commentators have grossly underestimated the value of the losses involved in lower money holdings, when comparing them with losses from increased unemployment, by ignoring two major factors. First, he argues, a temporary reduction in unemployment can only be gained at the expense of a permanent increase in inflation. Second, since the demand to hold money will grow with real income, the losses incurred by 'taxing' these holdings will grow year by year. Once you allow for the yearly growth in losses and their permanent

Table 13.2   The monetary cost of inflation

Annual rate of expected inflation (%)	Welfare loss as percentage of GDP*		
	$r_o = 1\%$	$r_o = 3\%$	$r_o = 5\%$
2	0.04	0.08	0.12
4	0.12	0.20	0.27
6	0.23	0.35	0.47
8	0.39	0.55	0.70
10	0.59	0.78	0.98
15	1.24	1.54	1.83
20	2.15	2.54	2.93
25	3.30	3.79	4.28
30	4.69	5.28	5.87

Source: Minford and Hilliard (1978)

Notes: *Calculated on the basis of 1976 (Quarter 3) GDP figures (as per Minford and Hilliard)
r_o = The real rate of interest
The nominal rate of interest equals r_o + the expected inflation rate.

nature, when discounted to the present the losses from higher inflation are enormous, one might even say fantastic. Indeed, on certain assumptions, according to Feldstein, the losses are infinite!

Finally, Minford and Hilliard have attempted to value the losses from lower money holdings for the UK. Their results are reproduced here as Table 13.2. Remarkable though it may seem, at any other than the lowest inflation rates, these losses are shown to be far greater than the losses from the various non-monetary sources. Indeed, the losses seem far greater than appears reasonable from one's own intuition and experience – they are simply not credible. Yet the difficulty of accepting the size of these estimates is mirrored by certain peculiar aspects of the theoretical analysis which are shared by other studies. Something appears to be wrong. The first thing that is wrong is the common fault of lumping together different sorts of assets into a category called money, which is apparently sharply different from other sorts of asset. Both Feldstein and Minford and Hilliard take an M1 definition of money, which includes both notes and coin and some bank deposits. Yet interest can be paid on bank current accounts, and we can be sure that if interest rates in the UK ever reached the level of 30 per cent mentioned by Minford and Hilliard, it would be. Once it is accepted, moreover, that interest can and would be paid on assets with a high degree of 'moneyness', the two potential worries raised by Laidler lose nearly all significance. Furthermore, it is highly questionable whether it would be appropriate to assume with regard to notes and coin, that demand will rise with real income. On the contrary, as financial technology advances, the demand to hold real cash balances could fall almost to zero.

But granted that for one reason or another, interest on M1 deposits does not keep pace with inflation, so that there is some incentive to economize on M1 as a whole rather than simply on notes and coin, substitution out of M1 deposits would tend to be a substitution into near monies, and in particular into other types of bank deposit. Although such substitution would undoubtedly cause wealth holders some inconvenience, it is difficult to believe that this would be consistent with the figures quoted in Table 13.2.

These results are debatable in that they derive from a particular model of money demand in the UK, and therefore from a particular assumption about interest elasticity, but this should not be the prime reason for scepticism about them. There is a much more serious theoretical problem concerning the use of the area ABCD in Figure 13.1 to measure the loss. The use of this area in analysis applying to any good, service, or asset, is strictly valid only on a number of key assumptions. Most notably in this case, it must be assumed that price is equal to marginal cost in the production of the assets which are close substitutes for money.[2]

With regard to assets, however, there are serious problems in assessing the costs of production, but if it can be assumed that the marginal costs of producing current accounts is zero, then it can surely be assumed that the marginal cost of producing deposit accounts is also zero. But in this case the area BCDE does not represent a loss at all. Although this area is lost for society as a whole on the 'production' of notes and coin and M1 deposits, it is compensated by a gain of approximately equal size on the 'production' of deposit accounts. Taking the whole area ABCD as a measure of the loss represents a gross overestimate.

CONCLUSIONS

Being against inflation is rather like being against sin – everyone agrees with you, but when you go on to define what you are talking about, and to propose action to deal with it, very real disagreement begins. What has been novel and controversial about the economic policy of the Thatcher and now Major administration is not its opposition to inflation, but rather the extent to which it has been prepared to subordinate other objectives to the aim of defeating inflation. Although it encounters opposition on the score of the costs which this policy entails in lost output, jobs, and investment, the Government is rarely challenged on the key assumption behind this policy, namely that the defeat of inflation is a necessary condition for the achievement of prosperity and economic progress. This is in large part due to the common tendency to associate inflation with the adverse shift of some key relative value such as wages relative to profits, or domestic costs relative to foreign costs, which in fact bear no necessary relationship to the overall rate of inflation. Indeed, it is probable that individuals' opposition to inflation is largely an opposition to price inflation, which erodes their real incomes, whilst companies' is largely an opposition to pay inflation, which erodes their profitability. There is then a real dispute about the allocation of the national cake, but while two different things are referred to by the same name, inflation, both interests seem united.

Another probable factor behind the strength of opposition to inflation is the desire for greater certainty. This is perfectly understandable, but it is by no means clear that lower rates of inflation would bring greater certainty to relative values. Stability of inflation would contribute much to reducing uncertainty about relative values, and the inflation rate may be more predictable when it turns out to be 10 per cent than when it turns out to be zero. The large costs often identified with attempts to stabilize rather than reduce inflation arise from the elusive loss from reduced money holdings whose theoretical basis and empirical measurement rest on dubious assumptions.

Of course, there are those who see inflation as a moral evil and its defeat as a moral imperative. It is not difficult to understand this view; inflation may bring great unfairness and injustice. Nevertheless, it is not so much the rate of inflation which measures the extent of these evils, but rather the degree to which it is anticipated and embodied in money values. The evils associated with inflation may be greater when the inflation rate is 5 per cent than when it is 15 per cent. Nor should we forget that combating inflation may involve moral evils as well, not least the infliction of suffering on a section of the population, the unemployed, who are not themselves responsible for the problem. Injustice and unfairness must take their place alongside economic efficiency and welfare in a judgement on anti-inflation policy, but it is far from clear in which direction they point.

Many commentators have doubted whether the UK Government will be able to achieve the reduction of inflation to low single figures which it would like, and many have questioned whether, having achieved this reduction, it would be able to sustain it once the economy returned to more normal levels of demand. Others have drawn attention to the enormous costs incurred in the attempt. These criticisms are powerful, but none of them identifies the most worrying feature of the current strategy – the dreadful prospect that, granted success against inflation, granted even continuing success, after all we have been through, and with a now much weaker economic base, the underlying problems of the British economy would remain much as they were, almost unaffected by what the Government would regard as a tremendous achievement.

NOTES

1. This is an abridged version of a paper that appeared in *The Three Banks Review*, December 1981.
2. The validity of the area above the cost line and below the demand curve (the welfare triangle) as a measure of the loss from some change depends on three key assumptions:

    (i)   that there are no income effects on the demand for the good in question from a change in the price of the good;
    (ii) that the prices of all other goods remain unchanged;
    (iii) that elsewhere in the economy price is equal to marginal cost.

In this case, the assumption that the marginal cost is zero means that it is appropriate to take the area ABCD rather than the triangle ABE, but the same analysis applies. Making due allowance for the issues raised in (i) and (ii) complicates the calculation of welfare loss considerably, but in this instance these factors do not present a substantive problem. The same, however, cannot be said for (iii). As argued in the text, the reasoning which supports inclusion of BCDE in the assessment grossly violates condition (iii).

REFERENCES

Bailey, M. J. L. (1956), 'The Welfare Cost of Inflationary Finance', *Journal of Political Economy*, April.

Feldstein, M. (1979), 'The Welfare Cost of Permanent Inflation and Optimal Short-Run Economic Policy', *Journal of Political Economy*, August.

Friedman, M. (1969), *The Optimum Quantity of Money*, Chicago: Aldine Press.

Gordon, R. J. (1971), 'Steady Anticipated Inflation: Mirage or Oasis', *Brookings Papers on Economic Activity*, No 2.

Hicks, J. R. (1974) 'Wages and Inflation', in *The Crisis in Keynesian Economics*, Oxford: Blackwell.

Laidler, D. (1977), 'The Welfare Costs of Inflation in Neo-Classical Theory', in E. Lundberg (ed.), *Inflation Theory and Anti-Inflation Policy*, London: Macmillan.

Minford, A. P. L. and Hilliard, G. W. (1978), 'The Costs of Variable Inflation', in M. J. Artis and A. R. Nobay, (eds), *Contemporary Economic Analysis*, London: Croom Helm.

Okun, A. N. (1975), 'Inflation: Its Mechanics and Welfare Costs', *Brookings Papers on Economic Activity*, 2.

FURTHER READING

There is a vast literature on inflation and in order to get a balanced view on the subject one therefore needs either a lot of time and energy or a sound survey of the material. Just such a survey is Richard Jackman, Charles Mulvey and James Trevithick, (1981) *The Economics of Inflation*, 2nd. edn, Oxford: Martin Robertson.

QUESTIONS FOR DISCUSSION

1. Will increased inflation lead to more or less unemployment, and why?
2. How do distortions to the structure of relative prices depend on the extent to which inflation is anticipated?
3. What is the relationship between the level and variability of inflation?
4. How significant are the costs of perfectly anticipated inflation?
5. What is the empirical and theoretical relationship between inflation and economic growth?
6. What policies would reduce the costs of unanticipated inflation and what problems, if any. are associated with such policies?

14. Monetary Policy in the 1980s

Barry Naisbitt[1]

As the UK economy enters the 1990s, base interest rates stand at 15 per
.cent and inflation at 7.7 per cent. These compare with rates of 17 per cent
and 18.4 per cent respectively at the start of the 1980s, see Figures 14.1 and
14.2. Despite ten years of monetary policy designed to control and reduce
inflation, the main concern of macroeconomic policy remains the problem
of inflation. This raises an obvious question: if ten years is not long
enough to reduce inflation to satisfactorily low levels, how long is? To
answer this question requires an examination of the policies that have
been followed to control inflationary pressures. Such an examination
needs to concentrate on the consistency and effectiveness of such policies.
Have a set of policies been tried and found wanting or have they not really
been tried?

The real thrust of anti-inflation policy in the early 1980s came from two

Figure 14.1   UK base rate

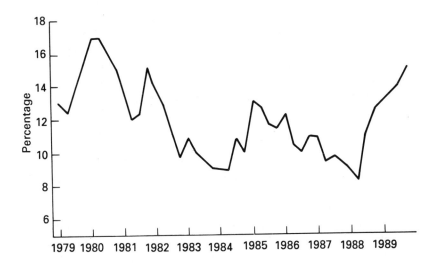

Figure 14.2   Retail price inflation

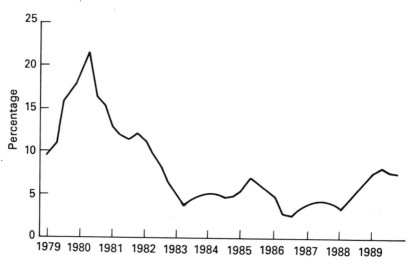

sources. First a medium-term strategy was instituted which set down
objectives, 'to bring down the rate of inflation and to create conditions for
a sustainable growth of output and employment' (Financial Statement
and Budget Report 1980–81). Plans were set for a progressive reduction in
the rate of growth of the money supply and a reduced borrowing
requirement for the public sector as a proportion of gross domestic
product. This was initially set out in detail in the 1980 Budget and called
the Medium Term Financial Strategy (MTFS). This strategy gave a clear
statement of medium-term intent to economic decision-makers at home
and abroad, both in industry and financial markets. The key part of the
strategy aimed at reducing inflation, was the setting of target growth rates
for key money supply measures. The second impetus followed from the
willingness of the government to use high interest rates to squeeze
economic activity and reduce inflationary pressures. In particular the 1981
Budget set the pace for a reduction in public sector borrowing as a
proportion of gross domestic product, by tightening fiscal policy in the
face of recession. The MTFS in the 1980 Budget set out a target growth
rate for the next financial year for £M3 (sterling M3) and further
indicative targets for the following three years. £M3 is one particular
measure of the money supply and is a broad measure of money which
includes notes and coin in circulation with the public and all sterling
deposits held by UK residents with the monetary sector (essentially banks
but not building societies). The basic notion underpinning the policy was
that by controlling this monetary growth measure and setting a declining

path for future targets, lower money supply growth would result in downward pressure on inflation.

Within a broad strategy the issue of monetary management falls into two categories; short-term tactics and possible changes in strategy. During any year between making announcements about the strategic overview, the problem of policy management becomes one of deciding what tactical policy choices to make in order to achieve a given target. The particular problem that the authorities had to face in the early 1980s was how to respond to monetary growth rates consistently above the target rates. In these circumstances, and having rejected monetary base control as a policy option, and determined against exchange control restrictions and direct control of credit creation, the key policy response that was considered was whether to raise interest rates to reduce monetary growth. As the publication of the next annual MTFS statement approached, the Government also faced each year the problem of whether to change the future target paths in the face of evidence of the past year. Tables 14.1 and 14.2 indicate that this was frequently done.

As the 1980s progressed the authorities argued that looking solely at £M3 growth did not provide sufficient information about overall monetary conditions. Thus in the 1981–82 FSBR the MTFS included a reference to the level of exchange rates and comments about asset price inflation as guiding judgements about the degree of tightness of monetary policy. Further to this, other money supply measures were added as target variables. The most controversial of these was narrow money (M0), which had earlier been rejected as a monetary target.[2] This was introduced in 1984 with the argument that 'other measures of narrow money, such as M0, are likely to be more satisfactory indicators of financial conditions'. (See Figure 14.3) The initial target range for M0 growth in the 1984–85 financial year was 4–8 per cent after it had grown by 5.7 per cent in the previous financial year. The FSBR also noted that 'broad and narrow money will have equal importance in the assessment of monetary conditions and interest rates'.

By the mid 1980s, and despite these changes to the strategy, policy seemed to be working. Inflation fell steadily from 18 per cent in 1980 to 4.7 per cent in 1983 and then, after a pick up in 1985, to 3.4 per cent in 1986, helped by the sharp fall in the price of oil. It is also interesting to note that £M3 growth had also fallen during the period – from 17.5 per cent in 1980/1 to 8.3 per cent in 1983/4. From the perspective of the mid 1980s it appeared as if monetary policy as embedded in the MTFS was indeed working. Indeed, the ratio of the PSBR to GDP fell back more rapidly than had been anticipated, to 1.6 per cent in 1985/6.

With hindsight, it appears that just when the policy was working it was

Table 14.1 MTFS targets: monetary growth

Target/projection Set in/for		Ranges for percentage growth in money supply measure												
		1980/1	1981/2	1982/3	1983/4	1984/5	1985/6	1986/7	1987/8	1988/9	1989/90	1990/1	1991/2	1992/3
March 1980	£M3	7–11	6–10	5–9	4–8									
March 1981	£M3		6–10	5–9	4–8									
March 1982	£M3*			8–12	7–11	6–10								
March 1983	£M3*				7–11	6–10	5–9							
March 1984	M0					4–8	3–7	2–6	1–5					
	£M3					6–10	5–9	4–8	3–7					
March 1985	M0						3–7	2–6	1–5	0–4				
	£M3						5–9	4–8	3–7	2–6				
March 1986	M0							2–6	2–6	1–5	1–5			
	£M3							11–15						
March 1987	M0								2–6	1–5				
March 1988	M0									1–5	1–5	0.4	0.4	
March 1989	M0										1–5	0.4	0.4	− 1.3
Out-turn	£M3	19.4	13.0	11.6	8.1	9.8	17.6	21.7	21.3	21.4				
	M0	6.9	2.5	4.8	5.5	5.4	3.3	4.3	6.0	6.6				

Note: *Targets were also set for M1 and PSL2 with the same growth rates as £M3.
Targets set for forthcoming year; illustrative ranges given for subsequent years.
Out-turns are measured by annualized growth rates over 14 month period from February to April the following year.

Table 14.2   MTFS targets: public sector borrowing requirement as a share of GDP (PSBR/GDP ratio (%))

Set in/for	1980/1	1981/2	1982/3	1983/4	1984/5	1985/6	1986/7	1987/8	1988/9	1989/90	1990/1	1991/2	1992/3
1980	3.75	3	2.25	1.50									
1981		4.25	3.25	2									
1982			3.50	2.75	2								
1983				2.75	2.50	2							
1984					2.25	2	2	1.75	1.75				
1985						2	2	1.75	1.75				
1986							1.75	1.75	1.50	1.50			
1987								1	1	1	1		
1988									-0.75	0	0	0	
1989										-2.75	-1.75	-1	-0.50
Out-turn	5.7	3.5	3.3	3.2	3.1	1.6	0.9	-0.75	-3.0				

Note: In the 1980 FSBR it was noted that 'the path for the PSBR is consistent with achieving the planned reduction in the growth of money supply over the medium term with lower interest rates'.

193

Figure 14.3   Money supply growth (annual percentage changes)

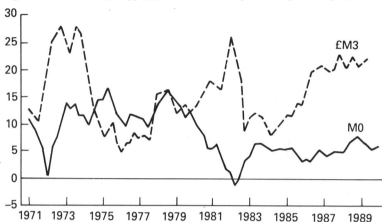

changed, and not for the better. Although it is not possible to pinpoint one particular factor and unequivocally state that it was the key to a change in monetary policy, in the middle of the decade there appears to have been a shift in policy emphasis from a reliance on purely domestic monetary targets towards an explicit consideration of external factors. As the exchange rate was starting to figure more prominently in the FSBR section detailing the MTFS, the Treasury pointed out that 'it will be necessary to judge the appropriate combination of monetary growth and the exchange rate needed to help financial policy on track; there is no mechanistic formula' (FSBR, 1985) to counter the development of 'rules' relating interest rate changes to exchange rate movements.

A major explanation for this change is that the behaviour of the broad money aggregate £M3 had proved difficult to interpret, with £M3 growth rising to 16.7 per cent in 1985/6. While the velocity of M0 had followed a relatively stable upward path during the 1980s, that of £M3 had fallen since 1979 after having risen since the early 1970s. In the 1985 Mansion House Speech, the Chancellor noted that the target for £M3 growth in that financial year 'had clearly been set too low'. The notions that financial innovation and liberalization, together with the high level of interest rates, had encouraged individuals and companies to hold £M3 assets as part of their wealth portfolios and had depressed the income velocity of £M3, gained currency.

By the 1986 Budget, the MTFS had clearly changed from its original manifestation. £M3 was no longer a target variable for succeeding years 'because the uncertainties surrounding its velocity trend are too great'. M0 growth of 2–6 per cent was set as a target for the current financial year and

Table 14.3   MTFS: nominal income growth assumptions (Nominal Income Growth (money GDP) annual % change)

Set in/for	1982/3	1983/4	1984/5	1985/6	1986/7	1987/8	1988/9	1989/90	1990/1	1991/2	1992/3
1982	12	9.75	9.50								
1983		7.75	8.75	6.75							
1984			8	7.50	6	5.75	5				
1985*				8.50	6.50	5.75	5				
1986					6.75	6.50	6	5.50			
1987						7.50	6.50	6	5.50		
1988							7.50	6.50	6	5.50	
1989								7.75	6	6	5.50
Out-turn	9.9	7.7	8.0	8.0	7.5	10.0	10.9				

Notes: *From 1985 projections for money GDP growth were included in the table giving money supply target ranges. The 1985 FSBR noted that 'within a given growth of money GDP, lower inflation will mean faster growth in real output'.

Table 14.4   MTFS: inflation assumptions (Inflation (GDP deflator), annual % change)

	1983/4	1984/5	1985/6	1986/7	1987/8	1988/9	1989/90	1990/1	1991/2	1992/3
1984		4.75	4.25	4						
1985			5	4.50	3.50	3				
1986				3.75	3.75	3.50	3			
1987					4.50	4	3.50	3		
1988						4.50	4	3.50	3	
1989							5.50	4	3	2.50
Out-turn	4.1	5.5	4.5	3.7	5.4	7.6				

Figure 14.4   Velocity of M0

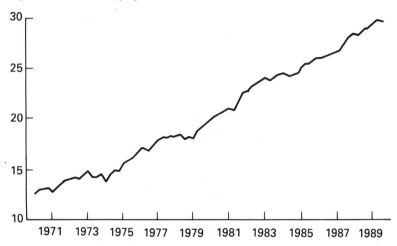

Figure 14.5   Velocity of sterling M3

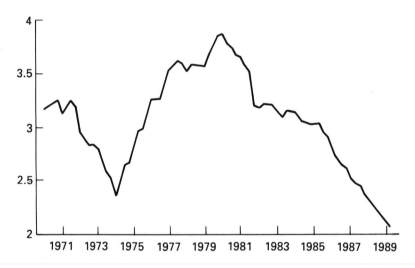

the same range was quoted as an 'illustrative range' for the following year, the first time a clear downward trend had not been published. The exchange rate had seemingly been elevated from the category of 'other relevant evidence' to a qualifying factor – 'a balance must be struck between the exchange rate and domestic monetary growth consistent with the government's aims for money GDP and inflation'.

A further, perhaps technical, twist was that at the same time as the broad money growth target was being dropped, the policy of overfunding the Public Sector Borrowing Requirement (PSBR) was abandoned. Overfunding is, in very simplistic terms, the sale of gilts to the UK private sector over and above the value of the public sector deficit. This reduces institutional cash flow and, since the bank deposits of non-bank financial institutions are part of the broad measure of money supply, reduces the rate of growth of the money supply. The operation of the policy of overfunding had offered an extra degree of flexibility in the control of £M3 but at the cost of a substantial build up of commercial bills at the Bank of England. The clear reversal of the policy was, however, indicative of a move away from the control of broad measures of money supply.

The next crucial period appears to have been in 1987 after the UK economy had adjusted successfully to the oil price shock. Sterling appreciated in early 1987 and there seemed to be evidence to point to the conclusion that monetary policy was too tight. As a result interest rates were reduced, but the Chancellor also chose to use interest rates to hold sterling at just below 3DM, with the result that subsequent upward pressure on sterling was resisted by base rate cuts. It is not clear-cut that the exchange rate constancy policy was wrong as such, rather it now appears that the level at which to hold the pound was incorrectly chosen (at too low a level) and, as a result, interest rates were reduced too far.

In retrospect it seems that domestic interest rates were reduced to a single digit figure too soon and that too much weight was given to the strength of sterling in allowing interest rates to fall. Some would argue that the government was too quick to chop and change its monetary targets and too willing to dismiss the behaviour of the broad money supply measures, thus withdrawing some of the confidence that financial markets had in the soundness of monetary policy. As Tables 14.1 and 14.2 show, the 1986–88 period was a key one for changes to the targets in the MTFS and, given the long and variable lags referred to by Friedman in the money-inflation process, these changes may have set in train a change in underlying inflationary conditions and in expectations.

It is of interest to examine the main transmission mechanism of monetary policy during this crucial period. While lower interest rates stimulated investment intentions and consumer spending directly, wealth effects appear to have been crucial. Initially the long bull market on the stock exchange led to asset price increases and increased wealth. Although some of the gains were wiped out in the October 1987 stock market crash, the subsequent easing of interest rates added to pressures from other asset prices. As interest rates fell and economic growth picked up, the housing market started to boom (see Table 14.5). On the basis of the steady rise in

Table 14.5   House prices in the UK (Annual percentage rates of house price inflation, fourth quarter on previous fourth quarter)

	1986 Q4	1987 Q4	1988 Q4	1989 Q4
North	5.6	7.1	19.6	32.7
Yorkshire & Humberside	5.1	9.4	40.4	24.2
North West	1.9	8.7	27.0	29.4
East Midlands	8.5	14.6	53.9	0.8
West Midlands	12.1	15.7	60.4	1.0
East Anglia	18.9	30.4	47.4	−16.3
South West	12.6	22.8	48.3	−9.7
South East	19.4	25.0	32.4	−10.8
Greater London	21.7	22.9	23.3	−8.5
Wales	3.5	8.5	46.3	10.4
Scotland	4.9	5.6	14.3	17.5
Northern Ireland	6.1	0.4	7.8	−0.6
UK	10.9	15.5	34.0	5.1

Source: Halifax Building Society press releases, all houses

real incomes and house prices (and hence housing wealth) since 1982, individuals realized that they had strong wealth positions. Home ownership offered not only consumption opportunities but also substantial capital gains and, at low interest rates – base rates reached a ten year low of 7.5 per cent in May 1988 (see Figure 14.1) – larger mortgages became more affordable. With a deregulated financial system there was increased competition to lend for house purchase. Banks had entered the mortgage market in a substantial way in the early 1980s and by the end of 1987 had a 19.5 per cent share of outstanding mortgage debt, after lending £10.1bn of the £29.8bn net advances for house purchase in 1987. Specialist mortgage lenders had also appeared, giving a further competitive thrust to the market.

The involvement of the banks in the mortgage lending boom clearly influenced the growth of their balance sheets and hence £M3 growth, which accelerated to 20 per cent in 1986/7. Increased economic activity and higher land values also impacted on the property industry more generally. An upsurge in construction activity in office, retail and industrial property led to increased borrowing by property and construction companies and the high rates of broad money supply growth continued in both 1988 and 1989.

At some stage during 1988 it is clear that government ministers felt compelled to re-examine their policy options in a fundamental manner. Although broad money supply was growing at a very rapid rate there was no longer any official target nor, following the breakdown of established econometric relationships, any clear guide as to what an 'appropriate' rate of growth should be. M0 targets remained in place but were consistently overshot. Ministers probably faced a choice between two main items.

The first was to re-introduce credit controls in some form. In the past these have usually taken the form of either controls on a particular type of borrowing – minimum deposits or maximum repayment periods for consumer credit purchases, for example – or controls in the form of a requirement for banks to hold a proportion of their deposits (or eligible liabilities) with the Bank of England. This latter form restricts the extent to which the sector controlled by the restriction can create credit by expanding its balance sheet. A deregulated financial environment, however, means that this form of control offers opportunities to the competitors of the controlled group – since in the past domestic banks have been the controlled sector this would mean building societies and specialist lenders for mortgage lending, and overseas banks for corporate borrowing – and makes the first type of control difficult to operate effectively because of the multiplicity of channels for borrowing. In a series of speeches, government ministers ruled out this particular change of direction and so the choice followed was to continue to use interest rates to control domestic economic activity and monetary growth.

Base rates therefore started rising, in a series of 0.5 per cent point stages, during the summer of 1988 and, in a later series of 1 per cent point increases, reached 15 per cent in October 1989. The key question concerns whether the present policy will actually succeed in reducing inflationary pressures. As the main transmission mechanism for interest rates in the consumer boom was through a wealth effect, with increased borrowing for house purchase (including any equity withdrawal element) which fuelled the house price boom, it is to this area that attention must first turn.

House prices have fallen in the southern regions in 1989 and are expected to fall more widely during 1990. There is a 'ripple effect' in house prices which spreads outward from the South East and this should work its way through the national house price picture. Thus borrowing for house purchase grew less quickly in 1989 than in 1988 and should slow further in 1990. High street spending growth has also been restrained, with spending on goods ancillary to house purchase also subdued.

Broad money growth has, however, remained high, fuelled on the company borrowing side by property and construction companies and by the continued merger/takeover boom. As the consumer squeeze bites and the housing and property market slows, so companies will rein back their investment plans and profit margins will be reduced. Borrowing for expansionary purposes will slow and broad money growth is likely to slow

Figure 14.6   Sterling exchange rates

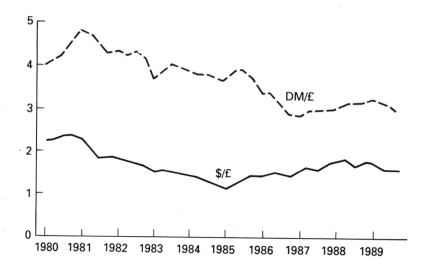

as a consequence. Narrow money growth temporarily moved into its
target range in September 1989 and many commentators expected it to fall
back consistently into the range by the end of 1989. It has not done so but,
with consumer spending growth expected to fall back further in 1990, M0
is likely to be back on target during 1990.

This policy of reliance on interest rates has been criticized as being that
of a 'one-club golfer'. While it is true that with only a putter one will get
round the course eventually, the score and time taken are likely to be high.
It makes obvious sense to leave the club house with a full bag of clubs to
use as appropriate. If credit controls, of any form, are ruled out, what can
the Chancellor do to reinforce his policy? A tight fiscal stance helps but,
with the Government already making a substantial repayment of the
National Debt, the scope for fiscal tightening at the present time is likely
to be restricted by fears of a recession and electoral considerations,
particularly given the long-term objective of lower personal tax rates.

One choice would be for the government to import an economic policy.
Joining the exchange rate mechanism (ERM) of the European Monetary
System (EMS) at a suitable exchange rate against the Deutschmark would
enable the government to cash in on the credibility of the Bundesbank as a
bastion of anti-inflationary policy (see Figure 14.6). This would offer
exchange rate stability against other EC currencies, a feature long-sought
by business, and offer an alternative underpinning for the MTFS. Both the

present government and the Labour Party have expressed their commitment to joining the ERM but only under certain conditions, one of which is that the UK inflation rate should be similar to that of the other major EC countries. With UK inflation more than double that in West Germany, early ERM membership would not appear consistent with economic statements by Government ministers. This makes continued reliance on the use of interest rates necessary.

An alternative would be for the Government to revive the MTFS, although it has clearly lost a degree of credibility, an erosion caused by too much chopping and changing of targets, and uncertainty about the role of exchange rates. There are perhaps two options. The first is to retain the existing system (M0 target only) and to use speeches to explain policy thinking more clearly and in particular to explain the interest rate/ exchange rate duality. This could be accompanied by setting tougher objectives for M0 and inflation for succeeding years to try to show a clear commitment. The second is to re-institute a broad money growth target and reinforce the M0 target.[3] Since the £M3 measure has been abolished for technical reasons (the conversion of Abbey National from a building society to a plc), the choice really lies between M4 and M5. Variations on this theme have been discussed in terms of an M2 or money index target, but the argument is the same – to widen the scope of and reinforce money growth targets and re-establish the 'monetarist' credentials of the Government.

The introduction of a target range for M4 would not, of itself, be expected to reduce inflation immediately. It may, however, reduce inflationary expectations and add credibility to the MTFS. For the latter to be effective might require a return to overfunding and a detailed consideration of the behaviour of the velocity of M4 is clearly an important issue for setting appropriate targets. Recent Bank of England research has related the long-run velocity movements in M4 to inflation and personal sector wealth, but not directly to interest rates, suggesting an indirect influence of interest rates via wealth effects. Whether the Government will choose to adopt broad money growth targets or to use ERM membership as the primary method of reinforcing counter-inflation policy credibility could be determined in part by the general move within the EC towards increased economic and monetary co-operation.

NOTES

1. The views expressed are those of the author and not necessarily those of Midland Bank plc.

2. Nigel Lawson, then the Financial Secretary to the Treasury and later Chancellor of the Exchequer, said

> for the purpose of setting the annual target for monetary growth, we have chosen broad money as the most useful guide. I believe we were, and remain, right to do so. Narrow money has the advantage of being easier to control, but it suffers from being almost too easy to control. A rise in interest rates will inevitably lead to a marked switch from non-interest bearing sight deposits to interest bearing time deposits, thus sharply depressing the growth of narrow money far beyond any true change in underlying monetary conditions. Nor can we forget that, under the Heath administration, the authorities were lulled into a false sense of security by the fact that the growth of narrow money was declining steadily throughout the government's lifetime. (Zurich, 14 January 1981)

3. In evidence to the Treasury and Civil Service Select Committee in November 1989, the Chancellor (John Major) noted that 'M0 is the best guide we have in an uncertain field and that is the one to which policy is geared at the moment'. This does not mean that it is the only one ever (see Note 2). For example, a return to a Domestic Credit Expansion (DCE) target could be possible.

REFERENCES

Artis, M. J. and Lewis, M. K. (1981), *Monetary Control in the United Kingdom*, London: Philip Allan.

Artis, M. J. and Taylor, M. P. (1988), 'Exchange Rates and the EMS: Assessing the Track Record' Centre for Economic Policy Research, Discussion paper No. 250.

Bank of England 'A New Monetary Aggregate', *Quarterly Bulletin*, **22**, 1982.

Fforde, J. S. (1983), 'Competition, Innovation and Regulation in British Banking' *Bank of England Quarterly Bulletin*, **20**.

Goodhart, C. A. E. (1984), *Monetary Theory and Practice*, London: Macmillan.

Goodhart, C. A. E. (1986), 'Financial Innovation and Monetary Control' *Oxford Review of Economic Policy*, **2**, (4).

Hall, S. G., Henry S. G. B. and Wilcox J. B. (1989), 'The Long-run Determination of the UK Monetary Aggregates', Bank of England Discussion Paper No 41.

H M Treasury, *Financial Statement and Budget Report* (various issues).

Llewellyn, D. T., Dennis, G. E. J., Hall, M. J. B. and Nellis, J. G. (1982), *The Framework of UK Monetary Policy*, London: Heinemann.

Midland Bank Economic Review, *Annual Monetary Survey* (various issues).

Rose, H. (1986), 'Change in Financial Intermediation in the UK' *Oxford Review of Economic Policy*, **2**, (4).

Temperton, P. (1986), *A Guide to UK Monetary Policy*, London: Macmillan.

Walton, D. and Westaway, P. (1989), 'M0 – The Return of the Prodigal Son', Goldman Sachs UK Economics Analyst, January.

QUESTIONS FOR DISCUSSION

1. Distinguish between alternative money supply measures and comment on their suitability as target variables.

2. To what extent can the fluctuations in the rate of inflation during the 1980s be explained by monetary policy measures?
3. Discuss the relationship between monetary policy and the exchange rate.
4. Examine the way in which monetary policy can affect the housing market, and the further implications that this might have on the macroeconomic performance of the economy.
5. To what extent do you think that the government should use fiscal policy and other measures to reinforce its interest rate approach?
6. How far does the experience of monetary policy in the 1980s suggest that economists still do not have a perfect understanding of all the relationships in the macroeconomy?

15. The International Co-ordination of Macroeconomic Policy

Graham Bird

A superficial glance at history seems to suggest that the world economy performs better when there is closer co-operation amongst individual countries. Periods when policies have been unco-ordinated, or even competitive, have been associated with generally unsatisfactory performance. The 1930s, characterized by beggar-thy-neighbour balance of payments policies, saw high levels of unemployment, slow rates of economic growth and stagnating world trade. Similarly the 1970s, following the breakdown of the Bretton Woods system, simultaneously experienced record rates of inflation, periods of economic recession and a slow down in the growth of world trade.

In contrast, the gold standard era of the late 1800s and early 1900s, when there were established 'rules of the game' for countries to follow, particularly with regard to allowing balance of payments disequilibria to influence domestic money supplies; and more recently the Bretton Woods era running through the 1950s and 1960s, when again countries had constraints imposed on their freedom of manoeuvre with respect to balance of payments policy, are in the minds of many seen as being responsible for sustained economic expansion and relatively low rates of inflation. Similarly, the supposed superior economic performance of those countries which are full members of the European Monetary System is yet again often attributed to the discipline imposed by belonging to the Exchange Rate Mechanism, which has the effect of discouraging governments from pursuing policies that result in serious misalignment of their currencies.

Economists are trained to be very wary of such casual empiricism. The lively debate that there has been over the performance of the UK economy during the years of the Thatcher administration illustrates clearly how difficult it is to come up with an agreed set of performance indicators, let alone an agreed way of *measuring* economic performance. How much more difficult it is to measure *global* economic performance. Moreover, even if the superiority of some eras over others could be established, the question remains of the extent to which such superiority may be attributed to individual causes. The existence of and compliance with some global code of economic policy practice may in principle be of little relevance in explaining economic performance. After all it is usually easier to comply with the rules of any game if you are winning! The Bretton Woods system, for instance, perhaps owed its durability to the stability of the world economy during the 1950s and 1960s rather than the other way about.

However, the perception that world economic performance has been unsatisfactory during the 1970s and 1980s, along with growing unease about flexible exchange rates, has resulted in increasing pressure to seek out some means of closer economic co-ordination amongst countries, in the belief that this will bring about an improvement. The argument that societies lose out from anarchy and benefit from co-operation and a framework of rules has a powerful common-sense appeal which many people see as being quite applicable to the sphere of macro (and indeed micro) economic policy.

Economic research frequently lags behind developments in the real world. But what we see now is a rapidly increasing amount of research dealing with various aspects of international policy co-ordination. Key questions that have arisen include the following:

1. What do we mean by the terms used? In particular what distinguishes co-ordination from co-operation?
2. What form might co-ordination take in principle, and what form has it taken in practice?
3. What are the arguments for co-ordination and from whence are the benefits derived?
4. What are the arguments against co-ordination?
5. If it is seen as offering net advantages, what are the main problems that need to be addressed in bringing greater co-ordination about?

TERMINOLOGY

The loose use of words normally gives rise to loose analysis. In the debate over policy co-ordination three terms have frequently been used: co-operation, co-ordination, and convergence. Although related, these terms remain analytically distinct.

1. *Co-operation* is a broad concept which can cover almost anything or everything. At one extreme it may involve merely the selective provi-

sion of information; at the other it may involve almost complete economic integration. Such broad concepts, although very useful to politicians, since it allows them to sound as if they are agreeing when in fact they vehemently disagree, tend to be of rather little use to economists.

2. *Co-ordination* is a narrower concept and occurs where national policies are modified in order to reflect international economic interdependencies. Through policy co-ordination countries are attempting to maximize some notion of 'joint' welfare; although policy co-ordination will rely on countries seeing it as a way of raising their own welfare.

3. *Convergence* is the process of becoming more similar, and is normally thought of as a consequence of co-ordination. However, care needs to be exercised in establishing clearly what it is that is converging: is it policies or performance? The difficulty here is that convergence of one of these may lead to divergence in the other. The co-ordination of policy in order to achieve greater convergence in economic performance may therefore require the pursuit of divergent policies. Furthermore, it is unwise to assume that convergence of performance is the ultimate objective. Who wants to converge towards uniformly high levels of unemployment and low levels of economic activity? The ultimate objective is to raise social welfare. While at the world level this may be undermined if economic performance in individual countries diverges too acutely, the central issue remains that of whether international policy co-ordination facilitates or improves the maximization of welfare.

FORMS OF POLICY CO-ORDINATION

Rules

Broadly speaking co-ordination can take two forms. One involves establishing a set of rules or guidelines for the conduct of economic policy. Once the rules have been agreed, countries do not need to discuss the details of policy but merely have to comply with the rules. An example of such an arrangement is to have a rule for maintaining exchange rates within agreed target zones. Although some proposals for such zones allow for them to be altered in order to eliminate currency misalignment and to maintain fundamental equilibrium exchange rates (FEERs), which are consistent with non-accelerating inflation rates of unemployment (NAIRU) and sustainable balance of payments current accounts in individual countries, exchange rate targets impose constraints on domestic economic management and imply therefore a measure of co-ordination.

However, just having an exchange rate target may be inadequate, and there may need to be supplementary rules covering the ways in which fiscal and monetary policies are to be used. Imagine, for example, a situation where a government's expansionary fiscal policy has led to deficit financing, which has in turn pushed up interest rates. This results in a capital inflow which more than offsets the deterioration in the current account. The exchange rate appreciates. To keep the value of the currency inside its predetermined target zone the government pursues expansionary monetary policy to lower the rate of interest, but this compounds the original policy error. It would have been more appropriate to reduce the fiscal deficit, or possibly to have encouraged other countries to pursue a greater measure of fiscal expansion. This suggests that a rather thicker rule book will be needed!

Discretion

The second form of co-ordination involves the discretionary use of policy. Under this system the performance of the world economy and of individual countries in it would be closely monitored. There would be an ongoing collection of data, covering performance indicators such as Gross National Product; domestic demand; inflation; unemployment; trade and the current account of the balance of payments; monetary growth; the fiscal balance; the exchange rate; the interest rate; and international reserves. Where global or individual performance is deemed to be unsatisfactory, a co-ordinated programme of policies would be undertaken. Here the constraint that co-ordination brings comes from joint decision-making, rather than from compliance with specified guidelines as it does in the 'rules' case. An example of the discretionary approach was the Bonn Economic Summit in 1978 which attempted to co-ordinate policy in a way that would avoid global recession. The strong economies were encouraged to act as a 'locomotive' to pull the world economy towards higher rates of economic growth.

As presented above, the discretionary approach to co-ordination attempts to improve the *general* macroeconomic performance of the world economy. However, in principle, it may also be directed towards *specific* problems and may operate on a more *ad hoc* basis. It may for example attempt to deal with the overvaluation of a particular currency or the problem of Third World debt. The more general and ambitious the discretionary approach, the more problematic it tends to become. This implies that from a practical point of view, policy co-ordination should be limited to a small number of countries and key areas of policy. Before going on to examine some of the problems with international policy co-ordination, let us briefly discuss the main arguments for and against it; although, as we shall see, part of the argument against it is that it is too difficult to implement in any effective form. What is desirable in principle may not be achievable in practice.

ARGUMENTS FOR POLICY CO-ORDINATION

The basic argument for policy co-ordination is that a better outcome in terms of world economic welfare may be achieved than would result from independent and unco-ordinated policy. To the extent that there is scope in the process for all countries to benefit, policy co-ordination is Pareto-efficient.

Many of the economic problems that individual countries encounter in terms of inflation, unemployment, recession, the balance of payments, and the environment are shared. There is a common-sense appeal to the idea that shared problems require shared solutions. Take the following example to illustrate the superiority of a shared solution. Imagine a country which is anxious to expand domestic demand in an attempt to counter recession and rising unemployment at home, but, at the same time, is concerned that independent demand expansion will result in balance of payments problems. It therefore accepts a lower level of domestic economic activity than it would ideally prefer. Fear of the balance of payments consequences means that unco-ordinated policy results in a sub-optimal outcome. If, on the other hand, expansion could be co-ordinated across countries, its balance of payments consequences would be neutralized since individual counries would experience an increase in their exports as well as their imports. In this set of circumstances unco-ordinated policy has a demand deflationary bias which may be avoided through policy co-ordination. On the other hand, failure to co-ordinate could conceivably lead to uniform expansion across countries which is excessive in respect of its global inflationary impact. Here again closer co-ordination of policy could confer benefits on all parties.

As another example, take the case of a country which is anxious to strengthen the current account of its balance of payments. In an attempt to do this it devalues its currency and deflates domestic demand. The purpose behind devaluation is to create price incentives which have the effect of expanding exports and contracting imports (depending on the values of key foreign trade elasticities). The deflation of demand may be necessary to generate spare capacity which is then used to meet the additional demand for home-produced goods; but it will also have the effect of lowering the demand for imports. If exports are regarded as given, the reduced demand for imports will translate into a strengthened current account. But can exports be regarded in this way? Since the imports of one country are the exports of others, a decline in one country's imports will mean a decline in the exports of other countries. Such a decline will, via the multiplier process, lead to a fall in national income in the exporting countries, and an induced fall in their imports. Some of these imports may come from the country which initiated the decline in demand with the result that the desired improvement in the balance of payments will not be achieved.

Furthermore, if countries share the desire to strengthen their own balance of payments and therefore endeavour to achieve this via managing domestic demand and depreciating the exchange rate the policies will be doomed to fail. There is a 'fallacy of composition' in the sense that what may work for one country on its own will not work for all countries together. All that will happen is that world economic activity and trade will fall and world unemployment will rise. In the zero sum world of the balance of payments the current account deficit of some countries may only fall if the surplus of others also falls; and this is likely to require the international orchestration of policy.

Lurking behind the above discussion of policy co-ordination are some fundamental features of the world economy in which we live. First, economies in the world are increasingly interdependent, both through trade and through financial markets; they are, in other words, increasingly 'open'.

Second, but leading on from this, what happens in one country, (especially if it is economically important), or one group of countries, has an impact on other countries; overspill effects, externalities and feedback effects therefore need to be recognized in the design of policy. Where externalities do not exist and an economy is completely closed, independent policy formulation is appropriate; but where they do exist, policy may need to be co-ordinated to allow for them. The situation is analogous to other aspects of society. Robinson Crusoe living on his island could behave much as he liked. In modern societies where the actions of one person affect others, we have rules which constrain our behaviour to comply with agreed norms; our behaviour is thereby co-ordinated. While some advocates of flexible exchange rates argued that they would allow such interdependencies to be eliminated and would allow countries to pursue independent policies, experience has shown that this represented a false prospectus. Although the details of the interdependence change with the nature of the exchange rate regime, it still exists. The appreciation in the value of the dollar in the first half of the 1980s implied a depreciation in the values of other currencies in the rest of the world, which in turn had an impact on both economic performance and economic policy in the rest of the world.

Third, economics suggests that the quality of decisions tends to improve as we have more information upon which to base them. Indeed one of the problems with atomistic competition relates to inadequate information about the behaviour of competitors; a problem which may be overcome to some extent by monopoly. Even if international policy co-operation were to be limited to the spread of information amongst governments concerning economic objectives and intentions, this could show up instances where domestic policies were *unsustainable* (as in the case where the build-up of debt via a fiscal deficit could not be internationally financed); *incompatible* (as in the case where balance of payments targets did not sum to zero or all countries hoped to generate a counter-inflationary effect through currency appreciation); or would result in policy *overkill* because global multipliers are higher than individual country multipliers.

The earlier reference to market structure is particularly apposite to a discussion of policy co-ordination, since analysis of the latter has drawn heavily on the theory of oligopoly and the related theory of games. Oligopoly is characterized by a few large sellers between whom there are significant interdependencies. Ignoring such interdependencies tends to result in what is a generally inferior 'Nash' equilibrium. Similarly in a world dominated by a few large interdependent countries or country groupings there will be scope for improving on the 'Nash' solution via policy co-ordination; with the distribution of the gains depending on the bargaining skill and strength of the participants in the game. Indeed as the world has evolved and the dominance of the United States has been reduced, the theory of oligopoly has become even more relevant.

Advocates of international policy co-ordination frequently point to the mismatch of fiscal policies during the 1980s between the United States on the one hand, and Europe and Japan on the other, as a practical example of where it could have helped. The large US fiscal deficit resulted in high interest rates, a large appreciation in the value of the dollar, and a rapid accumulation of debt in the US. The related depreciation of other currencies threatened additional inflation and led governments in other countries to raise interest rates and deflate demand. Currency misalignment fed on itself through the build-up of a speculative bubble, while high world interest rates, an overvalued dollar, and industrial recession contributed to the Third World debt crisis that came to the fore in 1982. Yet a reduction in the US fiscal deficit will involve a further recessionary threat, and a reduction in the US current account deficit will have to be accommodated by other countries, notably Japan. How much better it would have been, so advocates argue, if the imbalances could have been avoided in the first place by greater co-ordination of policy. Indeed, they argue, the severe overvaluation of the dollar was only ended by an agreement amongst the G3 countries (US, Japan & Germany) – the so-called Plaza Accord of 1985 – to bring down its value via co-ordinated interest rate policy and foreign exchange market intervention.

ARGUMENTS AGAINST POLICY CO-ORDINATION

Opponents of international policy co-ordination often start by stressing their support for international economic co-operation, and may even go as far as accepting that there are benefits from the greater sharing of economic information. Beyond that, however, their case incorporates a blend of practical and theoretical concerns, and ranges from the general to the specific.

Starting with a rather specific example, it is argued that the Louvre Accord in 1987 which was designed to stabilize exchange rates at the then existing levels impeded the decline in the value of the dollar which was in fact necessary to reduce the United States' current account deficit. Moreover it is claimed that an anticipated tightening in US monetary policy in order to defend an overvalued dollar was what sparked off the stock market crash of October 1987. Co-ordination is presented as getting in the way of appropriate policy, as limiting required adjustment and as causing financial instability.

More generally the argument is that the increased bureaucratization of decision-making will inevitably slow down necessary policy changes and will therefore impose (avoidable) welfare losses. Moreover, concern with the internationalization of policy will shift attention away from domestic policy and will encourage governments to claim that the solution to domestic problems lies elsewhere, and often beyond their direct control. It will enable governments which are preoccupied with re-election to avoid, or at least postpone, necessary but unpopular policies. More broadly it is argued that the economics of public choice provides little reason to believe that collusion by governments will result in increased economic welfare. Competition in policy formulation as elsewhere is seen as the preferred solution, since this will help to ensure that counter-inflationary policies are pursued.

While in principle critics claim that it would be misguided for them to do so, they also claim that in practice it is difficult for governments to deliver the necessary commitment with respect to policy co-ordination. This lack of ability to co-ordinate policy (as contrasted with a lack of willingness) follows in part from the fact that an individual country's own policy preferences may themselves represent the fragile consequence of domestic trade-offs and coalitions which could be undermined by the additional international dimension to policy formulation. Moreover critics, with particular reference to the US, have argued that there may be constitutional problems where the Administration cannot commit the US to fiscal policy independently of approval by the Congress.

Even where the international co-ordination of policy could be implemented and would have some advantages, critics argue that the benefits will, at best, be small in relation to the costs of co-ordination which include the high opportunity costs of the administrative time spent in negotiating any agreement.

A final argument against policy co-ordination is in fact a general argument against any attempt to manage aggregate demand through governmental policy irrespective of whether it is co-ordinated or unco-ordinated. The new classical macroeconomics (NCM) maintains that demand management policies will fail because they will induce offsetting changes in behaviour in the private sector and will therefore be crowded out. What is worse, according to NCM, is that while attempts to influence aggregate demand will turn out to be futile, they may still have an adverse effect on the supply side of the economy via the set of incentives (or disincentives) they create. For this reason as well, the international co-ordination of policy, which is usually presented as favouring demand management (even though in principle it could relate to supply side measures), is seen as being ill-conceived and, if anything, counter-productive.

AN OVERVIEW: ISSUES FOR FURTHER CONSIDERATION

As the review of the arguments for and against international policy co-ordination suggests, there must remain a degree of ambivalence about the gains from it. Unfortunately empirical evidence lends little further clarity. Although a growing number of studies have been published, their results are ambiguous. Even the confidence in which the results of individual studies may be held depends crucially on one's willingness to accept the often restrictive assumptions underpinning them. Neither analysis nor empirical evidence allows us to reach a firm conclusion. A great deal of further analytical and empirical work needs to be done before such a conclusion emerges. The views that individuals hold on the issue of policy co-ordination will therefore remain based on their own interpretation of the arguments and their own judgements as to the empirical issues involved. But what are the central questions that need to be examined further?

First, we need to improve our knowledge of how the world economy operates. What, for example, is the precise nature of the mechanisms through which economies are interrelated and what are the lags involved? While different governments believe in different models, agreement on the effects of policies and therefore on what policies are needed will be difficult to secure. However, whether the existence of *model uncertainty* eliminates any chance of gaining from co-ordination is more doubtful. Indeed some research suggests that it is precisely in conditions of uncertainty that co-ordination will be most beneficial. In addition there may be disagreement not only over the right model, but also over the objectives to be achieved. Co-ordination will be made easier where there are uniform objectives amongst the participants.

Second, what is to stop a government *reneging* on an agreement to pursue particular policies if it believes such action to be in its own best interests? The economics of international policy co-ordination raises the related questions of: *free riding, time inconsistency,* and *reputation.* Free riding will be possible if governments can avoid domestic policy changes and yet still benefit from policy changes elsewhere. Time inconsistency results where there is an incentive for governments not to implement policies since the mere announcement of the intention to implement them has in fact generated the ultimately desired response. Of course if governments are expected to renege on commitments or regularly fail to implement the policies they announce they will not be believed; they will lose credibility and reputation. In conducting economic policy governments therefore have to bear in mind their reputations. Although reneging may give short run gains, the associated loss of reputation may impose long run costs. However, rather than relying on governments choosing to honour commitments in order to defend their reputations it may be better to have a system for monitoring compliance and for penalizing non-compliance. Clearly policy co-ordination will only tend to work where participants act in a way that maintains their reputations.

Third, it may be easier to have monitoring and penalty arangements within a rule-based system of co-ordination than within a discretionary one; especially where the rules are fairly uncomplicated. However, rules not only need to be uncomplicated and clearly understood, they also need to be flexible enough to accommodate change and to give rise to a relatively symmetrical distribution of any adjustment burden; it was the lack of flexibility within both the gold standard and the Bretton Woods system, as well as an asymmetry in adjustment which led to their eventual demise. Moreover, the pursuit of simplicity can be taken too far. As noted earlier, it is unlikely that a rule-based system which relates only to exchange rates will be adequate. Correction of monetary and fiscal imbalances may be seen as at least equally important. It is significant that early proposals for the introduction of target zones have more recently been augmented by guidelines or blueprints for the conduct of macroeconomic policy; although it is also significant that a number of competing sets of guidelines are available.

Fourth, while an up-and-running system of rule-based co-ordination may on some counts be superior, a discretionary approach may still be needed to deal with global economic crises such as oil shocks, and to tackle specific problems such as Third World debt. There is certainly a body of opinion that argues that the resolution of this problem requires a more co-ordinated approach than has as yet emerged. Even without focusing specifically on the problem of debt, co-ordinated policy to reduce interest rates and avoid economic recession and encourage trade would benefit indebted nations. Furthermore, a discretionary approach may accommodate a broader agenda of co-ordination than would a rule-based system.

This brings us on to the fifth question. Just because the scope for Pareto efficient reform exists, can it be relied upon to occur? The short answer is, 'No'. Co-ordination is, in this respect, not unlike a public good. During the Bretton Woods era the United States was the hegemonic power and was a natural leader. Now the leadership role is apparently vacant. Some might argue that the public good aspects of co-ordination suggest that an inter-governmental agency such as the International Monetary Fund (IMF) should take the lead; but Fund policy is decided upon by its Executive Directors, who represent their country constituencies. Perhaps in some brave new world the IMF would be able to manage the supply of world money and manipulate global economic policy in a counter-cyclical fashion in order to sustain world economic growth and eliminate inflation and unemployment, but for the foreseeable future, and for as long as economists are unable to demonstrate empirically the gains from policy co-ordination, it is more likely that co-ordination will remain little more than a cosmetic exercise. Regular summits of the leaders of the industrialized economies may serve other purposes but will do little to bring about effective co-ordination of economic policy. The chances of progress are perhaps greater at the level of the European Community, although even here we have Mrs Thatcher's notorious delay in participating in the rule-based co-ordination which is associated with the Exchange Rate Mechanism, and the UK Government's apparent resistance to the more discretionary co-ordination of monetary and fiscal policy which might ultimately lead to establishing a European Central Bank, a European currency and common, or at least harmonized, tax policies. Evidence in other areas such as environmental protection, however, suggests that once a strong scientific consensus emerges, internationally co-ordinated policy action can sometimes quickly follow.

FURTHER READING

There are a number of useful surveys of international policy co-ordination now available. A readable review of the theory and practice is Michael Artis and Sylvia Ostry (1986), *International Economic Policy Co-ordination*, Chatham House Papers, 30, The Royal Institute of International Affairs and Routledge and Kegan Paul, London. Other excellent surveys are Jocelyn Horne and Paul R Masson (1988), 'Scope and Limits of International Economic Co-operation and Policy Co-ordination', *International Monetary Fund Staff Papers*, June; David Currie, (1990), 'International Macroeconomic Policy Co-ordination: Survey and Prognosis', in Graham Bird, (ed), *The International Financial Regime*, Surrey University Press with Academic Press; and Andrew Hughes Hallett, (1989), 'Macroeconomic Interdependence and the Co-ordination of Economic Policy', in David Greenaway, (ed), *Current Issues in Macroeconomics*, Macmillan, London. A lively presentation of a critic's view is to be found in Martin Feldstein, (1988), 'Thinking About International Economic Co-ordination', *Journal of Economic Perspectives*, Spring. A summary of one suggested set of policy criteria for the conduct of co-ordination may be found in John Williamson, (1990), 'The Blueprint Proposals for International Monetary Reform', in G Bird op. cit. Much quoted (and criticized) examples of attempts to measure the effects of policy co-ordination are Gilles Oudiz and J Sachs, (1984), 'Macroeconomic Policy Co-ordination among the Industrialised Economies', *Brooking Papers on Economic Activity*, and Jeffrey Frankel and K Rockett, (1988), 'International Macroeconomic Policy Co-ordination when Policy Makers Disagree on the Model', *American Economic Review*. Robert Putnam and Nicholas Boyle, (1987), *Hanging Together: Co-operation and Conflict in the Seven Power Summits*, Sage, provide an interesting discussion of the political economy of policy co-ordination.

QUESTIONS FOR DISCUSSION

1. How would you set about assessing the macroeconomic performance of the world economy, and what are the principal problems you will encounter?
2. If macroeconomic policy were to be co-ordinated internationally, how could this best be achieved?
3. What is meant by the argument that there are Pareto efficient gains from policy co-ordination?
4. Explain the connection between international economic interdependence and policy co-ordination.

5. In the debate over international policy co-ordination discuss the relevance of: games theory; model uncertainty; time inconsistency; and reputation.
6. Consider and comment on some practical examples of attempts to co-ordinate macroeconomic policy internationally.

16. The Rich and the Poor: Changes in Incomes of Developing Countries Since 1960

Sheila Page[1]

Most countries in the world are getting richer. Incomes in some countries which were previously regarded as 'developing' have now caught up with incomes in advanced countries. Yet incomes in other countries, particularly the poorest, have not improved and have therefore declined relative to the rest of the world. We are used to the idea of a 'North–South gap', but this concept is not helpful when trying to understand the meaning of income, wealth, welfare and poverty. Whatever terms are used, and however we measure them, the global range of incomes remains wide. Many of the poorest countries, particularly in Africa, have seen little improvement: their poverty clearly divides them from the rest of the world.

WHAT CAN COMPARING INCOMES TELL US?

The Purposes of Comparisons

Understanding income changes for one country or among a group of countries is crucial to national policy choices. The performance of different policies in achieving higher incomes or faster growth should be one crucial measure of the success of different strategies of development. Some types of development aid or access to special privileges are tied to particular levels of 'low income'. Have differences among 'developing countries' grown, so that it is no longer possible to think about the 'Third World' as a single category? Have the old boundaries between 'developed' and 'developing' changed? Has the gap between the richest and the poorest countries widened or narrowed? These changes have important implications for international policies on trade and capital flows.

The sluggish world growth of the 1980s, increasing debt service and expectations that these factors will continue to depress incomes have sharpened concern over standards of living in the developing countries in general. More dramatic events like drought and civil war have focused attention on some of the poorest. Falling incomes in poor countries or a failure to keep pace with those in the richer countries is contrary not only to the expectation that growth is normal, but also to the implicit purposes of the structural changes which are the essence of development, and to the explicit aims of aid programmes.

How to Make Comparisons

What is poverty? What do we mean by better living standards? We cannot answer these questions without first of all deciding whether to refer to relative or absolute standards of poverty. There will always be groups of people or countries which are in the bottom 10 per cent of any defined group, even though their identity may change over time. If poverty is defined relative to average income, then measurement of the rise or fall of certain groups' incomes will reflect individual changes and overall distribution of income. An absolute level is difficult to define because as the global level of income rises, standards of 'low' and 'acceptable' also rise.

A basic standard is gross domestic product (GDP), the fullest single measure of national income. GDP measures the value of all goods and services produced in a country, spending on them, and the income derived from this. For comparisons over time, all years are valued at one 'base' year's prices. This gives 'real' changes in GDP; figures for individual years (for example, GDP in 1985 measured by prices in 1980) can be called 'real' GDP to distinguish them from GDP measured by 1985 prices. To compare income in countries of different sizes, it can be divided by population to find the (real) GDP per capita. GDP includes government and other institutional income or spending, so GDP per capita includes the average value of this spending for each person. Conventional personal income is therefore lower than GDP per capita. On the other hand, the average income per household would be substantially higher because the figures relate to individuals, including children and the old who may not actually be earning.

The ethical, theoretical, and practical difficulties surrounding GDP measurement even for a single country can only be summarized here, emphasizing those most relevant to international comparisons:

GDP excludes, or measures inadequately, goods and services which are not sold. This omission may not be significant for a single country if non-marketed goods or services do not vary over short- or medium-term, or when comparisons are made among countries with similar non-market sectors. But for long-term assessments (say over 25 years) and for comparisons among countries with very different economic and social structures, it does. The distortions should therefore be minimized by adjusting carefully for known differences in prices and economic structure. A measurement of GDP will include everything that can be reliably measured. It is therefore a more accurate measurement of welfare than a measure of personal income or private consumption, which may or may not take into account those services (health and education are major examples) which are sometimes provided publicly and sometimes come out of personal spending.

This method of measurement could be criticized for failing to allow properly for permanent damage to non-renewable resources. In principle, an efficient pricing system should do this; in practice, it probably does not. In this case again, GDP still produces a better measurement than any practical alternative.

Some spending may be unproductive or even damaging; it may be needed to compensate for previous damaging expenditure (arms or some curative health spending are examples). But if we accept GDP as a measure of the potential capacity of a country's income, whether the income is 'wasted' or not is a question of judgement not entering into the measurement.

Further difficulties arise because of inequalities among groups of people and among regions. Comparing countries' average incomes may not give a good indicator of the differences between the most common incomes. If there have been large changes in income distribution, this could also affect interpretation of changes over time. These are not allowed for here because a country has the potential to change policies on distribution, and because of the practical difficulty of obtaining reliable and comparable measures of income inequality.

It is difficult therefore to collect data for the varied types of income (and spending) which can be compared effectively according to uniform measures, and any figures must be assumed to have a wide level of uncertainty. Making proper allowance for changes in prices and quality of goods and services poses major statistical difficulties, and frequently problems of judgement as well. The figures even for single countries therefore have a wide band of uncertainty.

The problems of comparing the 'real income' or 'welfare' of different groups with different patterns of income and expenditure are greater in a cross-country comparison than they are for different groups within one country. Variable exchange rates make measurement more difficult. When comparing incomes across time or across countries, figures must be adjusted for price differences. The practical difficulties of finding actual prices in one country include discounting, bargaining or parallel markets, and goods provided publicly at administered prices or without charge. Some goods are scarcer in some countries (for example machinery in developing countries, or personal services in rich but egalitarian countries). In addition, price rises and improvements in a product over time are difficult to distinguish. All these factors differ from country to country, and thus the problems of comparison are increased. No one set of relationships among prices is the 'right' one to use for measurement and the problem is compounded because spending patterns alter to avoid the more expensive goods.

International comparisons are based on two approaches. The first converts all national accounts in question (nominal or real) to the same currency (usually the US dollar) by using nominal exchange rates. If GDP is a measure of potential, the international value of a country's output is in some sense its 'real' value. This concept is useful when assessing a country's ability to meet international obligations, for example contributions to international institutions or repayment of debt.

The second approach avoids the use of exchange rates. In a period in which they fluctuate widely, countries' relative incomes appear to change drastically from year to year in a way which intuitively seems wrong. Most domestic prices and incomes are not immediately affected by exchange rate changes and people do not experience changes in income simply because their purchases have a changed value at international prices. Efforts have been made to construct at the international level the same type of product-by-product measures of prices and real income used for national time-series; the *UN International Comparisons Project* (ICP) was started in 1968 and full results for the fourth round have now been published. By looking at prices for a common range of individual goods and spending patterns within countries, this produces particularly useful figures. In each round the ICP makes cross-country comparisons for individual products for a 'benchmark year' (1970, 1973, 1975 and 1980; 1985 is the subject of phase five). The number of countries included in detail has increased to sixty for the 1980 study. These results have been used to construct series from 1950 to 1985 for 130 countries, at 1980 prices by using national accounts data and by allowing for spending patterns.

The data problems are clearly immense, but there is encouraging consistency between benchmark years. The estimates made by the project for the non-benchmark countries seem less reliable, but the increase in the number of countries covered in the survey (doubled between phases 3 and 4) has reduced the need for estimates. The countries included in our tables are mostly ICP benchmark countries, although some of the smaller ones were excluded, while Asian and African countries were added using the

ICP estimates. The major Middle Eastern oil exporters were not included in the benchmark countries so the ICP estimates for them are not used.

Any measure of income, however, remains an indirect measure of welfare, which is the basic objective of individuals and governments. Although it may be impossible to reach any consensus on what this means, or even on the measurable economic and social elements which it should include, most countries and observers would accept some basic indicators of health and education as objectives. These are similar to GDP in giving a measure of potential: of access to improved welfare, without specifying particular patterns of development or spending. If goods, services, or types of output (for example of manufacturing) were examined in greater detail, even though regular differences may appear between richer and poorer countries, the comparisons would reflect the political choices and priorities of different countries or their particular natural conditions, rather than an objective standard.

HOW INCOMES HAVE CHANGED

Average global income has risen because world GDP has grown faster than population. Income differences among most countries are not as great as simple comparisons suggest when better income figures and direct measures of health and education are used. In average and upper middle-income developing countries, incomes are starting to approach the level of rich countries. Even in 1960, a few developing countries, mainly in Latin America, had similar incomes to the poorer European countries. Since then, Asian countries have approached European levels. Up to the mid 1970s, differences between countries were probably diminishing, but this is less evident now (except in relation to health). Using any measure, there is a clear group of countries at the bottom, mainly in Africa, where there has been little absolute progress and a persistent decline in income relative to the rest of the world.

The 63 countries given in the tables here were chosen to represent a spread of incomes and to give a geographical range, and to include most large countries, and countries whose experience is particularly interesting. The tables clearly show, however, that results vary according to the way in which income is measured. Table 16.1 shows for 1985 the three measures of GDP per capita described above. Column 3 gives the national measure at 1985 prices, converted to dollars. Column 2 gives the same measure, but using 1980 prices and exchange rates. Although the different prices and exchange rates affect the ranking of countries, there are few dramatic changes in position. Column 1 uses the ICP figures (which adjust for

Table 16.1   Three measures of GDP per capita in 1985 (US dollars)

1 International or real national accounts 1980 international dollars	2 At 1980 prices and exchange rates conventional national accounts (US$)	3 At 1985 prices and exchange rates (US$)
Norway 12623	Norway 16413	US 16759
US 12532	Germany, FR 14235	Norway 13799
Canada 12196	France 12973	Canada 13431
Germany, FR 10708	US 12843	Japan 11014
France 9918	Belgium 12563	Australia 10481
Belgium 9717	Netherlands 12285	Germany, FR 10270
Japan 9447	Canada 11633	France 9466
Hong Kong 9093	Austria 11004	Austria 8692
Netherlands 9092	Australia 10968	Netherlands 8692
Austria 8929	Japan 10636	Belgium 8186
Australia 8850	UK 10384	UK 8127
UK 8655	Italy 8647	Italy 6224
Italy 7425	Hong Kong 6472	Hong Kong 6170
Spain 6437	Ireland 5947	Israel 5404
Israel 6270	Spain 5937	Ireland 4600
USSR 6266	Israel 5863	Spain 4204
Hungary 5765	Argentina 4599	Greece 3339
Ireland 5205	Greece 4315	Taiwan 3097
Yugoslavia 5063	Venezuela 3204	Venezuela 2750
Poland 4913	USSR 3037	USSR 2449
Greece 4464	Taiwan 2871	Argentina 2153
Mexico 3985	Yugoslavia 2818	South Korea 2039
South Africa 3885	South Africa 2591	Hungary 1936
Portugal 3729	Portugal 2576	Yugoslavia 1913
Taiwan 3581	Mexico 2569	Portugal 1909
Venezuela 3548	Hungary 2270	Poland 1894
Argentina 3486	Chile 2231	Mexico 1872
Chile 3486	South Korea 2192	Malaysia 1844
Malaysia 3415	Brazil 2028	South Africa 1600
Brazil 3282	Malaysia 2005	Brazil 1585

Table 16.1 Three measures of GDP per capita in 1985 (US dollars) – continued

1 International or real national accounts 1980 international dollars		2 At 1980 prices and exchange rates conventional national accounts (US$)		3 At 1985 prices and exchange rates (US$)	
South Korea	3056	Tunisia	1404	Ecuador	1578
Colombia	2599	Ecuador	1392	Guatemala	1363
Turkey	2533	Turkey	1388	Chile	1320
Ecuador	2387	Colombia	1295	Colombia	1160
Peru	2114	Ghana	1126	Tunisia	1151
Tunisia	2050	Cote d'Ivoire	1041	Turkey	1069
Thailand	1900	Guatemala	935	Bolivia	795
Guatemala	1608	Morocco	932	Nigeria	768
Sri Lanka	1539	Peru	847	Thailand	718
Philippines	1361	Thailand	832	Peru	708
Indonesia	1255	Zimbabwe	820	Cameroon	698
Morocco	1221	Nigeria	793	Cote d'Ivoire	641
Egypt	1188	Cameroon	791	Philippines	584
Pakistan	1153	Bolivia	691	Zimbabwe	583
Cameroon	1095	Egypt	621	Morocco	552
Bolivia	1089	Philippines	611	Egypt	529
Zimbabwe	948	Zambia	607	Indonesia	499
Cote d'Ivoire	920	Indonesia	552	Ghana	461
China	825	Kenya	399	Zambia	389
Senegal	754	Pakistan	339	Haiti	377
India	750	Madagascar	318	Sri Lanka	376
Kenya	698	Sri Lanka	313	Pakistan	337
Bangladesh	647	India	282	Tanzania	283
Haiti	631	China	273	Kenya	277
Zambia	584	Haiti	259	India	261
Nigeria	581	Tanzania	247	Madagascar	235
Madagascar	495	Zaire	215	China	222
Malawi	387	Malawi	193	Malawi	159
Mali	355	Bangladesh	157	Bangladesh	152
Tanzania	355	Ethiopia	112	Ethiopia	111
Ghana	349			Zaire	79
Ethiopia	310				
Zaire	210				

Table 16.2 Changes in national income over time

Income per capita (1980 international dollars)	1960	1965	1970	1975	1980	1985
Above 7,400	US	US	Canada Germany, FR US	Australia Belgium France Germany, FR Netherlands Norway US	Australia Austria Belgium Canada France Germany, FR Japan Netherlands Norway UK US	Australia Austria Belgium Canada France Germany, FR Hong Kong Italy Japan Netherlands Norway UK US
2,300–7,400	Argentina Australia Austria Belgium Canada Chile France Germany, FR Hungary Ireland Israel Italy Netherlands Norway Poland South Africa Spain UK USSR Venezuela	Argentina Australia Austria Belgium Canada Chile France Germany, FR Hong Kong Hungary Ireland Israel Italy Japan Mexico Netherlands Norway Poland South Africa Spain UK USSR Venezuela	Argentina Australia Austria Belgium France Greece Hong Kong Hungary Ireland Israel Italy Japan Mexico Netherlands Norway Poland Portugal South Africa Spain UK USSR Venezuela Yugoslavia	Argentina Austria Brazil Chile Greece Hong Kong Hungary Ireland Israel Italy Japan Mexico Peru Poland Portugal South Africa Spain UK USSR Venezuela Yugoslavia	Argentina Brazil Chile Colombia Ecuador Greece Hong Kong Hungary Ireland Israel Italy Malaysia Mexico Peru Poland Portugal South Africa South Korea Spain Taiwan USSR Venezuela Yugoslavia	Argentina Brazil Chile Colombia Ecuador Greece Hungary Ireland Israel Malaysia Mexico Poland Portugal South Africa South Korea Spain Taiwan Turkey USSR Venezuela Yugoslavia
1,200–2,300	Colombia Greece Guatemala Hong Kong	Brazil Colombia Ecuador Greece	Bolivia Brazil Colombia Ecuador	Bolivia Colombia Ecuador Guatemala	Bolivia Guatemala Morocco Philippines	Guatemala Indonesia Morocco Peru

Table 16.2 Changes in national income over time – continued

	1960	1965	1970	1975	1980	1985
1,200–2,300	Japan Mexico Peru Portugal Turkey Yugoslavia	Guatemala Malaysia Peru Portugal Turkey Yugoslavia	Guatemala Malaysia Peru South Korea Tunisia Turkey	Malaysia Philippines South Korea Taiwan Thailand Tunisia Turkey	Thailand Tunisia Turkey	Philippines Sri Lanka Thailand Tunisia
450,1,200	Bolivia Brazil Cameroon China Cote d'Ivoire Ecuador Egypt Ghana Guatemala Haiti India Indonesia Kenya Madagascar Malaysia Morocco Nigeria Pakistan Philippines Senegal South Korea Sri Lanka Taiwan Thailand Tunisia Zambia Zimbabwe	Bangladesh Bolivia Cameroon China Cote d'Ivoire Egypt Ghana Haiti India Indonesia Kenya Madagascar Morocco Nigeria Pakistan Philippines Senegal South Korea Sri Lanka Taiwan Thailand Tunisia Zambia Zimbabwe	Bangladesh Cameroon China Cote d'Ivoire Egypt Ghana Haiti India Indonesia Kenya Madagascar Morocco Nigeria Pakistan Philippines Senegal Sri Lanka Taiwan Thailand Zambia Zimbabwe	Bangladesh Cameroon China Cote d'Ivoire Egypt Ghana Haiti India Indonesia Kenya Madagascar Nigeria Pakistan Senegal Sri Lanka Zambia Zimbabwe	Bangladesh Cameroon China Cote d'Ivoire Egypt Haiti India Indonesia Kenya Madagascar Nigeria Pakistan Senegal Sri Lanka Zambia Zimbabwe	Bangladesh Bolivia Cameroon China Cote d'Ivoire Egypt Haiti India Kenya Madagascar Nigeria Pakistan Senegal Zambia Zimbabwe
Below 450	Bangladesh Ethiopia Malawi Mali Tanzania Zaire	Ethiopia Malawi Mali Tanzania Zaire	Ethiopia Malawi Mali Tanzania Zaire	Ethiopia Malawi Mali Tanzania Zaire	Ethiopia Ghana Malawi Mali Tanzania Zaire	Ethiopia Ghana Malawi Mali Tanzania Zaire

purchasing power), again with 1980 as a base. A striking result of this measurement comparison is the way in which ICP reduces the disparity between most low-income countries and the most advanced. Middle- to upper-middle-income countries' relative positions are changed, but the sub-Saharan African countries are less affected than the poorer Asian countries, and thus become more concentrated at the bottom of the column.

Poor and Rich Countries Today

If we look at the achievement of certain minimum and then higher, incomes as an indicator of a country's performance, column 3 of Table 16.1 provides the easiest way to apply our current perceptions of what income levels mean. These data have been used to define one possible division of countries into 'rich', 'poor', and upper and lower middle income groups, which is given in Table 16.2.

The lowest level corresponds closely to some international definitions of the poorest.[2] The median in Table 16.1, column 3 (that of the middle country in the ranking) is about $1600, the level of some major Latin American or Eastern European countries. The poorest countries are defined as below $400, which is a quarter of the median. The most advanced countries enjoy an income which is at least four times the median ($6400), slightly below the UK and close to Italy or Hong Kong. A band of roughly average countries is defined as $1000 to $2000. This leaves two intermediate groups: the richer developed and poorer European in the higher group, and the richer African and poorer Asian in the other. Using these definitions and 1980 prices, the 'rich' correspond to those with incomes above $7400, the poor to those with incomes below $450, and the middle to those with incomes between $1200 and $2300. The ICP figures (Table 16.1, column 1) give a similar group of 'rich' countries, but a much larger number of countries in the upper middle-income range: the middle country in this column has an income of $2600.

Changes in Income and Relative Income

Table 16.2 shows that the countries below the 'poverty line' have scarcely changed since 1960. Many of the countries in the middle three groups have moved up in at least one division, with some 'NIEs' (newly industrialized economies) advancing from 'lower' to 'upper' middle income. Many of the African countries, however, have remained 'lower middle' or poor.

The income range now occupied by the better performing Asian and Latin American countries corresponds to the 1960 level of the poorer European countries. South Korea and Brazil, for example, are now at a

Figure 16.1 Changes in income 1960–85 (1980 international dollars, log scale)

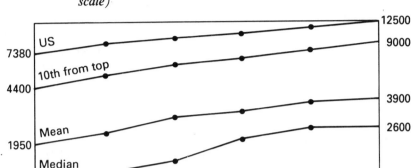

level similar to that of Italy in 1960, while Colombia or Turkey would occupy a position similar to that then occupied by Ireland or Spain.

Growth in the lowest category, and at the lower end of the countries with below-average income, has been much slower. Using data for national accounts (as in Table 16.1, column 2) the World Bank estimates growth rates for similar income groups: from 1965 to 1985, per capita income in low-income countries (under $400, excluding China and India) grew less than 0.5 per cent a year; in China and India at 3.5 per cent; in the lower-middle-income group ($400–$1600) at 2.6 per cent; and in the upper-middle-income group including only 'developing' countries ($1600–$7420) at 3.3 per cent. The differences in growth rate are greater than those indicated in Table 16.2, where for 1985 the 'low income' group does not include those who have grown out of that class. Figure 16.1 shows the general rise in real incomes over the past 25 years, with the increase in the mean (a simple average of the countries) relative to the median confirming the more rapid growth of the higher income countries. The figures for the tenth country from the top and from the bottom in each year indicate roughly the changes for the fairly rich and fairly poor (in relative terms). The greater rise for the rich is clear. It can also be seen how middle-income countries have 'caught up'. A country with income at the median level in 1985 would have been in the top quarter in 1960.

The US has the highest income in 1960. In 1985 it retained this position at 1985 exchange rates (the dollar was high), but not at 1980 exchange rates. This apparently confirms the observation in the 1975 ICP report of 'the general tendency for per capita income relative to the United States to rise through time for most countries'. But after 1975, although the richest countries continued to approach the US level, the middle-income groups' relative growth rate slowed, while that of the lowest-income group was never significant.

Education and Health

Life expectancy and infant mortality improved for all countries (except once again, for the poorest). The divisions in Tables 16.3 and 16.4 were chosen to indicate the typical situation now for rich and poor countries. In many of the lower-income countries, life expectancy increased by as much as ten years. The best improvements in the infant mortality rate have been in countries which moved from the lowest to the intermediate groups, although there has been clear progress at all levels.

The figures for primary school education (Table 16.5) shows that this is now effectively universal in all but the poorest countries; this was not the case even for some above-average income countries in 1960. Secondary enrolment also rose overall from some very low levels in 1960. More than two thirds of the countries had levels below 30 per cent in 1960, compared to only a quarter in 1985; only two countries had a level above 70 per cent in 1960; in 1985, however, a third of all countries had secondary enrolment at this level. The increases for many have been extremely large (Zimbabwe and Indonesia from 6 per cent to 39 per cent; Hong Kong and South Korea trebled from higher bases), but secondary enrolment figures for the poorest remain extremely low (under 15 per cent for Tanzania, Malawi, Mali and Ethiopia).

The infant mortality, life expectancy and enrolment statistics suggest that better progress has been made, especially by fairly poor countries, than the income measurements would suggest. But the contrast between the poorest and the rest is again stark. There are, however, many individual divergences. On all welfare measures, Sri Lanka is well above its income ranking, while some of the Latin American countries are seriously below, especially in relation to health. Income levels are not, therefore, an inescapable constraint on welfare growth.

SUMMARY AND CONCLUSIONS FOR POLICY

- Different methods of assessment produce different income levels or relative positions for a given country. Considerable caution must

Table 16.3 Life expectancy (years at birth)

70 and above		51-69		50 and below	
1960	1985	1960	1985	1960	1985
Australia	Argentina	Argentina	Bangladesh	Bangladesh	Ethiopia
Belgium	Australia	Austria	Bolivia	Bolivia	Malawi
Canada	Austria	Brazil	Brazil	Cameroon	Mali
France	Belgium	Chile	Cameroon	Cote d'Ivoire	Senegal
Netherlands	Canada	China	China	Egypt	
Norway	Chile	Colombia	Colombia	Ethiopia	
UK	France	Ecuador	Cote d'Ivoire	Ghana	
US	Germany, FR	Germany, FR	Ecuador	Guatemala	
	Hong Kong	Greece	Egypt	Haiti	
	Hungary	Hong Kong	Ghana	India	
	Ireland	Hungary	Greece	Indonesia	
	Israel	Ireland	Guatemala	Kenya	
	Italy	Israel	Haiti	Madagascar	
	Japan	Italy	India	Malawi	
	Netherlands	Japan	Indonesia	Mali	
	Norway	Malaysia	Kenya	Morocco	
	Poland	Mexico	Madagascar	Nigeria	
	Portugal	Poland	Malaysia	Pakistan	
	Spain	Portugal	Mexico	Peru	
	Taiwan	South Africa	Morocco	Philippines	
	UK	South Korea	Nigeria	Senegal	
	US	Spain	Pakistan	Tanzania	
	USSR	Sri Lanka	Peru	Thailand	
	Venezuela	Taiwan	Philippines	Tunisia	
	Yugoslavia	USSR	South Africa	Turkey	
		Venezuela	South Korea	Zaire	
		Yugoslavia	Sri Lanka	Zambia	
			Tanzania	Zimbabwe	
			Thailand		
			Tunisia		
			Turkey		
			Zaire		
			Zambia		
			Zimbabwe		

229

Table 16.4 Infant mortality (deaths per 1000)

15 or fewer		16-50		51-99		100 and above	
1960	1985	1960	1985	1960	1985	1960	1985
	Australia	Australia	Argentina	Argentina	Brazil	Bangladesh	Bangladesh
	Austria	Austria	Chile	Colombia	Cameroon	Bolivia	Bolivia
	Belgium	Belgium	China	Guatemala	Ecuador	Brazil	Cote d'Ivoire
	Canada	Canada	Colombia	Malaysia	Egypt	Cameroon	Ethiopia
	France	France	Greece	Mexico	Ghana	Chile	Haiti
	Germany, FR	Germany, FR	Hungary	Poland	Guatemala	China	Madagascar
	Hong Kong	Greece	Malaysia	Portugal	India	Cote d'Ivoire	Malawi
	Ireland	Hong Kong	Mexico	South Africa	Indonesia	Ecuador	Mali
	Israel	Hungary	Philippines	South Korea	Kenya	Egypt	Nigeria
	Italy	Ireland	Poland	Sri Lanka	Morocco	Ethiopia	Pakistan
	Japan	Israel	Portugal	Venezuela	Peru	Ghana	Senegal
	Netherlands	Italy	South Korea	Yugoslavia	South Africa	Haiti	Tanzania
	Norway	Japan	Sri Lanka		Tunisia	India	Zaire
	Spain	Netherlands	Thailand		Turkey	Indonesia	
	UK	Norway	USSR		Zambia	Kenya	
	US	Spain	Venezuela		Zimbabwe	Madagascar	
		UK	Yugoslavia			Malawi	
		US				Mali	
		USSR				Morocco	
						Nigeria	
						Pakistan	
						Peru	
						Philippines	
						Senegal	
						Tanzania	
						Thailand	
						Tunisia	
						Turkey	
						Zaire	
						Zambia	
						Zimbabwe	

Table 16.5 Primary school enrolment (%, relevant age group)

Effectively universal 95 or above		51–94		Less than 50	
1960	1984	1960	1984	1960	1984
Argentina	Argentina	Bolivia	Bangladesh	Bangladesh	Ethiopia
Australia	Australia	Cameroon	Bolivia	Cote d'Ivoire	Mali
Austria	Austria	Colombia	Cote d'Ivoire	Ethiopia	Pakistan
Belgium	Belgium	Ecuador	Egypt	Ghana	
Brazil	Brazil	Egypt	Ghana	Guatemala	
Canada	Cameroon	Hong Kong	Guatemala	Haiti	
Chile	Canada	India	Haiti	Kenya	
France	Chile	Indonesia	India	Mali	
Germany, FR	China	Madagascar	Malawi	Morocco	
Greece	Colombia	Malawi	Morocco	Nigeria	
Hungary	Ecuador	Mexico	Nigeria	Pakistan	
Ireland	France	Peru	Senegal	Senegal	
Israel	Germany, FR	South Africa	Tanzania	Tanzania	
Italy	Greece	South Korea	Zaire	Zambia	
Japan	Hong Kong	Thailand			
Malaysia	Hungary	Tunisia			
Netherlands	Indonesia	Turkey			
Norway	Ireland	Zaire			
Philippines	Israel				
Poland	Italy				
Portugal	Japan				
Spain	Kenya				
Sri Lanka	Madagascar				
UK	Malaysia				
US	Mexico				
USSR	Netherlands				
Venezuela	Norway				
Yugoslavia	Peru				
Zimbabwe	Philippines				
	Poland				
	Portugal				
	South Korea				
	Spain				
	Sri Lanka				
	Thailand				
	Tunisia				
	Turkey				
	UK				
	US				
	USSR				
	Venezuela				
	Yugoslavia				
	Zaire				
	Zambia				
	Zimbabwe				

therefore be exercised when attempting to classify countries, particularly when using conventional national accounts.

- Social, economic and financial indicators should be taken into account when measuring or monitoring a country's performance, its progress, regression or recovery.

- Some conventional terminology can be called into question:

    The 'Third World' is not a bloc in terms of income and wealth, but a very heterogeneous grouping of nations.

    Some countries in the 'South' overlap with those of the 'North'; not only have some of the former 'caught up' recently (particularly in East and S E Asia), but some in Latin America were already 'ahead' a generation ago.

- The achievement of high levels of income by some countries shows that it is possible to 'catch up' to the advanced level. These successes may provide evidence on which to base future domestic policies.

- There is a blurred boundary between 'advanced' and 'developing', and many countries which we call 'developing' are actually 'advanced' by 1960 standards. There is thus a case for examining how we perceive individual countries' roles in the international trade and financial system, since there is no obvious frontier between the 'developed' and the rest.

- The poorest countries can be identified, nonetheless, and treated differently. They are clearly separated from other developing countries by the level of their income, their rate of growth, or direct measures of health and education.

NOTES

1. This paper is an abridged version of an Overseas Development Institute Briefing Paper, June 1988. The assistance of Donald Roy is gratefully acknowledged.

2. The United Nations has defined a group of 41 Least Developed Countries using per capita income, share of manufacturing in output, and a social indicator. Most of these are too small, or cannot provide adequate data, to be included in these tables. We have, however, been able to include Malawi, Mali, Tanzania and Ethiopia (which have remained in the lowest income group) as well as Bangladesh and Haiti.

    The countries eligible for World Bank International Development Association credits (those with an income below $835 at 1986 prices) would fall below a level of about $2000 when assessed at 1980 prices, using ICP (Table 16.1, column 1). This suggests that the difference between using this and a $400 to $500 cut-off point is larger than the non-ICP measure indicates (Table 16.1, columns 2–3).

    Some other bilateral and multinational aid programmes use a level of around $1000 to $1300 to identify those eligible for some special treatment. Because the discrepancy between ICP and conventional measures decreases rapidly at this point, the difference is less marked on the ICP scale, which raises the cut-off point to a level around $2100.

REFERENCES

Heston, A. and Summers, R. (1982) *World Product and Income.*
Summers, R. and Heston A. (1988), 'A New Set of International Comparisons', *Review of Income and Wealth.*
Other data from IMF, UN, World Bank.

QUESTIONS FOR DISCUSSION

1. What problems are encountered when GDP is used as a measure of welfare? What alternative indicators could be used?
2. Why is it difficult to make GDP comparisons (*a*) across time, and (*b*) across countries? How might some of these difficulties be overcome?
3. To what extent does the choice of welfare indicator affect the ranking of countries? Which welfare indicators do you think should be used to determine the distribution of aid?
4. How useful are concepts such as: The Third World, The South etc?
5. Choose one (or more) country in each category (low, middle, high income and so on) and find out why it is ranked where it is. What aid does it receive/give? How swiftly is it developing, and why?
6. Identify some of the high growth countries which have recently 'caught up' with advanced countries. What is the source of their success? Why have many low income countries tended to grow more slowly than middle income countries recently? What could be done to help these poorest nations?

17. The Third World Debt 'Crisis': Causes and Cures

Graham Bird

INTRODUCTION

Third World debt has become one of the principal problems facing the world economy. It has been seen as threatening the stability of the entire international financial and banking system and as undermining the fragile foundations of democracy in some of the highly indebted developing countries. This chapter sets out to review, in a straightforward and uncomplicated way, the basic nature and causes of debt problems as well as the policy options that are, in principle, available. It will be seen that the use of simple economic concepts and analysis gets us a long way in understanding this often apparently intractable problem.

THE ECONOMICS OF DEBT

By relaxing the constraints imposed by domestic saving and foreign exchange, external borrowing allows countries to increase their rate of economic growth. The size and duration of this positive effect depends essentially on how the extra resources are used and on the marginal productivity of capital. However, even if borrowing is used purely to sustain or raise domestic consumption, there will at least be a short run benefit for the debtor's standard of living.

In the case of grants, that is financial inflows with a grant element of 100 per cent, there are no further problems. Although there will be debate over how the money should be used, the question of repaying the debt does not arise.

But most international financial flows are not grants. They are loans that have to be repaid with interest. By borrowing, countries are in effect trading off future domestic absorption (that is, consumption and investment expenditure) in favour of current absorption. Borrowers are relaxing current constraints at the cost of imposing future ones. Borrowing initially allows investment to exceed domestic saving and imports to exceed exports. However the crux of the debt problem is that in order to service loans, these inequalities have to be reversed to an extent and within a period of time determined by the conditions of the loans. In order to avoid a debt problem it is therefore necessary for a borrower to close the domestic savings gap and to go on to generate excess saving. However since loans normally have to be repaid in foreign exchange rather than in domestic currency, it is also necessary to convert this excess saving into foreign exchange, and to do this exports have to increase relative to imports.

Concentrating first of all on savings, and taking the simplest possible savings function where aggregate saving depends on the average propensity to save and the level of income, savings will increase if either the savings ratio or national income increases. Both changes may occur simultaneously if the marginal propensity to save exceeds the average propensity to save, and if the loan causes national income to rise. Assuming for a moment that the repayment of the principal of the loan can be financed by further borrowing, national income will rise provided the marginal productivity of the resources borrowed exceeds the rate of interest on the loan.[1]

Turning to the foreign exchange aspect of the problem, a borrower's holding of foreign exchange will increase either if exports expand, or if there is a substitution away from imports. What is required then is a shift of domestic resources into the tradeables sector of the economy. Relevant in this context is a whole range of both demand and supply side factors. Is it possible for the borrower to induce an increase in exports by altering the structure of prices via exchange rate policy or the use of subsidies and taxes, or is there a constraint on export growth imposed by the income elasticity of demand for exports and the growth of income in principal markets? Does the borrower's marginal propensity to import lie below the average propensity to import in which case the import coefficient will fall with economic growth, or is there scope for encouraging import substitution again through the exchange rate or fiscal system? And furthermore, will measures to increase the tradeables sector reduce economic growth as essential imports are foregone and essential domestic resources exported?

It is the inter-relationship between these various issues that makes debt a complex problem. Generally speaking, however, borrowers with a rising savings ratio, a low and falling incremental capital–output ratio (ICOR), rapid export growth potential relative to import growth, and paying relatively low interest rates should encounter few debt problems. On the other hand borrowers with falling saving ratios, high and rising ICORs, low export growth, little scope for import substitution other than of the type that adversely affects economic growth, and paying relatively high interest rates are likely to find difficulties; difficulties that will be compounded by the fact that debtors will then find it much more difficult to refinance their existing stock of debt.

A further aspect that complicates debt management relates to the time pattern of repayments. A borrower, while fulfilling the basic solvency criterion that the marginal productivity of the resources borrowed exceeds the rate of interest on the loan, may still encounter liquidity problems in particular years because of temporary shortages of foreign exchange. An additional difficulty here, however, is that what starts off as a liquidity problem may end up as a solvency one largely because of its effect on the expectations of lenders, who may become less keen on refinancing debt or may decide to increase the rate of interest charged. Furthermore, debtors may have to repay the debt in specific foreign currencies, yet their foreign exchange earnings may be in different currencies. Variations in exchange rates can therefore sometimes create debt difficulties if the earning power of exports falls when expressed in the particular currency required.

Why Do Debt Problems Arise?

From this discussion it is possible to identify a number of broad reasons why debt problems emerge. First, there may be factors that are exogenous to the debtor, such as falling export demand resulting from a world economic recession, or rising real interest rates, or unfavourable changes in exchange rates between third countries. Second, debt may have been poorly managed with the borrower borrowing too much given the capacity of the economy to repay, failing to choose the most appropriate sources of finance (possibly borrowing over a shorter term and at a higher cost than necessary), and failing to collect adequate information about the debt position. Third, and in addition to poor debt management, the economy itself may have been poorly managed. Failure by governments to undertake measures to increase domestic savings, by, for example, repressing financial markets and preventing domestic real interest rates from rising above very low or even negative levels, or by resisting the opportunity of raising saving compulsorily through the fiscal system, are likely to mean that the savings gap will not be closed. Furthermore, reluctance to reduce exchange rates that are greatly overvalued or to encourage export promotion in other ways will mean that the foreign exchange gap will not be closed.

However, other factors may also be at work in causing debt problems since these may be as much to do with creditors over-lending as with debtors over-borrowing. Certainly looking back at the 1970s, it appears now that the banks over-lent. With the benefit of hindsight such over-lending can be explained in a number of ways. With little evidence of country default the banks probably underestimated the risks of lending. Moreover, they tended to lack the information necessary to calculate such risks and may have misinterpreted what evidence they did have. They certainly seem to have miscalculated the impact of world recession and rising interest rates on the position of debtors. Beyond this, a belief that short term lending would enable them to extricate themselves if necessary, a confidence generated by the fact that other banks were also lending, and a belief that banks would not be allowed to go bust by national and international regulatory authorities, all had the effect of reducing their perceived risks.

In practice, of course, any specific country's debt problem will probably have arisen as a result of a combination of these reasons, even though one or other of them may dominate.

Once debt management problems emerge they frequently become increasingly difficult to control. Failure to service existing debt means that new debts are contracted in order to finance old ones, debt accumulates and the chances of being able to service it recede. Lenders, seeing the deteriorating debt position, regard the borrowers as less creditworthy and as a result it becomes yet harder for them to refinance outstanding loans.

However, saving and foreign exchange gaps which led to the acquisition of debt in the first place are *ex ante* phenomena; they can be closed *ex post* by means of countries simply failing to achieve their aspired growth rates. This would seem to suggest that, having once acquired debt, governments can avoid servicing problems provided only that they are prepared to pursue the necessary (deflationary) policies. But will they be willing to do so? The question of the willingness, as opposed to the ability, of debtor countries to meet their debt obligations is still broader than it appears from this. Even where full servicing of debt would imply relatively little in the way of restrictionary domestic policy, there may be pressures on debtor governments not to pay and instead to default on their debt or repudiate it.

The calculus of debt default is, in principle, quite straightforward, and simply involves comparing the probable costs and benefits of such action. Where there appears to be a net benefit from default then a rational debtor should repudiate its debt. In practice, the decision is more complicated. This is more to do with problems associated with calculating the costs of default than the benefits. The latter will rise with the volume of the debt and with the rate of interest, or, more generally, the severity of the terms.

The costs, however, depend crucially on certain behavioural responses which it may be difficult to predict with any degree of precision. How will creditors, for example, respond to default? It is perhaps reasonable to suppose that a defaulting country would lose access to new credit, including trade credit, for some period of time; might induce sanctions from the international community of creditors; and might encourage internal debtors to reconsider whether they should continue to meet outstanding obligations. But how significant would the responses be? If the defaulter were to lose access to international capital markets, for how long would the exclusion last? Given the uncertainty surrounding the costs of default, it may be assumed that a government's propensity to default will depend significantly on its degree of risk aversion. A risk-averse government may feel a moral obligation to meet outstanding commitments and may value an international reputation for honesty; this will also discourage default. Even so it needs to be recognized that anything which is perceived by the debtors as reducing the costs of default relative to the benefits will raise the probability that it will occur.

Just as the distinction between solvency and liquidity problems is sometimes difficult to sustain, so too the distinction between the ability and the willingness to service debt can become clouded, since in many cases the ability to pay exists if sufficient domestic sacrifice is made. In practical terms it seems likely that ability and willingness will be positively related. If, in fact, governments only become unwilling to meet their debt obligations as the size of the required sacrifice becomes unacceptable, then this suggests that policy designed to avoid default should concentrate on keeping the sacrifice of debtors (or the burden of adjustment) below this critical level. If, on the other hand, governments are actively seeking the optimal moment to default from the point of view of maximizing net benefits, then global anti-default policy needs to concentrate on maintaining, and indeed raising, the perceived costs of repudiation.

Debt Capacity

Given the problems associated with over-borrowing the concept of 'debt capacity' is clearly important. Unfortunately, it is a somewhat vague concept since it can be affected by changes in a number of factors such as the terms of trade, exchange rates and inflation. However, assuming that these variables do not change, a borrower's rate of debt accumulation will vary positively with the size of the savings gap and the interest rate on loans, and negatively with the rate of economic growth and thus the productivity of capital. If an initial savings gap is not closed, or indeed if saving exceeds investment by less than is required to make interest payments on existing loans, new borrowing will be needed if the target growth rate is to be achieved. Indebtedness will therefore increase.

If, on the other hand, saving increases so that it exceeds investment by an amount equal to interest payments, then net indebtedness will level off, and if by more, net indebtedness will fall.[2] By trying to calculate the difference between investment and saving in the future, borrowers can get some idea of their future capacity to service debt and thereby avoid the slide into further debt.

However, as noted above, such forecasts need to be complemented by considering what may happen to imports and exports, the terms of trade, interest rates and exchange rates. There is therefore no simple formula that allows debt capacity to be estimated with precision and full confidence. And in any case a borrower's capacity to service its debt is very closely related to the macroeconomic and microeconomic policies that it pursues, since many of the relevant variables can be influenced by governmental policy as well as by structural and behavioural change in the economy.

This analysis suggests that evaluating debt capacity is far from simple; each case needs to be examined on its own merits with many aspects of a country's economic and political structure being taken into account. However while no doubt recognizing this, lenders often find it more convenient to consult a more limited number of indicators of a country's debt position. Most of these indicators are at least loosely based on the analysis of debt capacity outlined above, but, as we shall see, on their own fail to provide a fully rounded picture. What are these indicators and in what ways are they deficient?

Debt Indicators

Outstanding debt
This indicator in fact indicates very little. Not only is there the problem of whether the debt is measured in nominal or real terms, but there is also the point that the measure says nothing about the capacity of economies to repay, and it is really this that creates the problem. Thus one country which has a large amount of outstanding debt may in fact be in a much stronger position than another country which, while having less debt, is less able to repay it. Furthermore, simply looking at the total amount of debt tells us nothing about the structure of the debt. Again a country with a lot of long term, but little short term debt may be in a stronger position than another country which, while possessing less debt overall, has more short term debt. The maturity of the debt as well as the interest charge on it will affect the debt service payments (repayment of principal, or amorti-

zation, and payment of interest) that have to be made, and it is the size of these in relation to the capacity of the economy to make them that is more important than the overall size of the debt.

Debt service ratio
This ratio expresses debt service payments as a proportion of export earnings. While there is always a temptation to select a particular value (say 20 per cent) for the debt service ratio as being some sort of threshold, this is misleading. Again some countries may be able to cope with much higher ratios while others are unable to cope with their debt even when the ratio is well below 20 per cent. The explanation of such differences arises from the fact that the debt service ratio is only a narrow measure of the debt problem. For example, it tells us nothing about the structure of the debt, the ability to service debt in the long run, the composition and commodity and geographical concentration of exports and the potential for export expansion, the instability of export receipts, the scope for import substitution as a way of increasing the net foreign exchange earnings associated with any given level of exports, the scope for balance of payments adjustment, or the level of foreign exchange reserves. On the other hand, the debt service ratio does indicate the degree of rigidity in a country's balance of payments and its vulnerability to problems caused by shortfalls in export receipts. It shows the extent to which there are prior claims on a borrower's foreign exchange earnings. Furthermore it does have the advantage of relating debt to what is probably the principal variable determining whether the debt can be repaid, namely export performance. Even so the debt service ratio may overstate the size of the debt problem and the constraints impinging on debtors, since borrowers may be able to reschedule the amortization of outstanding loans.

The ratio of interest payments to export earnings
Where the repayment of principal can be rolled over it is financing interest payments that creates the immediate problem. While the interest payments to exports ratio may indeed provide a more accurate reflection of the liquidity aspect of the debt problem it needs to be used with care. If, for example, it is possible to refinance interest payments from further borrowing does this mean that there is no debt problem? It would seem that the problem can almost be defined away. The fact is that, as we shall discuss later, further borrowing only defers debt service owed from current income; it does not eliminate servicing difficulties, unless in the intervening period the economy's capacity to repay debt can be increased. The benefit from a postponement depends on how productively the extra time is used.

One central aspect of the debt problem since the mid 1970s has been the use of floating interest rates on loans. The purpose behind these is to protect lenders from the fall in real interest rates that takes place when, with a given nominal interest rate, the rate of inflation accelerates. A difficulty for borrowers is that their foreign exchange earnings may not fully reflect variations in the global rate of inflation. The prices of different commodities move at different speeds and even in different directions. A situation may therefore arise where a borrower, heavily dependent on one export, experiences a fall in the price of this commodity as well as an increase in nominal interest payments on debt. Even where the export price is rising, the rate of increase may well be below the average rate for imports and the country's terms of trade will therefore deteriorate.

Another aspect of floating rates is that since actual interest payments usually include a component reflecting the negative effect of inflation on the real value of the loan, it is amortized at a faster speed in real terms than was agreed when the loan was taken out. This assimilation of some amortization into interest payments can clearly distort the interest payment ratio as a consistent indicator of the size of the debt problem.[3]

Ratio of debt service payments to new disbursements: net transfer
In a sense this ratio is of more interest to the borrower than the lender since it basically says in which direction the resource flow is going. If outgoings on old debt exceed new borrowing there will be negative net transfer, and the pattern of capital flows will at this time be serving to widen the foreign exchange gap and will therefore be constraining economic development unless domestic saving, exports and the productivity of capital can be increased. While this is clearly of concern to borrowers it is also of concern to lenders since, as we have already seen, in the long run it is through economic growth that debts may be repaid. Lenders do not wish to see the countries to which they have lent stagnating. Moreover the existence of negative net transfers increases the probability of default.

Global Aspects of Debt

Up to now we have looked at the debt problem from the perspective of the individual borrower, implying thereby that debt problems are in some way self-contained. This is far from the truth. To illustrate the point consider two possibilities. The first is that when faced with an unmanageable debt problem a major borrower decides to default. Given the structure of bank lending this could easily result in difficulties for those banks whose lending was heavily concentrated in that country. Given that banking systems rely crucially on confidence, a default of this kind would certainly result in a crisis of confidence which would have ramifications for both the countries in which the lenders were located, as well as for other borrowers, since the supply of loans would undoubtedly fall. It is difficult to estimate precisely the effects of such defaults but it is clear that the consequences would be global and not country-specific.

The second possibility is that the borrower pursues a programme of economic policies designed to reduce imports and shift the current account of the balance of payments into surplus. But again the outside world would not be unaffected by such measures. A fall in one country's imports means a fall in other countries' exports. Given a simple income expenditure model this implies a multiplied decline in income in the exporting countries and in turn a fall in imports. This means a further fall in other countries' exports. World trade shrinks, economic growth slows down, unemployment rises. Again the debt problem is shown to be a global phenomenon. Precisely how significant these trading interrelationships are depends on a range of import, export and saving coefficients, and a sophisticated model would be needed to calculate them. However one estimate that has been made suggests that a moderate (say 1 per cent) uniform reduction in the real rate of economic growth of developing countries would lower the rate of economic growth in industrial countries by approaching 1 per cent. The closer are the trading relationships between the countries involved, the more marked the interlinking effect is likely to be. The overall conclusion may be drawn from this that there is a mutuality of interest in avoiding severe debt problems.

THE SIZE OF THE DEBT PROBLEM: SOME FACTS AND FIGURES

The foregoing discussion identifies a number of variables that might help to indicate the size and nature of the debt problem. From our analysis of debt capacity it emerges that the chances of being able to service debt rise with the growth of output and exports. It is to be expected then that in an environment of slow growth and stagnating export performance debt will become more difficult to manage, especially if at the same time, the terms of lending harden with rising interest rates and falling maturities. However it also needs to be stressed that mechanically referring to a series of debt indicators can easily lead to misinterpretation since whether a given debt situation constitutes a problem depends crucially on the economic and political circumstances of individual countries. Debt is but one aspect of the much broader problem of economic management and should not be viewed in isolation.

Examination of data on debt reveals a number of developments since the early 1970s. The most important of these can be listed and discussed quite briefly. First, there has been a big increase in the nominal amount of external debt. From 1972 to 1982, for instance, the volume of outstanding medium term and long term debt held by developing countries increased some fivefold as these countries endeavoured to maintain their rates of economic growth in spite of a deteriorating external environment. However, much of this increase reflected the rapid inflation that occurred during the 1970s. Indeed when measured in real terms or in relation to other economic magnitudes such as exports, the debt situation at the end of the 1970s was not substantially different from that at the beginning of the decade. But in the early 1980s the debt situation deteriorated. Not only did real debt continue to increase, but even where there was a decline in the rate at which indebtedness was growing, this was more than offset by a reduced rate of export growth. As a result both debt/export and debt service ratios increased significantly for most important debtors. Thus the debt/export ratio for the 21 major LDC borrowers rose from less than 125 per cent in 1980 to nearly 180 per cent in 1982.

Second, within this overall picture there was a large shift away from public debt towards private debt. Between 1976 and 1981 for instance, about two thirds of the increase in long term and medium term debt was to private banks, mostly as a result of syndicated lending, and by 1983 more than a quarter of total external debt was short term. With short term debt included the increasing share of the private sector was probably much sharper. Whereas the convention had been to exclude short term debt from the discussion of debt problems, since it was usually assumed to be trade-related and rolled over automatically, this was no longer the case by the beginning of the 1980s. Many borrowers resorted to short term borrowing in order to finance longer term payments deficits, and an implication of this was that the roll-over of such short term credits was no longer automatic. Indeed the need to refinance or reschedule short term debt became a pressing aspect of the entire debt problem. The move towards borrowing from the banks brought with it a hardening of the terms of overall debt, as the average maturity of the debt shortened and interest payments on it increased. These developments in the structure of debt meant that for any given amount of debt there was a more severe debt problem, especially in terms of liquidity. The use of floating interest rates and their volatility also meant that the size of the debt problem could suddenly increase as interest rates increased. Between 1980 and 1982 net interest payments more than doubled. Of course where borrowers also hold substantial overseas deposits there will be a benefit from higher interest rates and the adverse effect on debt will be neutralized.

Third, and largely because banks only lend to countries they deem creditworthy, the shift over to the private sector served to increase the concentration of debt. One's perception of the global debt problem has therefore become increasingly influenced by what happens in a relatively small number of countries. Meanwhile, the debts of developing countries have also been quite heavily concentrated in the hands of relatively few banks and this again has increased the fragility of the entire system of international capital flows.

Fourth, the vicious circle of debt came more into play in the 1980s. Problems of debt management in some countries reduced the confidence of the banks and their willingness to expand lending. At the same time lending from other sources failed to expand to fill the gap that this left. The difficulty of refinancing or rolling over to which this gave rise, itself created further debt problems.

One indicator of the deteriorating debt situation is the number of reschedulings that occur; agreements between debtors and creditors to rearrange and effectively postpone debt repayments, particularly repayments of principal but occasionally payments of interest as well. By the end of 1983, reschedulings had increased dramatically.

Before discussing policy to deal with debt let us briefly examine whether the evidence allows us to say what the main causes of debt problems were in the early 1980s. The data in fact reveal both a shortfall in export receipts as well as a dramatic increase in real interest rates. The combined impact of these two factors was to raise the developing countries' debt service ratio from 18 per cent in 1980 to 25 per cent in 1982. It might appear that a rapidly deteriorating external environment was the principal cause of the debt crisis of the early 1980s.

But are things that simple? The short answer is 'No', for while these external or global factors affected many borrowers, not all of them encountered crises. Thus, while Korea held the third largest amount of debt with the banks, it was able to escape debt rescheduling. Other developing countries with less debt, even in relation to the size of their economies, however, had to seek debt renegotiations. One potential explanation is that global factors may affect different countries in different ways, depending, for example, on the structure of their trade. Another potential answer, and one that seems to have some empirical support, is that some countries were better able to adjust their economies in such a way as to accommodate global changes, without encountering debt crises. If this is true, it means that although external factors were the underlying cause of debt-related problems in the 1980s, the extent to which these problems led to a debt crisis depended on domestic economic management. This conclusion emphasizes two points relevant to the assessment of default risk. The first is the vulnerability of an economy to external factors, such as falling export demand or rising real interest rates. The second is the scope for domestic adjustment in response to a deteriorating global economic environment.

POLICIES FOR DEALING WITH DEBT

Once debt problems have arisen, whether caused by internal or external factors or a combination of the two, the question of how to cope with them has to be answered. Basically there are four broad approaches to dealing with the problem of debt.

The Market Solution

This approach, which appears to have been much favoured in some political circles, particularly before the Mexican debt crisis in 1982, says that market forces should be allowed to operate. If debtors cannot meet their obligations then they should default. The market will penalize both the debtors and creditors. Debtors will find it harder to gain access to loans in the future and creditors will incur losses. The market will thereby police both overborrowing and overlending.

The problem with this approach arises if, for some reason, the market fails. A conventional cause of market failure relates to externalities, and a market solution to the debt probem will indeed involve such externalities. The external costs will fall on the populations of debtor countries as their creditworthiness is adversely affected. For the international banking system, the failure of banks that might result from either formal or informal default could have far-reaching consequences, with, ultimately, the stability of the system itself being threatened, which could have adverse consequences for creditor countries. It was the eventual acceptance of the undesirability of some of these externalities which pushed the world away from fully implementing the market solution to the debt problem.

Economic Adjustment in Debtors

In principle, adjustment may take a number of forms. Where its purpose is to free foreign exchange which may then be used to meet debt obligations, the options are either to expand exports or to contract imports. Although governments may, through appropriate policy, stimulate export growth, the extent to which this will occur will be constrained by the state of the market for developing countries' exports. If the governments of industrial countries are pursuing anti-inflationary policies which restrain the growth of demand in their economies and, at the same time, are pursuing protectionist measures to limit imports and avoid payments deficits, then the environment will not be conducive to export expansion by the debtor nations. In these circumstances, and where debtors are under international pressure to turn their own balance of payments around over a relatively short time span, there is little effective option open to them other than to reduce imports either by deflating domestic demand or by imposing their own controls on imports.

Such an adjustment strategy, however, raises a number of further issues. First, there will again be externalities associated with it. Living standards or, at best, the rate of growth of living standards in the debtor countries will fall, and there may be limits on the domestic acceptability of this. One possible externality is, therefore, social and political unrest within the debtor countries which could result in the undermining of democracy. Second, rapid adjustment is unlikely to induce the structural changes which may be required and it may therefore be anti-developmental. Here, it needs to be recognized that economic growth within the debtors provides the greatest opportunity for them to be able to meet their debt obligations. An inter-temporal inconsistency can easily arise between measures that are pursued in the short run and those that are required in the long run. Creditors may well be anxious to observe that governments are prepared to make domestic sacrifices to service their debts. On the other hand, they will not be pleased to see a scenario for the debtors which involves falling economic growth and declining export prospects due to shortages of required imported goods. Thus, while deflationary adjustment programmes may increase the confidence of creditors in the short run they will probably fail to raise confidence in the long run unless the growth of output and exports picks up. And this may itself be made less likely by a deflationary programme of adjustment.

The third issue associated with deflationary or protectionist adjustment in the debtor countries relates to the causes of the problem. Is it reasonable to expect debtor countries to shoulder the burden of adjustment if it may be demonstrated that policies in industrial countries were largely responsible for causing the debt problem in the first place? Simple macroeconomic theory suggests that the simultaneous rise in world interest rates along with a decline in the demand for developing countries' exports, as was observed in the early 1980s, may be explained by the pursuit of contractionary monetary policy in a number of important industrial economies at that time. If this explanation of events is accepted, not only would emphasis on adjustment within the debtors represent an inequitable distribution of the adjustment burden, but it would also be inefficient in the sense that it would fail to make full use of the world's productive potential.

Adjustment in Other Countries

For reasons implied by the above discussion, this appears to be an attractive alternative strategy for alleviating the debt problem. A policy of expansion across the industrial countries could, for example, reduce world interest rates and enhance the export prospects of debtor countries. But even here, things are not as straightforward as they might initially seem. First, a question hangs over the appropriate form of expansion: to what extent should it rely on fiscal or monetary policy? Clearly too much emphasis on expansionary fiscal policy could lead to rising interest rates, and this would not be to the advantage of the debtors. Second, if the expansion were to be unco-ordinated, the benefits to different debtors would depend on their individual patterns of trade. Moreover, in as much as unco-ordinated expansion results in exchange rate instability, this could be to the disadvantage of developing and indebted nations. Third, there remains the fundamental problem of how to put pressure on industrial countries to expand their economies, particularly in a co-ordinated fashion. While the international economic system affords some opportunity to exert pressure on deficit countries to adjust – although even here not all deficit countries are uniformly treated – it has yet to come up with a satisfactory mechanism by which surplus countries can be encouraged to expand their economies.

Rescheduling

The main idea with rescheduling is to allow debtor countries more time to service and repay their debt by spreading out their existing obligations. With a relatively high discount rate in debtor countries, rescheduling serves to reduce the present value of a given stock of debt obligations. However, the principal appeal of rescheduling exists if the debt problem is of the liquidity type. In this case time is the problem, and it is time that rescheduling provides. Where the problems are more fundamental and are more of an insolvency nature, the benefit from rescheduling depends crucially on how the time provided is used. Where rescheduling enables appropriate structural adjustment to be carried through, it can clearly make an important contribution towards solving an insolvency problem. Much rests on the superiority of gradualism and structural adjustment programmes over 'shock' short-run adjustment programmes. Indeed, if it can be argued that a short, sharp shock is what is needed, then it follows that rescheduling, which enables such policies to be avoided, is undesirable.

From this menu of choice, options one and three have been largely, though not totally, rejected. Banks have suffered some losses as a result of their lending to developing countries and have not been completely insulated from the market; moreover, in 1984, economic expansion in the USA enabled some Latin American debtors to increase their export earnings – although US policy also had the effect of keeping interest rates high. But, in the main, the debt problem has been handled by a combination, and usually a formal combination of adjustment in the debtor countries and rescheduling. The adjustment has normally been conducted under the auspices of the International Monetary Fund, but with the World Bank taking on an increasingly significant role in policy conditionality. Although elements relating to the supply side have crept into some Fund-supported programmes, the conventional emphasis on demand restraint and devaluation of the exchange rate has been maintained. After an initial period of strictness, rescheduling terms were gradually liberalized across a number of areas.

Whether one assesses the approach that has *de facto* been adopted as a success or as a failure depends very much on the particular perspective adopted. Certainly, mass default and the collapse of the international banking system has been avoided. Indeed, it could be argued that the banks have had to undertake relatively little adjustment and have made relatively few sacrifices. From this perspective the approach has worked. However, from the perspective of the debtor countries, where it might be supposed greater attention will be focused on domestic living standards rather than the stability of the international banking system, things appear somewhat different. In any event, the question arises as to whether techniques that have been used in the past will prove adequate in the future. It is to a consideration of the future that we now turn.

Recent Trends and Prospects

The data in Table 17.1 provide some indication of recent trends in the size of the developing country debt crisis and the related performance of highly indebted countries. Lines 1 and 2 take two common debt indicators discussed earlier. Each of these shows the quite dramatic increase in the size of the debt problem in 1982. But they also suggest that by 1988 the problem had yet to be overcome, with the debt ratio standing at almost 300 per cent and the debt service ratio at 40 per cent. An indication of a deteriorating debt situation has been the move from positive to negative

Table 17.1 Debt and performance indicators of highly indebted developing countries (US $ billions or percentages)

	1970–79	1979–81	1982	1983	1984	1985	1986	1987	1988
Debt ratio	160.0	185.0	268.3	291.9	271.3	288.3	348.7	338.7	299.8
Debt service ratio	27.3	35.7	51.9	41.8	41.7	40.7	45.3	35.5	39.6
Net transfer	5.9	13.2	9.3	−21.2	−38.0	−37.3	−17.3	−23.3	−27.8
Real per capita income growth	4.0	1.3	−4.5	−6.5	0.1	1.0	0.6	0.1	–
Investment ratio	23.9	24.4	21.6	17.1	16.0	16.8	17.2	17.4	17.0
Export volume growth	2.1	4.6	−5.0	5.6	8.7	2.3	−2.5	5.6	10.8
Import volume growth	8.8	6.4	−16.3	−21.3	−2.2	1.2	−0.9	0.5	7.7

Source: World Bank and IMF

net transfers. For the period since 1983, debtor countries have been paying back more in the form of servicing old loans than they have been receiving in the form of new ones. Although in one sense anyone taking on debt must anticipate a future negative net transfer, in the case of the indebted developing countries the turn-around has been achieved at the cost of domestic investment and imports which hold the key to economic growth. It is growth that has tended to be sacrificed in favour of net repayments. Yet it is only through growth that repayments can be sustained in the long run. Moreover, negative net transfers increase the incentive for debtors to default, since the financial gains from such action rise relative to the losses.

Pressures for default also result from the stagnating living standards revealed in line 4. Indeed it is this line which most aptly shows the sacrifices that the debtor countries have made in order to release foreign exchange to meet their debt obligations. Although there has been some growth in export volume over the period covered by the Table this has been substantially neutralized by deteriorating terms of trade, with the result that countries have been forced to cut back on imports even though these are frequently vital inputs into exports.

In short, Table 17.1 provides little suggestion that the policies pursued during the 1980s did much to cure the debt crisis. Indeed much of the data suggest that the situation was worse at the end of the 1980s than it was in 1982 when the debt crisis first became a subject of popular concern. So what will happen in the future? The possibility that the crisis will be cured by economic growth amongst industrialized countries, rising commodity demand and prices, and falling interest rates seems slim. Indeed the current outlook is one of slow growth, high interest rates and rising protectionism – not a set of circumstances designed to relieve the crisis. With falling living standards, negative net transfers, and low rates of investment and imports threatening sustained economic development in the indebted nations, the prospects may point more towards debtor default. But given this scenario what alternative policies might be put in place?

CONCLUDING REMARKS: QUESTIONS FOR THE FUTURE

In trying to find a cure for the problem of developing country debt numerous proposals have been put forward. However, instead of examining these it may be more useful to try and identify the broader questions with which reform will have to deal.

First, any strategy for dealing with debt will have to involve a combination of adjustment and financing. But what is the appropriate *blend*? In part, the answer to this question will depend on the *type* of adjustment. To what extent can adjustment be achieved within a framework of sustained economic growth? It is likely that adjustment related to the supply side of the economy will be preferable on these grounds, but structural adjustment takes more time to implement and this increases the need for international financing. From where will the necessary finance come? Not only may finance be necessary to support debtors' attempts to raise their long term servicing capacity, but it may also be required to help handle liquidity crises; so through what mechanisms should such short term assistance be provided?

Second, on the creditors' side, both the private commercial sector and the international financial institutions have historically been involved with the debt crisis. In seeking to provide a cure what should be their respective roles? Should the emphasis be placed on market-related reforms such as debt sales in the secondary market and debt-equity swaps, or should it instead be placed on the official sector with, for example, an international agency taking over loans from the banks. Is there more reason to worry about 'market failure' or 'government failure' in this context? Within the official sector what should be the division of labour between the International Monetary Fund and the World Bank?

Third, to the extent that additional financial support for debtors is deemed necessary, is this best provided by means of new money or debt relief? In either event, from where is the financial support to come? While relief should help reduce the debt overhang, what can be done to help close the future financing gap that developing countries are likely to encounter, assuming that they aim to achieve even modest increases in living standards? What new financial instruments and financing mechanisms will secure the flow of longer term developmental assistance?

Fourth, in considering the pattern of developmental assistance sight should not be lost of international equity. Total preoccupation with alleviating the problems of the highly indebted developing countries of Latin America could crowd out financial flows to less well-off countries in Africa and Asia.

Fifth, even the most ambitious schemes will not help to cure the crisis if they remain unadopted. Attention therefore needs to be paid to making any scheme attractive to those whose approval is required. The political economy of Third World debt needs to be addressed.

Finally, can the richer countries of the world contribute more to solving the Third World debt crisis by means of supporting and financing schemes for relief, or by pursuing policies within their own economies to create a global economic environment that facilitates a cure? It may be noted here that debt problems are not the exclusive preserve of the Third World. Most notoriously, by financing its fiscal deficit through borrowing, the United States has become a major international debtor. Debt acquisition by the US not only tends to crowd out other borrowers from international capital markets but also tends to keep world interest rates at a high level.

NOTES

1. Given that a proportion of future domestic saving goes on paying the interest on external borrowing, the rate of economic growth at this stage will clearly tend to be lower than it would have been without such payments. Yet by enabling countries to overcome financial constraints on growth and allowing their economies to 'take-off', they may still enjoy a higher standard of living even when they are repaying loans than if they had not borrowed in the first place. It all depends on how productively the borrowed resources are used. If borrowing leads to an increase in income and this in turn leads to an increase in savings, after allowing for the saving that goes as interest payments, growth will clearly rise as a result of borrowing.
2. What happens to debt as a proportion of national income depends basically on the relative sizes of the rate of interest and rate of growth of income. Given conditions where both indebtedness and income are increasing, this debt ratio will tend to rise if the rate of interest exceeds the rate of income growth.
3. Although we have discussed the debt ratios using exports as the denominator, the size of debt service payments or interest payments can also be judged against the size of GDP. While this measure can provide additional insights it does suffer from the fact that, in the short run at least, not all sources of national income can be used to service debt. Furthermore there is the question of what exchange rate to use in order to convert domestic currency GDP into GDP expressed in the currency in which debt is measured. Changing the exchange rate can change the apparent size of the debt problem.

FURTHER READING

There are many books and articles available which explore much more fully the issues raised in this chapter. A useful review of many of them may be found in Graham Bird, (ed) (1989), *Third World Debt: The Search for a Solution*, Aldershot: Edward Elgar. Another useful review is Stephany Griffith-Jones, (1985), 'Ways Forward from the Debt Crisis', *Oxford Review of Economic Policy*, Winter. The causes of debt servicing problems are investigated in Donal Donovan, (1984), 'Nature and Origins of Debt Servicing Difficulties', *Finance and Development*, December, and, in greater depth, by Peter Nunnenkamp, (1986), *The International Debt Crisis of the Third World*, Brighton: Wheatsheaf Books. The political economy of debt provides the focus of Benjamin J. Cohen's (1989), 'Developing Country Debt: A Middle way', *Essays in International Finance*, No. 173, Princeton University, May. Meanwhile a full and detailed analysis of debt relief is given by John Williamson (1988), in his 'Voluntary Approaches to Debt Relief', *Policy Analyses in International Economics*, No. 25, Institute for International Economics, Washington DC, September.

SOME QUESTIONS FOR DISCUSSION

1. What factors determine whether the acquisition of debt by a country results in a debt problem?
2. What difficulties are associated with the use of conventional 'debt indicators' to measure the size of debt problems?
3. What is the calculus of debt repudiation?
4. To what extent does the Third World debt problem depend on the economic policies pursued in the major industrial countries?
5. What are the merits and demerits of refinancing and rescheduling as compared with debt relief?
6. In the light of recent trends what policies would you advocate in seeking to resolve the problem of Third World debt?

18. The European Community: Trade, Factor Mobility and Exchange Rates

Christopher Flockton

Economic integration, or the combining of separate national economies into larger economic regions, is far from being solely a European phenomenon: rather, we find integration arrangements across the globe, in much of Latin America, Africa and among the Eastern bloc countries, where the process followed principles of socialist integration. In East and West perhaps the main driving force behind integration movements is political cohesion, but there are clear and strong economic motives for abolishing national frontiers within a grouping. If barriers to trade in goods and services and likewise to the mobility of labour, capital and entrepreneurship are abolished, then competitive forces will promote enhanced resource allocation with a consequent rise in welfare. In the case of the European Community, which has achieved the most advanced stage of integration among such groupings, many of these barriers have been removed: where they still exist, such as in the case of non-tariff barriers or restrictions to factor mobility, the Single Market programme, or '1992', addresses their removal. This process of market integration sets in train a dynamic of integration which extends into the macroeconomic policy field, raising the question of economic and monetary union (EMU). We propose in this chapter to study the trade and factor mobility aspects of a common market and to look at exchange rate arrangements (the European Monetary System), which are sometimes argued to be an essential accompaniment of market integration.

Although moves are again under way in the form of the Delors Report (1989), to push the European Community much closer towards economic and monetary union, much still remains to be done to complete the customs union and common market. At this initial stage, some definitions are in order. One may compare a free trade area with a customs union and then proceed to explain a common market as a more advanced form of the latter. In a free trade area, member states engage in free trade (in specified products) among themselves, with no tariff barriers, quota restrictions or competition-distorting subsidies to pose an obstacle. Member states are free, however, to follow an independent commercial policy *vis-à-vis* third countries, and so trade policy with the rest of the world will vary from one member state to another. Here lies the crucial distinction with a customs union, for in the latter, not only does the free trade regime hold within the union, but participating countries adopt a common tariff and trading regime with third countries. Hence there is a single 'tariff wall' of the same height around the customs union, and trade policy with non-members is centrally-negotiated. In practice also, a customs union may embrace all sectors of the economy. While, logically, a customs union should also include the free (unhindered) supply of services, in practice barriers to this can be associated with factor immobility, and so services trade is linked partly to the establishment of a common market. A common market extends beyond a customs union to embrace factor mobility – of labour, capital and entrepreneurship. The unhindered mobility of these resources to flow where factor returns are greatest would clearly promote allocative efficiency and growth. The promotion of services trade is an allied question, since the freedom to establish a business, to have professional qualifications recognized or to offer financial services requiring capital movements, all pertain to factor market integration. As a final point, it can readily be seen that once member states' economies are completely open to each other in this way, and capital can move freely, then the degree of interdependence calls for close macroeconomic policy harmonization, and perhaps for the institution of a single currency to benefit to the fullest from the single market.

Before we turn to the theoretical underpinnings of these forms of integration, let us briefly survey the attainments among the twelve members of the EC. The Treaty of Rome, which was signed by the original six members in 1957, provided for a customs union and common market, together with the introduction of common policies in some sectors, chiefly agriculture, but also in transport and vocational training. (Energy was covered by the 1951 Treaty of Paris and the 1957 Euratom Treaty.) The fact that integration was to be promoted by competitive trade interpenetration is apparent from Article 3 of the Treaty. This specified not only the minimum requirements for establishing a common market, namely, elimination of internal trade barriers, erection of a common external tariff (CET) and abolition of obstacles to factor movement, but it forbade distortions of competition which would impede the process of market integration. Responsibility for a common commercial policy and for preferential trade agreements with colonies and ex-colonies was to be in the hands of the Council of Ministers and the Brussels Commission. The fact that more than just a common market was envisaged is evident not only from the provisions concerning common sectoral policies, but also from the clauses concerning the establishment of funds for the improvement of the standard of living of workers, and for the development of less developed regions. The provisions concerning the harmonization of national macroeconomic policies were, however, circumscribed: co-ordination was required to facilitate the open trading regime within the common market.

The customs union was completed eighteen months ahead of schedule in 1968, and concurrently with the abolition of trade barriers within the Six, a common external tariff was imposed in stages, representing the unweighted average of the six countries' external protection. It was subsequently cut by three GATT tariff rounds. With the first enlargement in 1973, when the UK was admitted, a five-year transition period was allowed: Greece had a similar period upon joining in 1981 and Spain and Portugal have a seven year transition from 1986. The degree of reorientation of member states' trading links can be seen from the fact that intra-Community exports as a proportion of total exports of the Six have reached well over 50 per cent, after initial levels of about 30 per cent. The UK has also shown a rapid geographical reorientation of its trade structure such that this (though not in volume or in surpluses!) is comparable now to that of Germany. In other areas, the results are mixed. For good or ill, only the common agricultural policy has developed as a true common sectoral policy. And, although the first attempts at an ambitious economic and monetary union (EMU) were begun in 1969, the only lasting outcome to date has been the EMS, which is a much more modest adjustable peg exchange rate system.

THE THEORY OF CUSTOMS UNIONS

What is the theoretical basis for establishing a customs union? For reasons that will become apparent, this offers only a second-best option compared with universal free trade, but it can nevertheless afford net welfare gains to the union as a whole. The advantages are clearly those of trade liberalization, namely, that if trade protection within the grouping is eliminated, each country would specialize in the production of those goods in which it had a comparative advantage, covering its needs for other goods through trade. In the grouping as a whole, greater welfare would result. However, we have left out of account the fact that the union maintains protection against third country imports by means of a CET. To the extent that more efficient and lower cost external suppliers are excluded, the resource allo-

Figure 18.1   Welfare costs of a tariff

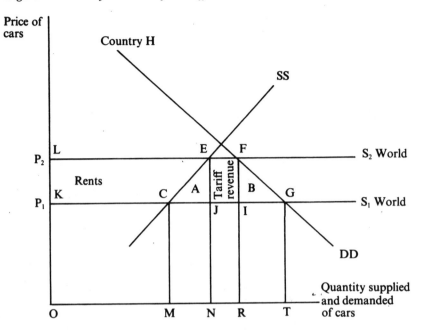

cation gains, and gains to the consumer are reduced. It is because of the external protection that we consider customs unions to be a second best option in comparison with free trade.

To understand the theoretical argument we commence with a discussion of the welfare effects of a tariff reduction. In Figure 18.1, we show the domestic supply and demand curves for cars in the home country H. A specific import duty raises the world price from P_1 to P_2, at which the rest of the world supplies H. We assume a perfectly elastic world supply (in other words, the importation of the good by country H has no terms of trade effects). In these circumstances, at intersection F, OR is the equilibrium quantity of cars at P_2. Imports amount to NR, and ON is supplied by domestic producers. We note first that the tariff affords a rent to domestic producers of KLEC in the form of an excess of revenue over production cost. The tariff revenue accruing to government is JEFI. The benefits which accrue as a result of tariff abolition are as follows. At the new price level P_1, intersection G now gives an equilibrium quantity T, with (increased) imports now totalling MT. Home production is cut back to OM. If we divide up area KLFG into four sections, two represent transfers and two give positive welfare gains as a result of the eradication of the 'deadweight' burdens of the tariff. The rents are eliminated and

Figure 18.2   Trade creation and trade diversion

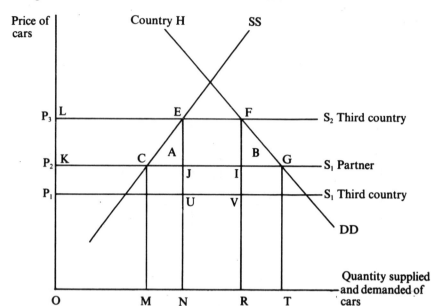

represent a transfer from home producers to consumers, while the tariff revenue is lost to government, but this is to the benefit of consumers in the form of lower prices. Triangle A is a production gain arising from the elimination of less efficient home production: it is assumed that MCEN resources are transferred costlessly to alternative home production. Triangle B represents a consumption gain. Consumer surplus is represented by the area under the demand curve in excess of the consumer expenditure. Comparing the two intersections F and G, reveals a net consumer gain equivalent to triangle B. The total welfare gain is therefore shown by our production and consumption gains, the Marshallian triangles A and B.

This argument for tariff abolition is of course an argument for free trade rather than just for a customs union. If we assume that, after formation of the union, a partner country can supply at P_1, that is, at the world price, then the customs union produces pure 'trade creation' in the case of cars. Imports from the partner displace less efficient home production. However, the existence of a common external tariff implies that the world trade price for the good in question is lower than the community price and that cheaper imports from the rest of the world may be displaced by dearer union sources of supply upon creation of the union. In Figure 18.2, we see the effects of both trade creation and trade diversion: in this latter case, cheaper imports from the rest of the world are displaced by imports from a partner country made possible by the existence of the tariff. The fact that the third country is the more efficient producer is shown by its supply price P_1, which is raised by a tariff to P_3. Before creation of the customs union, the home country imports from the third country. At intersection F, domestic production is ON and imports, NR. The creation of a customs union favours the partner country as supplier, even though it is a less efficient producer than the third country. If the CET ensures a world supply price level of P_3, then the partner country in the union will now supply a part of home demand at P_2. At intersection G, home production is OM, and imports from the partner, MT. Trade creation brings the production and consumption gains denoted by the triangles A and B, but there is also a welfare loss denoted by rectangle JIVU. Previously, tariff revenues of EFVU were raised on imports from the world, but the loss of this source of supply, and the absence of such revenues on intra-union trade involves a net loss of JIVU, which has arisen through trade diversion.

The previous argumentation implies that customs unions are not unambiguously beneficial, though net trade creation (the surplus of trade creation over trade diversion, that is, $A + B - (JIVU)$) denotes the welfare gain arising. There are obviously other benefits which argue in favour of a second-best strategy. These generally are political in nature, though some further economic arguments can be adduced. Firstly, the structure of the common external tariff may reflect a coalition of interests between member countries which are trading off relative degrees of protection for specific branches. Each state may achieve a 'public goods' benefit by ensuring protection of a favoured branch. There is also a terms of trade argument. So far we have assumed that world supply is perfectly price elastic. However, if the world supply curve is upward sloping, then the imposition of a tariff will ensure that the reduced quantity imported is acquired at a lower import price. Certainly, in the case of a large trading bloc such as the EC, the assumption of perfect elasticity is unreasonable.

So far, the analysis has been static, as the welfare gains are once for all gains. So-called 'dynamic gains', associated with the creation of a large market, are not considered by orthodox trade theory. There are three types of such gain – economies of scale, greater competition and increased investment. As we shall see, our previous concepts of 'trade creation' and 'trade diversion' remain valid in the presence of significant economies of scale, but they require supplementation. Let us assume that the rest of the world producers produce at constant costs, but that within the union, production at decreasing unit costs is available to firms:

1. Trade creation will occur if a producer in a partner country expands

output and undercuts the producer supply price in the home country. Gains through trade creation will occur in the home country, and there will be benefits arising in the partner country. These are benefits from cost reduction, a consumption gain, and the partner benefits from selling at a higher level than the world price into the home market.

2. Trade diversion will occur in the home country if, as a result of customs union formation, a partner country producer expands output and drives a cheaper rest of world supplier out of the home country market. The benefits to the partner are as in 1 above.

3. Trade suppression may occur if a new producer (efficient in union terms only) establishes in the partner country once cheaper rest of world suppliers are displaced by customs union formation. (Robson 1987).

It should also be borne in mind that there may be some likelihood of monopolistic behaviour in the presence of scale economies.

The remaining two dynamic factors concern enhanced competition and a rise in the investment rate. Under the first, the so-called 'cold shower' effect of competition among previously more protected producers should raise technical efficiency by better factor utilization in the firm. This concerns in effect the eradication of so-called 'X-inefficiency'. Finally, market enlargement may induce greater investment in capacity widening and in a greater R&D effort, which may justify itself over longer production runs.

EMPIRICAL STUDIES

Empirical findings on the static and dynamic effects of customs union formation must be treated with some caution, particularly as such effects are not well captured by statistical analysis. Studies of the static effects look at trade flows, rather than at the production and consumption gains, and the dynamic effects are far from easy to specify and test. Concerning trade creation and trade diversion, Davenport (1982) points to an extensive literature covering the experience in the 1960s of the original Six. In spite of divergences between these studies in terms of their methodology and timescale, Davenport sees a clustering in the results: he concludes that we might take trade creation at $10 billion for 1970 and trade diversion at $1 billion. The net gain represents 10 per cent of combined Community goods imports at that time or 2 per cent of Community GDP. Of course, this represents trade flows, not the Marshallian welfare gains. Net welfare gains may, in Davenport's view, amount to less than 1 per cent of Community GNP, such that the static gains from trade in a customs union may not be great. The reasons are not hard to find: only tradeables are concerned here, and the relatively small beneficial impact merely illustrates that the most costly trade barriers have already been eliminated so as to enjoy the benefits to trade.

The dynamic gains are doubtless far greater, but are difficult to analyse quantitatively. To recap, these involve returns to scale in a larger market, the gains from enhanced competition and the spur to investment. Davenport (1982) surveys the difficulties involved in any assessment. The impact of tariff abolition on scale economies requires a modelling of the counter-factual situation where tariffs are retained: it also requires industry-by-industry surveys which seek to separate scale economies from other dynamic factors, in a context of open trade. The competitive gains concern the eradication of so-called 'X-inefficiency', which is difficult to capture statistically. Finally, the increment to growth which arises from increased investment relates to the two preceding dynamic factors. Of course, there will also be a reduction in investment in branches in certain countries which suffer increased import competition. Estimates of the consequential net increase in growth are fraught with difficulties.

It is clear, however, that while the customs union in aggregate should reap the gains from trade, there is no reason to believe that these will be equally distributed among member states, with the industrially more competitive partners tending to benefit at the expense of the weaker. This brings us to studies of the impact of Community membership on the UK, which of course has seen a rising industrial goods trade deficit with the EC especially since 1979. On the face of things, the poorly competitive British manufacturers would appear to have capitulated in the face of strong import competition from the rest of the EC. Of course, two key questions which dominated successive UK negotiations for entry concerned Britain's net budget contribution and its adoption of the high price, protectionist Common Agricultural Policy (CAP). This latter would replace the low food price system in Britain under which foodstuffs entered the country at the world price. The adoption of the CAP naturally formed a classic example of trade diversion, with an important balance of payments cost for Britain. However, much attention has been devoted to industrial goods trade, in relation to which the UK lost Commonwealth Preference for its exports, lost its own tariff protection against continental producers, and had to adopt a CET which generally afforded the UK lower protection against non-preferential third countries.

A highly influential study by Featherston, Moore and Rhodes (FMR) (1979) gave a very wide range of estimates of the effects on British manufactures trade in the period 1973–77, but their preferred estimate was of a net import effect of £1.1 billion arising from EC membership. This huge loss of domestic market share by UK manufacturers created in the view of the authors an overwhelming balance of payments constraint on macroeconomic policy. They see it as the cause of the deflationary strategies adopted almost continuously in the mid and late 1970s. Including the direct budgetary contribution to Brussels, they estimate the associated loss of potential output by 1977/8 at 15 per cent of real GNP. Winters (1987), in a survey of this and other work points to methodological shortcomings and offers an alternative assessment. We may note his comments that the FMR study attributes all the deflation of the period to this balance of payments constraint, when rampant domestic inflation or structural weaknesses in British manufacturing must have had a strong influence on policy. It is also the case that consumption gains are intimately associated with a corresponding production loss by the previous supplier. To put this trade problem into some perspective, the UK's manufacturing trade deteriorated in like manner with the rest of the OECD, and a large share of the UK goods trade deficit with the EC is made up of car imports by multinational companies, sensitive to exchange rate changes and productivity differentials.

WELFARE GAINS FROM FACTOR MOBILITY

In moving from the framework of a customs union to that of a common market, we relax the central assumption in static trade theory of factor immobility. A common market requires the integration of factor markets: not simply through the abolition of obstacles to free movement, but in practice through a certain harmonization of regulations governing the markets for capital, labour and enterprise. In a common market, we may for example expect underemployed Portuguese workers to migrate to the Federal Republic and for German capital and enterprise to be attracted to Portuguese locations. If there exist differences between member states in the marginal social productivity of each factor, then disparities will subsist in wage and profit rates, which, in the competitive model equal these productivities. The migration of less well-rewarded or unemployed factors will lead to an equalization of the marginal social productivities and this will be accompanied by a narrowing of the differences in factor earnings between member states. Hence we might expect, in a neo-classical world, a reduction of regional income disparities within a common market.

If we turn first to the capital market, then the freeing of capital movements by the abolition of capital controls, as provided in the Rome

Treaty, will lead to capital flows to the higher-yielding country (that is, with the higher marginal productivity of capital). These flows will cease once this marginal productivity is equalized union-wide. (We omit the 'polarization' case, where, in the presence of externalities and technological change, growth regions continue to grow at the expense of declining regions). We may conclude that such capital flows benefit both donor and recipient countries. Both enjoy a net increase in national income, the first in the form of a 'rentier' income, the second through an expansion of output. Robson (1987) extends the discussion considerably to include the operation of foreign (that is non-union) capital and multinational companies, which leads to a much more nuanced result.

Swann (1988) details the achievements of the Community in terms of capital market liberalization. Article 67 and subsequent articles govern the abolition of restrictions on capital movements. These cover payments in foreign currency for current transactions (imports), forbidding discrimination by nationality in rules governing credit and capital markets, and capital movements. It is in the latter that most difficulties have arisen, since a number of governments (notably France and Italy) have had recourse to exchange control on a permanent or semi-permanent basis. This has served to support their currencies and enabled them to pursue a more independent monetary policy. In brief, the Commission issued directives in 1960 and 1962 which set out categories of capital movement subject to different degrees of required liberalization. In particular, financial and commercial credits, opening of deposit accounts, non-listed securities transactions, were either not subject to liberalization or only to conditional liberalization. In the mid 1980s, further capital liberalization measures were agreed, and indeed complete liberalization will be essential for the free supply of financial services under the 1992 programme. France abandoned its remaining exchange controls in January 1990, and Italy must conform by 1 July 1990, the commencement of Phase 1 of the Delors plan.

The second area of factor mobility concerns the free movement of labour. Discrimination against a national from another Community state is forbidden with regard to employment, remuneration and other conditions of work. Hence Community nationals have equal rights in applying for vacancies, and have equal treatment in their country of residence as regards social security, taxation, trade union rights and workers' housing. Since July 1968, Community nationals have required only a residence permit, not a work permit, to work anywhere in the EC, and their accumulated social security rights are transferable.

Lastly, in the case of the right of establishment and the freedom to supply services, these are secured in principle by Articles 52–66 of the

Rome Treaty, and confirmed by two decisions of the European Court of Justice. Giving practical effect to them is however much more complicated. In the matter of the right to practice by professionals such as doctors and lawyers, the recognition of training standards is a wearisome process. Much more has been achieved in the case of the right of establishment of firms, in spite of the two decade delay in agreement over the European Company Statute. In the services sector, a foreign subsidiary offering insurance for example, must meet the legal requirements of the host country, which may be quite at variance with those of the home country. Finally, the thorniest question concerns the export of services from one member state to another. The conflicting state regulations governing sectors such as insurance, banking, telecommunications, transport, have effectively ruled out much inter-state supply of services, thereby granting considerable protection to the home industry. The eradication of these non-tariff barriers is of course a major feature of the Single Market programme.

THE EUROPEAN MONETARY SYSTEM (EMS)

Economic and monetary union was first announced as an objective for the Community in 1969 and the Werner Report of 1970 set out how such a union might be approached in stages. If economic union implies close economic policy co-ordination, in addition to a single unified market, then monetary union involves the immutable fixing of exchange rates and freeing of capital movements, so as to benefit to the full from this market integration. Under such a regime, a very high degree of monetary policy co-ordination would be imposed, including convergence on a union-level inflation rate. It is clear that the costs are those associated with the loss of the exchange rate as a policy instrument, together with the inability to pursue an independent monetary policy course. The benefits would have to be substantial in compensation. Greater exchange rate stability (especially in the real exchange rate) is said to promote trade and investment, and a regime of fixed exchange rates leads to greater price stability, in part through the greater financial stability it imposes. Savings involve economies in the use of international reserves, and in the abolition of currency hedging costs.

Little came of the ambitious Werner Report plans for an EMU by 1980. The ill-starred 'snake in the tunnel' which represented Phase 1 of the plan, became transformed into a Deutschmark-dominated bloc, as weaker currencies left the exchange rate mechanism in the post-oil shock years. In 1978, Chancellor Schmidt and President Giscard d'Estaing conceived of the EMS to remedy failings in international monetary arrangements. Their version was motivated by practical concerns – currency instability harmed the CAP, floating exchange rates magnified inflation differentials and seemed to harm trade, the Deutschmark appreciated inexorably against a collapsing dollar. New monetary arrangements in the form of an EMS seemed to promise a zone of monetary stability in Europe, and a rekindling of trade and investment there. In themselves, the EMS plans were more modest than the earlier EMU conception.

The strategy for the system involved a two-stage implementation: as a first stage, the three elements of the system as we now know it – the European Currency Unit (ECU), the Exchange Rate Mechanism (ERM) and the European Monetary Cooperation Fund (EMCF) currency intervention arrangements – would be instituted. The second or 'institutional' phase envisaged the creation of a European Monetary Fund which would take over permanently the reserves of participating countries, acting like a central bank. In addition, the ECU would be fully utilized as a reserve asset and as a means of settlement. This latter, institutional phase was ambitious and too supranational for acceptance during the post second oil shock years, and so we have been left with the three main EMS elements. In brief, these are as follows:

1. The ECU is a composite currency comprising the participating states' currencies, with a specified weighting for each. The weighting of a currency depends on the respective member state's share of collective GNP, on its share of collective exports and on its size. The Ecu has a central role in the system as *numeraire* for the ERM, as a denominator for currency intervention operations, and as a means of settlement between central banks and a reserve asset. It is created by the deposit of gold and foreign currency reserves at the EMCF.

2. The ERM is the parity grid, and it is in this that the UK has until October 1990 refused to participate. Each participating currency has a central rate expressed in Ecus, and cross rates, namely the parities between individual currencies, are derived from these Ecu rates. Around the cross rate is a permissible margin of fluctuation of ±2.25 per cent, with a wider band of ±6 per cent for Italy and Spain. If a currency hits the ceiling or floor of its band, intervention is obligatory on all participating central banks. If the French franc were weak against the Deutschmark (DM), the Bank of France would borrow DM from the Bundesbank for intervention to support the franc, and could repay in Ecu. A final characteristic is the 'divergence indicator' which operates as a warning bell when a currency has moved 75 per cent of the width of the band away from the central rate with the Ecu.

There is a presumption that the respective government and central bank will then take countervailing action in support of their currency. Of course this applies also in the case of a strengthening currency, and so it is said that the divergence indicator imposes symmetry, namely, obligations in respect of strong and weak currencies alike. As a final point, currency realignments are permitted, but are agreed multilaterally by all participating states.

3. The EMCF manages the intervention mechanisms of the system and issues drawing rights in Ecu against the deposits of gold and currency reserves. Credits of short- and medium-term duration for currency intervention purposes are available to member states, subject to corresponding policy commitments.

How has the EMS worked in practice? In the period 1979–86, there were no fewer than 11 realignments in the parity grid, but eight of these took place in the years to 1983, when economic performance and policy in member states diverged markedly in the wake of the second oil shock. In this earlier period therefore, membership of this fixed but adjustable exchange rate system imposed no lasting financial discipline on members. In practice, the succession of realignments helped to restore the purchasing power parity of the currencies of relatively high inflation countries. It is in the more recent period that the EMS can be said to have achieved some of its objectives.

The 1983–89 period has been one of relative exchange rate stability in the ERM. Volatility of nominal exchange rates has been notably reduced. Of more importance for trade and growth, however, is the movement of real exchange rates. Misalignments, whereby nominal exchange rates move in the opposite direction from that required by purchasing power parity, so marking a loss of competitiveness, have not been substantial or long-lasting. But some rise in the real exchange rate has been accepted by higher-inflation countries for its counter-inflation effect.

Some evidence of the influence of the ERM in imposing financial discipline can be detected in inflation rates, and in convergence of other aspects of economic performance. In terms of inflation, the ERM average for 1986 was 2.5 per cent, with a small dispersion around this figure. Whether of course it was ERM membership that exerted greatest influence here, or the impact of recession and falling dollar oil prices, is open to debate. In terms of growth rates, there is evidence of convergence on the low German figure for this period, which hints at the disinflationary strategies pursued. Of course, convergence of growth rates in itself may not be desirable, but a wide spread of rates would probably make a fixed currency system unsustainable.

One reason why there seems to have been a convergence towards both German inflation and growth rates concerns the asymmetry of the system in practice. The system has operated as a DM-dominated bloc because the Bundesbank has refused to conduct intervention buying of weaker currencies on any scale. In other words, it has avoided the issuing of Deutschmarks and the attendant rise in the DM money supply, associated with such operations. While maintaining a tighter monetary stance itself, it has obliged weaker currency countries to adopt more restrictive macroeconomic policies – with the expected results for inflation and economic growth. Germany's ERM partners have until recently accepted this 'deflationary bias' in the system, and have been seen to commit themselves to the maintenance of a parity with the low-inflation DM, easing their own domestic costs of disinflation (the required real interest rates may be lower and the losses to the real economy fewer). However, the 1987 Basle–Nyborg agreement was designed to redress this asymmetry, at the insistence of France and Italy, which now seek a more expansionary course, having accomplished a phase of disinflation. There are many who view the so-called Delors plan (1989) for economic and monetary union as a means of substituting a more co-operative and expansionist European Central Bank for the present Bundesbank domination of the EMS.

Was the time ripe for Britain to join the ERM, as it had been legally committed to doing under the 1986 Single European Act? The traditional arguments marshalled against entry had been losing force. The antithesis between a fixed exchange rate and a money supply target matters less now that the instability of the demand for money has been acknowledged. The 'bi-polarity' argument which postulated a fundamental tension between sterling and the DM arising from their status as reserve currencies and from their inverse reactions to an oil price change, is now less important – the UK is less oil-dependent, and sterling has a reduced reserve role. Exchange controls, which buttressed the franc and lira within the EMS, have for several years now been progressively relaxed, with no evident effects on the system. Other arguments relate more generally to the loss of policy autonomy over the sterling exchange rate – what if the pound became misaligned and what if we were forced to give priority to price stability over employment, as the Germans do? One might point out that, had sterling been an ERM participant it would have suffered far less from overshooting (misalignment) and the employment costs of getting the relatively high UK inflation rate down might have been and still be less than under a floating rate regime. Finally, as the UK's geographic structure of trade becomes heavily weighted towards the EC, and as its openness to the EC increases, so the argument for a fixed parity in the ERM gained force.

REFERENCES AND FURTHER READING

Davenport, M. (1982), 'Economic impact of the EEC', ch. 8 in A. Boltho 'The European Economy', Oxford: Oxford University Press.

Featherston, M., Moore, B and Rhodes, J. (1979), 'EEC Membership and UK Trade in Manufactures', *Cambridge Journal of Economics*, December.

Harrop, J. (1989), *Political Economy of European Integration*, Aldershot: Elgar.

Hitiris, T. (1988), *European Community Economics*, London: Harvester .

Robson, P. (1987), *Economics of International Integration*, London: Allen and Unwin.

Swann, D. (1988), *Economics of the Common Market*, 6th edn, London: Pelican.

Winters, L. A. (1987), 'Britain in Europe: a survey of quantitative trade studies', *Journal of Common Market Studies*, **XXV** (4), pp 315–35.

QUESTIONS FOR DISCUSSION

1. Outline the basic theory of a customs union and common market.
2. With reference to the experience of the EC, discuss the current stage of completion of the common market.
3. Why is the programme for a Single Unified Market by the end of 1992 necessary?
4. What are the main elements of the EMS adjustable peg system?
5. Outline the advantages and constraints of an adjustable peg system.
6. Should the UK participate in the exchange rate mechanism of the EMS?

19.   The Economics of Perestroika

S. M. Murshed

INTRODUCTION

Arguably the most interesting events of our time are the political and economic reforms sweeping through Eastern Europe, in the areas comprising the (former) Soviet Bloc. The shape of these changes, labelled Perestroika (literally, reconstructing or transformation) are quite different and diverse in the different parts of Eastern Europe. This makes generalization about reform hazardous. One cannot hope to capture the various minutiae regarding changes in the economies of Eastern Europe; the heterogeneity amongst the various nations in Eastern Europe makes this task particularly difficult. One can, however, make some broad general statements about the nature and direction of economic reform in Eastern Europe. In this chapter, I present some of the principal features of the typical 'Eastern' economy, argue that many problems are still unresolved and discuss some related issues.

It is convenient to begin by briefly pointing out some of the differences between the various nations in Eastern Europe affected by Perestroika. The largest economy is the Soviet Union which is also the most autarkic. In addition to being a major agricultural producer, it has also a large industrial sector and is a very large repository of natural resources. The role of military production in its industrial sector is substantial and it is also one of the world's major arms exporters. The Soviet Union is also the country where *economic* reforms associated with Perestroika have been the most minimal. Indeed it has been pointed out that in the Soviet Union Perestroika has meant *political* (and not yet economic) reform. Notwithstanding the conversion of some military production units into civilian use, the inflexible and bureaucratic nature of Soviet society makes economic reform difficult. By contrast, economic reform has been well under way in Hungary for some time. It is *the* economy in Eastern Europe where the consumer goods sector is most developed. It, like Poland, has large international debts. It is also in the vanguard of foreign (direct and collaborative) investment, making its production process perhaps the

269

most efficient in Eastern Europe. Czechoslovakia besides being one of the most industrialized countries in Eastern Europe, is also the least likely nation in the region to encounter serious balance of payments problems. East Germany is very likely to cede being a nation state in the near future. The most interesting question surrounding its imminent re-unification with its richer and larger neighbour concerns wage differentials. The other issue is monetary union between the two regions. It is also the country in Eastern Europe where the principle of pure uncertainty as to future events applies most. Bulgaria and Rumania are the least developed and least industrialized countries in the (old) Soviet bloc, although Rumania is reputed to have a food surplus. Of great interest to theoretical economists is the Polish economy. Not only does Poland employ the services of prominent Western macroeconomists like Jeffrey Sachs of Harvard University, but it is also the country where economic reform has been most drastic. In the recent past Poland was notable for having a thriving private agricultural sector and dual exchange rates. The pace of reform in Poland makes her an interesting case for study by macroeconomists; whereas the Hungarian economy is of interest to theorists of foreign direct investment.

MEASURING PERFORMANCE

There are two serious problems in measuring the performance of most East European economies. The first is related to prices, and the second to quantities. Traditionally in centrally planned economies, prices do not play a central role in the allocative process, that is, they do not provide the signals about production decisions which they do in decentralized market economies. Furthermore, it is not their function to equilibrate supply and demand, that is, to clear markets. Nor do prices necessarily reflect the cost of production (related to the Marxian transformation problem of convert- ing values into prices). To a large extent prices had been administered in Eastern Europe. Production was traditionally of a command variety based on social necessity rather than market signals. This created the classic incentive incompatibility problem. Abstracting from problems of what actually constitutes the social optimum, the planner or decision- maker may not have had the incentives to bring about a socially optimal level of production. Thus the symmetry, alleged by some, between a decentralized (market) and a planned economy in terms of the reaction to the same economic signals breaks down if the planner has no incentive to carry out the action necessitated by the signal, whereas the market retains the incentive. Regarding the measurement of quantities the problem appears less acute. Here the concept of net material product, which emphasizes physical production and ignores the value of many services, has usually been employed in measuring national income. The conventions used to arrive at these figures are, in some cases, at variance with Western methods of calculating national income. The problem of making output comparisons with the West is (was) tedious although not insuperable.

We are used to regarding the traditional Eastern European production process as inefficient. This raises the question of the source of this inefficiency. It can be best described in the words of the famous Hungarian economist Janos Kornai as the phenomenon arising from the shortage economy (see Kornai, 1980). Thus the distinguishing feature of East European production was the chronic paucity of inputs. According to Kornai, "... shortage is a consequence of the economic mechanism and of the institutional framework ... even if household demand is tightly managed, ... the state and firms have also unlimited demand for inputs". (Kornai, 1982, pp 103–4). Generalized shortage arises out of the phenomenon of the 'soft budget constraint' (see Kornai, 1986). An economic organization or firm faced with a soft budget constraint is not strictly required to match outlays (costs) with revenues. (Many would argue that although more widespread this was not an exclusive feature of planned economies.) If the enterprise knows it can incur losses, and will always be subsidized by the state, this implies that it does not have to maximize profit or minimize cost. It will produce *inefficiently*: the direct source of the inefficiency arises out of the fact that the firm has no incentive to make an *optimal* use of the inputs currently available to it. If it does not use those available inputs optimally it will always feel short of inputs. To summarize, it is the soft budget constraint faced by economic enterprises which engenders the shortage of inputs and the resultant inefficiency in production.

THE MACROECONOMY

The chronic shortage of inputs felt by individual firms will constrain aggregate supply. On the aggregate demand side, planned or notional expenditures are frustrated by the inability of the supply side to meet them. The Eastern macroeconomy can be described as a supply constrained excess demand regime. If demand exceeds supply it implies disequilibrium and a tendency for inflation. Inflation can be repressed by explicit rationing of aggregate demand. (Rationing is a device to deal with excess demand, by somehow allocating the quantity of the good in short supply by means other than price.) But rationing merely disguises a fundamental disequilibrium. In the East European macroeconomy it is aggregate supply which constrains output production. This contrasts with the Keynesian view of the Western economy where it is the lack of effective demand which constrains output (there is excess capacity).

THE ROLE OF PLANNING

One function of planning is to allocate rationed goods, especially when these goods are inputs into the production process. The other function is to take production and pricing decisions. Thus the value of national income is determined by the planning agency. In taking output decisions one would expect the planner to 'optimize' subject to the constraints he faces. One constraint is the shortage of inputs. Another could be the need to maintain full employment. Thus the planner, when making decisions about how much to produce, would not be able to vary labour input, rather his choice would have to relate to wage rates and administratively fixed prices. This introduces an additional source of inefficiency in the production process. With regards to full employment, even if there is no open unemployment, there could be disguised unemployment.

Although it has been argued that prices do not play a central role in the planned economy there are two important exceptions. First, in the area of some consumer goods, especially food and second-hand durables, there was a limited 'free' market in many East European economies, even if only via a black (illegal) market. Freer markets implies that prices clear markets. Second, in the exportable sector, demand factors in the rest of the world, especially the West, caused prices to respond to market forces.

INTERDEPENDENCE BETWEEN THE WEST AND THE EAST?

Although interdependence exists, it is asymmetrical, as the West wields the greater economic power. One source of interdependence comes from the fact that Eastern goods are sensitive in terms of price and quality to Western demand. The other is that the East, faced with a paucity of inputs in its production process, has had to turn to the West to help make good this shortage. This is particularly true of high technology, but is also true of less sophisticated technical intermediate inputs. Quite obviously the ability of each East European economy to import these technical inputs is limited by the amount they export to the West and the foreign exchange (hard currency) they can borrow. This balance of payments constraint limits outputs and its growth in the East.

DUAL SECTORAL STRUCTURE AND STRUCTURAL INFLATION

Before turning to the macroeconomic effects of Perestroika it is worthwhile dichotomizing the typical East European economy into two broad sectors. One is the consumer good and/or agricultural sector, where to some extent the prices are adjusted to clear markets (the so called flexprice sector). The other is the industrial and/or investment goods sector, in which state control was greatest and where inefficiency in production due to soft budget constraints might be most expected. In this sector, the paucity of inputs and technological dependence on the West would be most severe, and rationing would be greatest. Prices would reflect the administered cost of domestic inputs, imported intermediate inputs and subsidies. One could refer to this industrial investment sector as the fixprice sector of the economy. Although this two sector aggregative view of the economy contains simplification it is not unrealistic.

Especially in Poland, but to a more limited extent elsewhere, Perestroika frees the agricultural or consumer goods sector's 'market' mechanism, ends quantity rationing in the industrial/investment goods sector, and makes wages determined more by market and trade union bargaining processes. But does this eliminate the disequilibrium nature of the previous regime? The effect of the regime switch is to convert repressed inflation into *open inflation* but with the fundamental problem of disequilibrium still remaining. But this begs the question as to how disequilibrium can persist when markets have been liberalized and prices become more flexible. It is more in the sense of *ex ante* or notional demand that disequilibrium continues. Even though *ex post* or effective demand is equal to supply, what is bought must necessarily equal what is sold; planned or notional demand is greater than supply, except with this excess demand no longer repressed. Thus in the typical Eastern economy static disequilibrium is replaced by *dynamic* disequilibrium. Expected future unification of Eastern with Western Germany can exacerbate the inflationary process. This tendency will be heightened by the announcement that for private savers in East Germany, savings in Ostmarks will be equivalent to Deutschmarks on a one to one parity, much more favourable than the market rate of exchange. This could provide a massive source of demand inflation.

It is clear that this sort of inflation is unsustainable in the long-run and in the case of Poland the problem is being tackled with unpleasant effects in terms of unemployment and declining living standards. In other countries the problem is yet to appear. But how can this type of inflation persist in the short to medium-run? There could be a price–wage–price spiral sustaining it. Suppose there is excess demand for consumer goods due to pent up demand being released as households dishoard, or as a result of transfers from abroad. As the cost of living rises it could lead to wage increases which would raise the cost of production in the industrial sector that then passes on these increases. One can visualize a steady state inflation with prices in different sectors rising at similar rates.

If industrial enterprises cannot pass on higher costs they would be bankrupted and disguised unemployment would become open unemployment. To avoid this the government could step in, printing more money to bale out firms. This would amount to a monetized fiscal (budget) deficit. Such a policy, which was pursued quite explicitly in Poland until the recent change of heart, would avoid open unemployment but would be inflationary. Many would argue that this was one of the major roles of government expenditure in many East European economies. Attempts to raise real wages by some workers would also cause unemployment, as partial or wholly market orientated enterprises would be forced to economize on labour input, especially if the commitment to full employment is abandoned. Some economists argue that a pool of unemployment may be required to make labour supply elastic, and readily available to the new growing market economies. In fact it is difficult to see how far this would actually help, given that skill mismatches are likely to appear. The type of inflation described above is best termed *structural* inflation. Here it is the underlying structure of society, specifically some form of structural disequilibrium or conflict, which causes the inflation, rather than increases in the money supply which plays a passive role where it accommodates and facilitates the interactions of the real side of the economy. In a tautological sense inflation is a monetary phenomenon as long as paper (fiat) money is the unit of account. This sort of inflation led by agricultural price increases has an historical counterpart in the Soviet Union and a similar phenomenon occurred in the 1920s during the days of the New Economic Policy; a period associated with economic liberalization. It was labelled the 'scissors crisis'. Agricultural and industrial prices were likened to the blades of a pair of scissors which at that time were moving further apart. It is salutary to note that the failure of the relatively liberal economic order during the New Economic Policy was greatly due to the scissors crisis and resulted in the Stalinist economic system of collectivization and rigid central planning. A rigid command economy existed before the New Economic Policy, during the civil war between the communists and the 'white' Russians. This phase in Soviet economic history (1918–21) is referred to as War Communism. It is worth noting that in virtually all wartime economies the supply of output is to a large extent geared to the needs of war and dictated by the state; shortages, excess demand and black markets appear, and the consequent inflationary pressures can be repressed by rationing. If so, could one view the Soviet economic system from Stalin to Gorbachev as representative of an economic siege mentality; and could economic Perestroika, when it does fully emerge, be interpreted as marking the end of this second (final) phase of War Communism?

What is the way out of the problems arising from disequilibrium in East European economies, which recent reforms have brought out into the open rather than resolved? There are two fundamental problems. One is generalized excess demand causing open inflation. This leads to the second and perhaps more serious problem which is related to the economics of shortage – the fact that production in Eastern Europe fails to respond to demand and is carried out inefficiently. We have to distinguish between the different countries in Eastern Europe – in Hungary production is arguably the most efficient and thus this problem is not acute; East Germany and Czechoslovakia are also quite efficient; making the Soviet Union one of the worst offenders in this respect. There will also be differences in the extent of excess demand across countries. The solutions are related to the problems. Demand reduction by reducing government expenditure would reduce open inflation but with unpleasant consequences in terms of unemployment, the standard of living, and the provision of basic needs. But above all, on the supply side an improvement in productivity is required, which would result in more effective use of available inputs and thus get away from the shortage syndrome. This could require a major overhaul of the production process and technology. The important point here is that demand side measures aimed at expenditure reduction (belt tightening) will ultimately prove useless unless the supply side is improved. This is because unless the economy is able to organize production more efficiently, the spectre of inflation will reappear once the iron grip on expenditure is relaxed.

FOREIGN AID

What role would transfers from the West, a new Marshall plan, play in the process of reform? Certainly transfers in the form of aid or lending from the West to the East would make more resources available and alleviate the shortages in the production process, and are therefore desirable. But they cannot act as a substitute for, or succeed in the absence of reform measures to improve especially the supply side of Eastern economies. There are also potential gains from economic policy co-ordination between governments in East and West. Co-ordination implies acting jointly rather than independently. The problem as far as transfers are concerned is the lack of funds. Huge trade deficits in several developed Western countries, notably the USA, mean there is less in terms of savings from trade surpluses for other countries to absorb. Furthermore there is no single large locomotive engine in the world economy, as the United States was in the immediate post-war era, dubbed the golden age (1945–70), which will lead global expansion.

Unlike in the golden age, when economic growth in one country or region was never at the expense of another, we live in a period of conflicting (competing) rather than complementary interests. As far as the West is concerned, Eastern Europe is much more likely to be complementary (non-conflicting) to its interests due to physical proximity, unlike the growing threats posed by competing Asian and Latin American manufactured exports. The losers from transfers to the East will be the Third World.

FURTHER ISSUES

Currency Convertibility

A freely convertable currency at some fixed rate of exchange will require a large initial stock of foreign exchange reserves. It is unlikely, in the near future, that a convertible Eastern European currency will be treated as a financial asset held for speculative purposes, and most international transactions with Eastern Europe are likely to be conducted in Western hard currencies. Competitive devaluation against Western currencies may not always help the country concerned, as devaluation, while making exports cheaper abroad, raises the domestic cost of imported intermediate goods, hurting production and the supply side of the economy. If a more flexible, market clearing rate of exchange is gradually adopted by some Eastern European countries, it would become important to reduce exchange rate volatility, as uncertainty about forward rates of exchange do little to facilitate trade. Here association with the European monetary system would help.

German Monetary Union and Unification

Great interest has been aroused by the prospect of monetary union between East and West Germany. Although this issue is fraught with uncertainty, it has raised (exaggerated) fears of increased interest rate needed to sustain the new unified currency. In the German context the monetary and financial sector mainly exists to service industrial production and is not an end in itself, unlike American and British financial institutions which appear to have an independent *raison d'être*. It is thus natural to have monetary union as a prelude to full economic union and the movements of West German banks eastward offering full financial packages to sustain production is in anticipation of unification. Of greater long-term interest, is the future role of West German trade surpluses, part of which will be transferred to the East. West Germany's transfers to its Eastern half to buy West German goods could result in extra inflation in West Germany, reduce German trade with the rest of the world, and reduce its capital exports elsewhere. The more rapid the unification process, the greater is the possible dislocation to world trade and payments.

Microeconomic Policy

The Hungarian and Polish experience suggests that moves to a more *uniform* non-discretionary taxation system would increase welfare. As far as industrial organization is concerned a mere switch to market forces in many East European economies could create a situation of widespread monopoly rather than competition. Given the highly concentrated structure of East European industry and the presence of special interest groups (as in any other country) there is a great danger of making a transition from state socialism to monopoly capitalism. Monopolistic structures characterized by special interest groups (directly unproductive activities) result in market failure as the socially beneficial signals of the price mechanism are ignored, especially those regarding entry into and exit from industries. Nor is it absolutely clear that privatization and Western models of stock markets would ensure improved capital markets.

The differences between the East European and Soviet experience needs re-emphasizing. Economic reform has been slowest in the Soviet Union where bureaucratic resistance to change is perhaps the major obstacle towards more decentralized decision making. Notwithstanding recent announcements, the fact that the Soviet Union does not have a balance of payments problem and has a huge store of natural resources is likely to slow down the process of change and heighten inertia.

CONCLUSIONS

In summary, the principal problem of the Eastern European economy lies in the inefficiency of its production process. This resulted in demand always exceeding supply. The resultant inflationary tendency used to be suppressed, but recent reforms have made it more open. Belt tightening and austerity can reduce inflation at a substantial social cost, unemployment being one of the main social costs of disinflation. But the fundamental problem of disequilibrium, caused by supply falling short of demand, will remain as long as the soft budget constraint is not relaxed and old production processes are employed. The transition from a soft budget constraint, associated with the old centrally planned regime, to a hard budget constraint linked to market and competitive forces is bound to have gainers and losers. Market forces, and not socialist principles, are likely to dictate the distribution of income and, unlike even a short time ago, the transition seems likely to go beyond market socialism to fully fledged capitalism in many East European economies. Assistance from the West is unlikely to be adequate for (or at least below the expectations) of most Eastern European countries. As part of Perestroika, Eastern Europe is likely to swap the problems of centrally planned economies for those of Western economies, such as inequality and unemployment. No amount of tinkering with the system will do any good unless the fundamental problem of productivity on the supply side is tackled, enabling these economies to be more dynamic. Otherwise the reform process will, like faith without charity, come to nothing.

REFERENCES AND FURTHER READING

The following references develop and extend some of the ideas and concepts introduced in this chapter:

Desai, P. (1987), *The Soviet Economy: Problems and Prospects*, Oxford: Blackwell.
Kornai, J. (1980), *Economics of Shortage*, Amsterdam: North Holland.
Kornai, J. (1982), 'Shortage as a Fundamental Problem of Centrally Planned Economies and Hungarian Reform', an interview with A Jutta-Pietsch in *Economics of Planning*, 18, pp. 103–13.
Kornai, J. (1986), 'The Soft Budget Constraint', *Kyklos*, 39, pp. 3–30.
Nove, A. (1969), *An Economic History of the USSR*, Harmondsworth: Penguin.
Nuti, D. M. (1988), 'Perestroika: Transition From Central Planning to Market Socialism', *Economic Policy*, October, pp 355–89.

An additional useful review is to be found in Paul G Hare, (1990) 'From Central Planning to Market Economy: Some Microeconomic Issues', *Economic Journal*, June.

QUESTIONS FOR DISCUSSION

1.   What is Perestroika?
2.   To what extent are economic and political liberalization connected?

3. What is meant by the concepts of (*a*) a shortage economy, and (*b*) a soft budget constraint?

4. What are the implications of Perestroika for inflation and unemployment in Eastern Europe? What are the inflationary effects of German unification?

5. In terms of economic structure and reforms what are the principle differences between the major economies of Eastern Europe?

6. Is a Marshall plan (large transfers of aid) needed for Eastern Europe, and who are likely to be the main gainers and losers from such transfers?

Index